Money, Morality
&
The Machine

D1506362

Also by
Craig R. Smith

Rediscovering Gold in the 21st Century:
The Complete Guide to the Next Gold Rush

Black Gold Stranglehold:
The Myth of Scarcity and the Politics of Oil
(co-authored with Jerome R. Corsi)

Also Co-Authored by
Craig R. Smith and Lowell Ponte

Crashing the Dollar:
How to Survive a Global Currency Collapse

The Uses of Inflation:
Monetary Policy and Governance in the 21st Century

Re-Making Money:
Ways to Restore America's Optimistic Golden Age

The Inflation Deception:
Six Ways Government Tricks Us...And Seven Ways to Stop It!

The Great Debasement:
The 100-Year Dying of the Dollar
and How to Get America's Money Back

The Great Withdrawal:
How the Progressives' 100-Year Debasement
of America and the Dollar Ends

Don't Bank On It!
The Unsafe World of 21st Century Banking

We Have Seen The Future And It Looks Like Baltimore:
American Dream vs. Progressive Dream

Money, Morality & The Machine

Smith's Law in an Unethical, Over-Governed Age

By Craig R. Smith

and Lowell Ponte

Foreword by Pat Boone

P2 Publishing
Phoenix, Arizona

Money, Morality & The Machine

Smith's Law in an Unethical, Over-Governed Age

Cover art by Dustin D. Brown
Editing by Ellen L. Ponte

Portions of this book originally appeared in the following projects by
Craig R. Smith and Lowell Ponte: *We Have Seen the Future and It
Looks Like Baltimore: American Dream vs. Progressive Dream; Don't
Bank On It! The Unsafe World of 21st Century Banking;
The Great Debasement: The 100-Year Dying
of the Dollar and How to Get America's Money Back;
Crashing the Dollar: How to Survive a Global Currency Collapse* and
*The Great Withdrawal: How the Progressives' 100-Year
Debasement of America and the Dollar Ends;*
as well as in various White Papers and Studies.
Copyright © 2010, 2011, 2012, 2013, 2014 by Idea Factory Press.
Copyright © 2015, 2016 by P2 Publishing.
All Rights Reserved.

Library of Congress Data
ISBN Number 978-0-9968476-3-6
First Edition — September 2016

P2 Publishing
15018 North Tatum Boulevard
Phoenix, Arizona 85032

Table of Contents

Dedication

To my wonderful wife and best friend
Melissa Smith, who makes me better
each day and raised our daughters
Holly and Katie to love the Lord
with all their hearts.
Also to my Pastor Tommy Barnett,
who taught me that doing the right thing
is always the right thing to do,
and to always hold onto the vision.

Foreword
by Pat Boone

"A false balance is abomination to the Lord:
but a just weight is his delight."

– Proverbs 11: 1 [KJV]

In ancient times merchants used a scale and weights to measure how much was sold and paid. Cheating often happened, and the Bible has many condemnations of those who use crooked scales and dishonest weights as a way to steal from others.

In this book my long-trusted friend and advisor Craig Smith and former *Reader's Digest* Roving Editor Lowell Ponte look at what has happened to our values since politicians switched Constitutional dollars backed by precious metal for today's paper dollars backed by…nothing.

A nation's currency has consequences, they show. Bad, debased money drives good morals out of society, causing a downward money-and-morality spiral that goes on debasing our money and its users.

We are paying a terrible price for this not only in our pocketbooks but also in social insecurity, fear, expanding government, and shrinking faith, trust, integrity, work, and freedom. Our dollar, which says "In God We Trust," is being "weighed in the balances and found wanting."

Craig and Lowell show how each of us can return to honest money, and how this could help restore America's national defense and future.

– PAT BOONE

President Dwight David Eisenhower
Farewell Address
January 17, 1961
(Excerpt) [1]

"Progress toward...noble goals is persistently threatened by the conflict now engulfing the world. It commands our whole attention, absorbs our very beings. We face a hostile ideology — global in scope, atheistic in character, ruthless in purpose, and insidious in method. Unhappily the danger it poses promises to be of indefinite duration....

A vital element in keeping the peace is our military establishment. Our arms must be mighty, ready for instant action, so that no potential aggressor may be tempted to risk his own destruction.

Our military organization today bears little relation to that known by any of my predecessors in peacetime.... We have been compelled to create a permanent armaments industry of vast proportions. Added to this, three and a half million men and women are directly engaged in the defense establishment. We annually spend on military security more than the net income of all United States corporations.

This conjunction of an immense military establishment and a large arms industry is new in the American experience. The total influence — economic, political, even spiritual — is felt in every city, every State house, every office of the Federal government.

We recognize the imperative need for this development. Yet we must not fail to comprehend its grave implications. Our toil, resources and livelihood are all involved; so is the very structure of our society.

In the councils of government, we must guard against the acquisition of unwarranted influence, whether sought or unsought, by the military-industrial complex. The potential for the disastrous rise of misplaced power exists and will persist.

We must never let the weight of this combination endanger our liberties or democratic processes.... Only an alert and knowledgeable citizenry can compel the proper meshing of the huge industrial and military machinery of defense with our peaceful methods and goals, so that security and liberty may prosper together..."

Introduction
by Craig R. Smith

"We shape our tools,
and thereafter our tools shape us."

– Marshall McLuhan

When I was a boy, banks were the pillars of a community; bastions of strength and stability; institutions staffed by honorable bankers who could be trusted.

Sadly, this no longer rings true. The banks have manipulated the financial system to suit their own ends and our faith in their integrity has all but evaporated. The money for which we labor, save for college and retirement, and use to fund this great experiment we call America is no longer honest.

Since Nixon closed the gold window in 1971 — essentially ending sound money and ushering in "elastic money" — we have seen an accelerated deterioration of our society as a whole. Fear, greed and apathy are the new normal instead of vices to avoid. Buying and selling of favors has replaced moral fortitude and personal responsibility. I have long been of the opinion that every ill we face as a nation today has its roots in the devaluation of our currency.

In this book we will explore the nexus between Money, Morals and The Machine. We shaped The Machine, and it has debased our money and morals, shaping us. Our challenge now is to undo this.

Gresham's Law states that bad money forces out good money. As the government has produced promises to pay in the form of paper money, honest money — gold and silver coins — has been forced out of the system and out of the hands of citizens.

Smith's Law states that as the value of money deteriorates, morals deteriorate, and as morals deteriorate, so does the value of money. Bad money drives out good values.

As these two laws play out, both here and abroad, those in power are willing to ignore morality in pursuit of riches. The government is hard-pressed to condemn this mindset because the Federal Reserve can, and does, merely push a button to create a trillion dollars of "wealth." It takes many millions of hours of labor by the citizens to earn the same "wealth."

When our Founders set in motion the principles that made America great, they planned for the possibility that men might become more motivated by greed and avarice than love of country or fellow citizen. They drafted a Constitution to ensure the rule of law would be equally applied to all. Slowly, that same Constitution has become more of a minor annoyance to those in power instead of the overarching compass it was intended to be.

This shift has allowed the creation of a Machine more powerful and corrupt than our Founders likely ever conceived. A system which rewards extortion and greed. A nation in which free markets, integrity and hard work are trumped by unscrupulous lawyers, back channel lobbyists, central bankers, and unethical politicians who can make consequences disappear; just ask Marc Rich.

In these pages we will expose The Machine for what it truly is and how it came to be so all-consuming. We will describe how it survives today and most importantly how to stop it and bring honesty, integrity and morality back to America.

In Chapter One we show why Great Britain, once the world's greatest empire, voted to "Brexit," to escape being colonized by a new rising empire called the European Union.

In Chapter Two we discover how the United States, which declared its own independence from the British Empire in 1776, turned from being a republic, free of entangling alliances, into an empire.

In Chapter Three we see how The Machine has taken control and imperils our Republic, our currency, our values and future.

In Chapter Four we explain Smith's Law and how "de-facing" and debasing our money has debased our morality and strength.

In Chapter Five we show how the escape hatches are being closed all around us, who is doing this, what it means, and how to break free.

In Chapter Six we see how our democratic Republic, our freedom of speech, and our other rights are are being foreclosed.

In Chapters Seven and Eight we look to the future in both technology and science fiction to glimpse a dawning Age of Zero — zero cash, zero jobs, zero economic growth, zero privacy, and perhaps zero freedom.

In our Epilogue we offer ways you can still create a more secure and prosperous future for your family, as well as for our nation and world.

This book does not prescribe an easy, quick fix.

It took decades for this decay to gnaw away at the character of the nation and it will take time and sacrifice to right our ship, but we can. It will require a shift in our thinking and a willingness to challenge the status quo.

I'm excited about America. We will recover and we will return the nation to its rightful owners (We the People) and to the Constitution which guides it. Rule of law equally applied can bring accountability back to our institutions that have lost the trust of the people — the Congress, the presidency, the banks, and our manipulated markets.

A country that has been through dozens of economic calamities, two world wars, recessions, historic inflation and even depressions will overcome. Our setbacks are opportunities to get the great engine back on the track.

Will you join me on this journey? If so, read on and become part of the solution.

– CRAIG R. SMITH

*"We have no government, armed with power,
capable of contending with human passions,
unbridled by morality and religion.*

*Avarice, ambition, revenge and licentiousness
would break the strongest cords of our Constitution,
as a whale goes through a net.*

*Our Constitution was made only
for a moral and religious people.
It is wholly inadequate
to the government of any other."*

– President John Adams
1798

Part One

Declarations of Independence

Chapter One

Breaking Free

"I want my country back."

– Frederick Forsyth
British Novelist / Journalist [1]

A major revolution shook the world on June 23, 2016...the latest of many such efforts to come as people and nations strive to break free from the tyranny now growing around us.

The world's ruling elite, who are part of the "Deep State," expected the United Kingdom vote to leave the European Union to fail.

The referendum, known as Brexit for "British Exit," instead won by 52-48 percent.

This triggered a worldwide seismic shockwave that on Friday, June 24 wiped out more than $2 Trillion from global markets. This shock for a time halted stock trading in Asia, sent Dow futures plunging by more than 700 points, drove the 10-year Treasury bond yield to modern record lows, and sent gold surging upwards by more than $80. [2]

By July 1, the U.S. Dollar had gained nearly 12 percent against the British Pound and about 2.5 percent against the Euro as investors rushed to move their money from both the United Kingdom and European Union.

This crisis seemed small, however, compared to the anti-Brexit propaganda campaign nicknamed "Project Fear" that warned of literal doomsday if the referendum passed — predicting that food supplies would dry up, the economy would collapse, and Western Civilization itself would disintegrate.

Far more frightening is what pro-Brexit investigators discovered about the foe they are fighting. The United States today faces essentially this same enemy in many different disguises. This book exposes these forces and shows how you can help protect your family and nation against them.

Forsyth's Saga

One of Brexit's most outspoken supporters is the renowned writer and journalist Frederick Forsyth, whose novels include *The Day of the Jackal* and *The Odessa File* and have sold more than 70 million copies.

Forsyth is an independent-minded skeptic about both the European Union and claims of manmade global climatic warming.

When he turned his investigative skills to understanding the European Union, the findings he published in the U.K. *Daily Express* and elsewhere opened many eyes.

The Founding Father of the European Union, he found, was a French intellectual named Jean Monnet. In the wake of World War II Monnet became obsessed with two ideas.

The first was that Europe should be united into a single "Superstate" so that such a terrible war could never again happen.

The second was that German voters had elected a criminally insane demagogue to rule over them, and therefore democracy should never again be trusted to select the European Superstate's rulers.

After studying Jean Monnet's public and private writings, Forsyth wrote:

"How could the various peoples ever be persuaded to hand over their countries from democracy to oligarchy, the government of the elite? Let me quote from what [Monnet] wrote:

"'Europe's nations should be guided towards the Super-state without their people understanding what is happening. This can be accomplished by successive steps, each disguised as having an economic purpose, but which will eventually and irreversibly lead to federation.'" [3]

"The referendum decision of June 23 will be the last ever, the decision permanent. So this is your choice," wrote Forsyth.

"This is about the country in which we will spend the rest of our lives, the land we will pass on to our children and grandchildren."

"What kind of a country, what kind of a governmental system? People's democracy or officialdom's empire? Our right to hold power to account or just two duties: to pay and obey?"

EUrocrats

Why were a majority of U.K. voters eager to secede from the European Union?

In today's Great Britain, nearly 62 percent of its laws and regulations originate not in the Parliament in London but in Brussels, Belgium, from an army of "Eurocrats" and members of the European Parliament.

These rules and laws range from the sublime to the ridiculous, such as creating guidelines as to how much "bend" a supermarket banana may have before being declared illegal to sell.

The Brits even had their own Boston Tea Party-like protests when EU nanny statist rules ordered them to stop using electric tea kettles because of their energy inefficiency.

The highest United Kingdom courts could be overruled by the highest EU court in Strasbourg.

The United Kingdom could no longer refuse admittance to a traveler from the EU, nor deny that person welfare payments for life if he or she found no satisfactory job.

And with each passing day this spider web of EU rules, controls, mandates and costs to taxpayers grows a bit bigger.

How would it feel if we were in a binding union with the nations of Latin America, which outvote us and can impose their laws and rules in the United States? Imagine, says one pro-Brexit member of Britain's Parliament, that a worker from any of these Latino countries has an automatic legal right to move to the United States and, if he fails to find a satisfactory job, is entitled to welfare that American taxpayers are required to pay him.

The EU imposed a $1.5 Billion fine on Poland for refusing to accept vast numbers of Muslim refugees.

Member nations in many ways lose control of their borders, sovereignty, and laws — and pay hundreds of billions to the EU for the privilege.

Nations such as Great Britain that once colonized others are being turned into colonies of the rising European Union megastate empire.

Come to think of it, this sounds similar to what President Barack Obama has been imposing on Americans.

No wonder that Mr. Obama prior to the vote visited Great Britain and spoke out almost threateningly against Brexit, implying that it might move the United States closer to the EU and farther from the United Kingdom in our alliances.

But Americans can at least still pretend we are a sovereign nation, not the pawn or serf of a globalist union of foreign nations possessing the power to replace our laws with their arbitrary ideology.

And as the Brexit debates brought to light, the European Union has routinely lied to the people and lawmakers of the United Kingdom. The Brits in April learned, for example, that the European Union has secretly been preparing an EU military. [4]

An EU Secret Army?

Other investigators found evidence of an even more ominous side to the European Union.

Kept out of public sight prior to the Brexit vote were internal EU documents, including EU foreign policy chief Federica Mogherini's *Global Strategy* declaration, that offer glimpses of a European Union with its own independent military. As the U.K. *Daily Express* reported, this could provide a "credible European defence" that would let the EU "act autonomously if and when necessary." [5]

A large number of European Union nations are also members of NATO, the North Atlantic Treaty Organization, which gives them military protection under America's nuclear umbrella.

As we have explored in previous books, joining NATO thereby saved our Western European allies much of the cost of defending themselves against Soviet invasion. They then used much of the money that Uncle Sam's generosity saved them to build welfare states.

By treaty, these allies are supposed to be contributing a mere two percent of their Gross Domestic Product (GDP) to help pay for their national defense, but only one or two of the European Union's NATO members are doing so. The United States pays less than 16 percent of its total annual federal budget for national defense, including our NATO defense commitments.

Yet if these recent documents are right, the same nations that Republican presidential candidate Donald Trump criticizes for not meeting their minimum NATO defense commitments might soon be funding a separate European Union military that can operate independently of NATO.

The U.K. *Daily Express* has also reported evidence that "the foreign ministers of France and Germany are due to reveal a blueprint to effectively do away with individual member states in what is being described as an 'ultimatum.' "

Imperial Ambitions?

"Under the radical proposals EU countries will lose the right to have their own army, criminal law, taxation system or central bank, with all those powers being transferred to Brussels," the U.K. *Daily Express* reported. [6]

Why would the European Union want or need its own military, separate from those of member states and allies such as the United States in NATO?

Could it be that the EU has its own imperial ambitions to project military power beyond Europe's current borders and into the Middle East and sub-Saharan Africa or beyond?

Could European Union Eurocrats envision themselves as military rulers of an empire, the likes of which several European nations each possessed in previous centuries?

Or, as some British voters feared, will this incipient military force be able to impose its will on disarmed member countries and potentially prevent their secession from its imperial grasp?

"Stealth, Deceit and Intimidation"

"[T]he reality of Britain's membership [in] the EU is that we are no longer a free, independent nation governed by politicians who are accountable to us at the ballot box," writes prominent British journalist Leo McKinstry in the U.K. *Daily Express*.

"Instead we are a regional province of an empire ruled by a self-serving, unelected oligarachy."

"The Eurocrats like to see themselves as progressive," McKinstry continues, "but in truth they are profoundly reactionary, a throwback to the pre-20th Century days of governance by a privileged, parasitic elite."

"They despise the concept of popular opinion because they regard it as a barrier to the creation of a unified European superstate. They know that they have little support for their federalist ideology so they have to impose their dogma by stealth, deceit and intimidation…. Hatred of the people's will infuses the entire pro-EU cause."

It is, McKinstry writes, an "anti-democratic impulse." [7]

He is equally passionate about the torrent of immigrants that the EU has let in, along with giving them the right to move anywhere in its countries.

"The EU's catastrophic decision to open the floodgates led to the arrival of more than 1.1 million migrants, most of them fit, young men," McKinstry writes.

"Amidst mounting social disintegration and division, this anarchic policy has fuelled the import of violent misogyny, welfare dependency and jihadist extremism...."

"But, utterly unembarrassed, the Brussels federalists see the migration crisis as a perfect opportunity to pursue their agenda of political unification," writes McKinstry.

"Under the guise of sorting out the mess, they aim to grab more power, thereby further reducing the member states to the status of provinces in their empire."

"[N]othing in the EU plans involves bringing back internal borders or strengthening external frontiers," writes McKinstry. Instead, the EU has offered two schemes, both of which give Brussels more authority for "redistributing migrants," one of which would let the EU set "quotas based on the wealth and population of each member state."

"In accordance with federalist dogma," he writes, "both schemes involve a massive increase in EU power and a further erosion of national sovereignty." [8]

"I Am Not British!"

The opposition to Brexit was also ferocious and fearful.

"I am not British! I am European!" read one young protestor's sign in London. It made clear that this was a vote of political allegiance, like those of Leftists who want to see America's southern border simply erased.

Polls suggest that the young in the U.K. want Europe to merge into one borderless entity. Many want the right to travel and work freely anywhere in the European Union.

How odd this is, since prior to the Brexit vote the economy was far better and unemployment was dramatically lower in the United Kingdom than in most of the European Union.

Many young people also prefer the Euro-socialist welfare states to a culturally more conservative, old-fashioned Britain still rooted in the past with capitalism and the late Prime Minister Margaret Thatcher.

As Thatcher's name reminds us, she was able to roll back much of the leftward drift of her nation and, as she liked to say, "put the GREAT back in Great Britain."

Much of the fear these protestors felt for the Brexit vote was not just about their country — but also for the risk that if Brexit succeeded it could prompt similar referendums in other nations and perhaps cause the entire collectivist European Union to unravel.

Polls already have shown that if French voters were permitted such a vote, a majority would support leaving the EU. France's socialist President François Hollande has turned down a request by the populist leader Marine Le Pen of the National Front party to hold such a referendum.

Facing Brexit

Britain's exit from the European Union was opposed by Conservative Party Prime Minister David Cameron and other anti-Brexit forces through a barrage of scare tactics, as we noted. Among these claims: Brexit will cost every British family thousands of Pounds by denying Britain access to European markets; it will cause economic chaos; and Britain returning to its independent sovereign status of 45 years ago might even lead to "the end of Western Civilization."

Cameron and others are serving business interests that have enriched themselves via European Union trade with Europe. But more than 40 pro-Brexit Tory members of Parliament opposed ousting Cameron, in part to deal with Scotland and Northern Ireland, and in part because Cameron kept his promise to call such a referendum. Nevertheless, Cameron resigned and was promptly replaced by 59-year-old Theresa May, a centrist conservative who quietly opposed Brexit.

Scottish voters two years ago came close to voting for independence from Great Britain. With Britain leaving the EU, will Scotland vote to separate from the United Kingdom and then join the European Union as its own independent country? Northern Ireland, which voted against Brexit, might likewise secede from the United Kingdom and join EU member Ireland.

(Few countries are rushing to join the European Union at the moment, with its crushing regulations and other high costs of membership. Days before the June 23 referendum, Switzerland withdrew its application to join the EU.)

Around Europe are dozens of secession movements. Many Venetians want to become a nation independent of Italy. A likely majority of Catalans around Barcelona want independence from Spain. In Austria a populist leader narrowly lost an election with all other major parties cooperating to defeat him; a re-vote was called in this odd case. The successful Brexit vote will fuel many such movements around the world.

Donald Trump is not a secessionist, but his anti-establishment populist rhetoric is part of a global phenomenon whose activists are winning votes in France, Germany, Italy and many other countries. People are simply fed up with old-line oppressive political leaders.

The world has decided that the status quo no longer deserves automatic support. People want to be heard, and they are tired of politicians, crony capitalists, and big business elites calling the shots. People want liberty. They want to be free. And they want to be left alone.

Globalists Afraid

At a late July 2016 meeting of the G-20 — the richest business nations in the world — leaders reluctantly agreed to adopt less harsh measures against nations where populist opposition movements are growing. Their fear that the globalist ideology is in trouble was all too evident. [9]

In North America, independent socialist Senator Bernie Sanders of Vermont has led a surprisingly successful rebellion to move the Democratic Party even farther leftward. A movement in Vermont continues to call for separating from the United States — and perhaps becoming a province of Canada. Many in Quebec, meanwhile, still want to separate from the rest of Canada.

Also in the United States, independence movements in Alaska and Texas [4] want their own Brexit-like referendums.

Historically, politics around the world involve forcing things together under bigger governments, or forcing them apart into smaller nations. The British people's Declaration of Independence vote will help roll back the globalist government direction of the European Union and similar Progressive collectivist entities.

A vote against Brexit, its supporters argue, could have made Britain's decline permanent, because the people would never again have been allowed to regain their freedom with a ballot.

Government regulators and central banks such as the Federal Reserve might have "stepped in," in the wake of the Brexit vote, to manipulate markets and protect the old order. They did this in 2008 and created the longest recession in American history.

They should release the free market to work without political interference in order to restore genuine health and growth to our economy. And, indeed, by mid-August 2016 European stock markets had regained their confidence and mostly returned to pre-Brexit trading levels.

The world wants change that will bring back freedom, personal responsibility and individualism, and will end collectivism. People are hungry to return to small government, free markets and honest money.

British voters have taken a brave and noble step to push back against those who are trying to turn our nations into conquered provinces of their socialist empires.

Trying to Overthrow Brexit

In shaken London, the immediate response of sore losers has been to try to negate this Brexit vote of Britons fed up with seeing the European Union's globalism destroy their nation.

Nearly five million anti-Brexit voters purportedly signed an Internet petition declaring the referendum vote invalid, despite its 72.2 percent voter turnout, because that near-record turnout fell short of 75 percent.

Many of these signatures apparently were fraudulent. The *London Telegraph* reported that nearly 24,000 may have come from Communist North Korea, where few have Internet access. More than 39,000 appear to have come from Vatican City, which has a resident population of fewer than 800. Welcome to the new Progressive "democracy." [10]

Fair's fair. If we are going to move the goalposts and change the rules retroactively after the game — something that nearly all legal scholars in Great Britain reject — then so be it.

In 1975, U.K. voters approved their nation's membership in what was then called the European Community (or European Economic Community) after being promised that this entity would confine itself to trade matters, not attempt to become a political entity that expands its powers to steal the sovereignty of member nations.

What was the voter turnout for this 1975 referendum? Answer: 64.6 percent — far less than the turnout for the June 23, 2016 Brexit referendum.

So, according to the new rule proposed by those eager to retroactively erase the Brexit vote they lost, we should declare that the United Kingdom's 1975 vote failed to reach the 75 percent threshold they claim is needed to make the earlier pro-EU referendum valid.

(Mind you, we are all for extending to voters what lawmakers must achieve to pass any valid law — a Quorum, usually 50 percent plus 1 of members present in the legislative body.

This would overcome the sneaky local U.S. referendums put on ballots for voter approval in late spring or summer when most voters are on vacation.

Many measures thus become law with only 10 or 15 percent of registered voters casting a ballot.)

Scotland has not had a voter turnout of 75 percent since 1992, but its legislature's First Minister Nicola Sturgeon rushed to the microphones to warn that Scotland's parliament might be "in a position to block Brexit."

In Scotland, where golf and its duffer "do-over" were born, 62 percent — roughly 1.66 million — voted against Brexit but could not overcome the vastly larger 17 million British 53.4 percent pro-Brexit vote in England.

"We have to respect the vote…even if we don't like it," said Scottish Secretary David Mundell. After being united for three centuries, Scotland rejected a breakup with England. Many supporters of Scottish independence assumed the U.K. would remain in the European Union.

Opposing Democracy

In London, its newly-elected Labour Party Muslim Mayor Sadiq Khan said his city would continue to welcome immigrants. A separate online petition declared London to be "an international city, and we want to remain at the heart of Europe." Londoners voted 59.9 percent against Brexit, and the petition has reportedly gathered 100,000 signatures to declare this ancient capital independent of the United Kingdom. Although Khan's words were not secessionist, some critics took them to be a declaration that London might become what in the U.S. is called a "sanctuary city."

One EU-loving globalist, James Traub of the journal *Foreign Policy*, haughtily said: "It's time for the elites to rise up against the ignorant masses." [11]

And in what might be the ugliest gesture of all, Brexit opponents who said it won because of the votes of old, bigoted and stupid people have proposed changing the laws to prevent anyone over a certain age — say, 65 — from voting at all.

In effect, they want to tilt future elections as was done more than a century ago in America's segregated South with literacy tests that denied votes to those who think differently.

One EU former bureaucrat, Fraser Cameron, went even farther, declaring that because referendums of the people might cause "problems," they should be forbidden entirely. People from outside the ruling elite simply cannot be trusted with a vote over EU government policy. [12]

Never forget that the Founding Father of the European Union wanted ultimately to abolish democracy and, like the ancient Greek philosopher Plato in his work *The Republic*, envisioned a society ruled by an unelected elite of "philosopher kings" who would make all decisions for the people — even, wrote Plato, what music people would be permitted to hear.

This is the European ideal that so many socialists want to impose in America.

If nothing else, Brexit has inspired an ironic passion among its opponents for breaking big government up into smaller entities.

Brexit, said now-former Prime Minister Cameron, was a "once in a generation, once in a lifetime" decision. The now-Disunited Kingdom has had "referendums, not neverendums." But many twists lie ahead as the world turns away from entrenched nanny statist globalism.

Clearly, a majority of voters, sick of the European rot that has been destroying the Great in Great Britain, pushed back — and history changed.

In 2016, America's Fourth of July fireworks took on new meaning. This is our celebration of declaring and winning independence from the British Empire.

The United Kingdom is at last "a nation again," asserting its freedom from an even larger oppressive empire. We salute them as a fellow free revolutionary people.

In the U.S., this same populist impulse can be seen in the popularity of anti-establishment politician Donald Trump, who backed Brexit.

The then-presumptive Democratic candidate Hillary Clinton and President Barack Obama urged those in the United Kingdom to submit to the socialist collectivism of the European Union.

We Americans will have our chance to reject such values this November, and to renew our own American Revolution.

Memory and Money

"As a union of medium-to-small sized countries," says the public 2016 EU *Global Strategy* overview, "we have a shared European interest in facing the world together."

How could the little United Kingdom and its mere 64 million people dare to brave the world on its own by voting for Brexit, by leaving the European Union?

The answer is that Britons woke up and smelled the coffee...no, tea... and suddenly remembered who they were and what their little island had accomplished in human history.

As recently as 1927, within living memory, roughly a quarter of our world's population was in one way or another ruled by the British Empire, a domain so vast around our planet that on it the sun never set. The British and their Scottish warriors conquered and ruled a quarter of the world with a smaller population than they have today.

You are reading this right now in English, the world's official language of diplomacy, trade, business, science and global air traffic control, because of their empire. [13]

Little Luxembourg and its half-million people might need the EU, but even after losing millions of its finest soldiers in two nightmarish world wars, and even after losing the British Empire (except for a few outposts such as Gibraltar on the southern coast of Spain, which ironically may legally remain a member of the EU even after the U.K. Brexits) following World War II, the United Kingdom remains far more than "a medium-to-small" country.

Just by itself, the United Kingdom today is the world's fifth largest economy. Subtract this one nation from the 28 countries of the EU and the European Union tumbles from being the world's second most successful economic bloc to third place. Even after Brexit, London will continue to be one of the world's largest economic centers.

Just by itself, the United Kingdom today — depending on how one calculates — ranks between fifth and ninth among the world's military powers. It is a declared nuclear weapon power with 225 such weapons. In the EU only France can rival this, with a declared 300 atomic weapons.

(Nuclear weapons exist in several European nations, of course, but these are American weapons under command and control of the U.S. military. The U.K. and French weapons are under their control.)

What Britons scarcely whispered during the public debate over Brexit was this: Because they for centuries were colonizers, they understood how to subdue and rule a foreign people. And they recognized that the European Union was itself a rising empire using those same ancient tactics to colonize them.

Bad "Samaritans"

The Britons remembered their Bible and Jesus' parable of the Good Samaritan. Many Jews two thousand years ago hated the Samaritans because they were alien. Ancient empires such as the Assyrians and Babylonians ruled conquered peoples by moving them, by moving defeated Israelites to Babylon and herding another captive people, the Samaritans, to Israel — making it easier to rule both uprooted peoples.

The United Kingdom had joined the proto-European Union, which then was supposedly just a group to make trading easier. But by 2016 Britons watched as the EU was forcing them to take in hundreds of thousands of foreigners, and requiring U.K. taxpayers to support such immigrants with never-ending welfare payments.

In effect, the EU was erasing the United Kingdom's borders and flooding it with immigrants of alien values and ideas — Samaritans, who would soon be able to outvote and control Britons.

The European Union was permanently transforming the United Kingdom by using a flood of foreign immigrants to create alien nations inside the country. No wonder so many Britons felt alienated.

The ancient Roman Empire, like the British Empire, mastered this technique. It was no accident when both drew new national boundaries that put long-rival tribes inside the same country.

These tactics are historically called "divide and conquer." By pitting these little Balkanized sub-nations and tribes against one another, a small Roman or British force could rule merely by controlling the balance of power among them.

No wonder that older Britons who remembered their empire were horrified to see such tactics used against them by the European Union.

They recognized what could happen.

Rule, Britannia!

British oldsters also grew up singing a beloved imperial song titled "Rule, Britannia!":

> Rule Britannia!
> Britannia, rule the waves.
> Britons never shall be slaves…
>
> The nations, not so blessed as thee,
> Must in their turn to tyrants fall…
> While thou shalt flourish…great and free,
> The dread and envy of them all.

Its sea-based empire had been to Great Britain what the western frontier and Manifest Destiny had been to the United States. Both nations believed that they had a destiny to fulfill, and regarded their success as evidence that God favored their enterprise.

The centuries-old belief that they had won the highest prize in life by being born British had been beaten down by a century of Leftist propaganda telling them that all cultures were equal and imperialism was evil.

The Leftists who continue to heap shame on Christian, capitalist Great Britain, however, saw nothing wrong with the imperial Soviet Union enslaving Eastern Europe and Cuba and Vietnam, nor with imperial Communist China conquering and destroying human rights in Tibet.

These Leftists seldom mentioned that Karl Marx had praised the British Empire for bringing modern ideas and technology to many backward nations. When Marx's freedom of expression was threatened in Europe, the father of Communism found safety in the British public library.

The campaign over Brexit reminded millions of Britons of the greatness of their culture and history. It reminded them that they were effectively still one of the world's top five powers economically and militarily, even without EU membership.

It also alerted them to the very real danger that, having been the world's greatest colonizer, they should recognize that they were now being colonized by a new empire called the European Union.

Fabians

Those familiar with a type of socialism created in Great Britain a century ago will recognize the pattern.

Fabian socialism, named for the Roman general who defeated Hannibal by relentless small hit-and-run attacks, planned to overthrow capitalism not by one huge revolution. Instead, it would achieve this by small, incremental rules, regulations, taxes and "social reforms" that would slowly bleed capitalist enterprises and bring them bit by bit under full government control.

Fabian socialism was promoted by Sidney and Beatrice Webb and their fashionable friends in the Bloomsbury circle. Among the members of this circle was the British economist whose ideas in America guide our central bank, the Federal Reserve, and the circle of economic advisors around President Barack Obama. This economist's name is John Maynard Keynes.

Fabians would also found the London School of Economics, where Rolling Stone Mick Jagger would someday study, and a philosopher named Karl

Popper taught. Popper would become the dominant intellectual influence on a radical currency trader named George Soros, who in 1992 gained billions by becoming "the man who broke the Bank of London."

Jean Monnet's European Union, a machine designed to use deception to incrementally enslave Europeans, appears to be planned and run on the same cunning model as Fabian socialism.

Fabianism aims to socialize nations as in the tale of frogs in a pot of water heated very slowly; by the time they recognize the danger and try to jump to freedom, they are already cooked. Every year the government adds a few new regulations here and taxes there until businesses awaken one day to find themselves immobilized and bankrupt from this slow-motion socialist takeover.

Wither Brexit?

The fear now is that, despite the attempt of Britons to jump out of the EU via Brexit, they might have waited too long.

The new U.K. Prime Minister Theresa May promises that "Brexit means Brexit" and that no new referendum will be permitted to overturn the 2016 vote of the people. Like Margaret Thatcher, whose father was a shopkeeper, May comes from Britain's middle class and a father who was a minister.

But by late July, Ms. May was already saying that the request to start a two-year negotiation clock will not be submitted until 2017, which means that the actual separation of the United Kingdom and European Union might not happen until late 2019…and could be delayed beyond that.

At least one British pundit now assumes that neither side will be happy with the compromises likely to be struck in EU-U.K. negotiations. The clean break Brexit enthusiasts hoped for may, in the end, leave Britain still entangled in various EU rules as a price of trading with EU countries.

Or the political winds may shift and a new referendum may be arranged that simply blows Brexit away. In past years when countries such as Ireland failed to vote for European Union membership, they were simply required to vote again and again and again until they complied — at which point any such voting that might have undone EU membership was halted.

As Forsyth discovered, one of the two objectives of the European Union was to abolish democracy, to prevent the people from having a say in their governance. After the EU replaces their indigenous governments, Europe will hold no more elections at all — except for members of the European Parliament of the EU, which effectively has almost no power.

Euro Zoned

One other thing that likely helped reawaken pro-Brexit voters was the paper in their pocket.

Of the 28 nations seduced into joining the European Union, 19 replaced their own currency with the new money, the Euro.

Europeans could now travel freely from one EU nation to another, and they could buy and sell without needing to seek out a bank or *cambio* to convert their nation's currency into that of another. Such exchanges almost always came with a conversion cost attached.

Little did those in the Eurozone know, as we have explained in previous books, that the Euro was not really a new currency. In effect, it was the German Deutsche Mark in disguise.

Because of its dominant economic power in the heart of Europe, Germany had an oversized influence on the new European Central Bank (ECB), its interest rates, and how many Euros it issued.

Europe has been in a slow civil war for more than four centuries over which country or empire will unify the continent under its rule, as things had been under the Roman Empire two thousand years ago.

(Some might date this struggle for unity in Europe to the crowning of Charlemagne in 800 A.D. as head of the Holy Roman Empire, which as historians like to joke was neither holy, nor Roman, nor an empire.)

Napoleon attempted to take control of Europe two centuries ago. And Germany likewise tried and failed to unify Europe twice in World War I and II, producing horrifying bloodshed both times.

The Euro, we have argued, was issued by the ECB in 1999 as what, in essence, was Germany's third attempt in the 20ᵗʰ Century to conquer Europe — this time through a currency that gave Germany trading and other advantages with other European countries, thereby creating an invisible imperial relationship that turned these other countries into secret colonies of Germany.

Germany, however, made a crucial miscalculation. By allowing profligate nations, for example Greece, to join the Eurozone based on phony Greek financial documents, Germany did the equivalent of giving teenage boys whiskey, car keys, and a No Limit credit card.

Once Greece was admitted to the Eurozone, bankers in much of the world — and especially in Germany — assumed that this country had been given a huge credit line by the German government, the *de facto* co-signer on loans by Greece.

Germany would have to make good on any Greek loan, many bankers reasoned, because a Greek default could wreck the reputation of the new Euro and the Eurozone.

Given the opportunity to borrow huge amounts of money, Greek officials borrowed every Euro they could, running up debts that Germany has bailed out again and again to the tune of most of a trillion Euros. Such is the price of trying to rule Europe with a manipulated currency.

Euro-nations

One major economist who has lost respect for the Euro is Joseph Stiglitz — Nobel Laureate, former Chairman of President Bill Clinton's Council of Economic Advisors, former Chief Economist at the World Bank, and a professor at Columbia University.

In his August 2016 book *The Euro: How a Common Currency Threatens the Future of Europe*, Stiglitz explains how in its 17 years this ill-conceived currency that was supposed to unify Europe has instead polarized it into debtors vs. creditors who distrust and dislike one another. [14]

Dr. Stiglitz, a man of the Left and a globalist, now believes the Euro has damaged Greece and other nations, hurt workers, increased the amount of economic inequality in Europe, and been used by giant companies to undermine small competitors in smaller nations.

Stiglitz fears that if EU hard-liners like the head of the European Commission Jean-Claude Juncker try to get very tough on the United Kingdom to make other nations afraid to consider their own Brexit, this will have bad consequences.

"To me that was shocking," Stiglitz told the *New York Times*. "You hope that people want to stay in the E.U. because it's delivering benefits, because there's a belief in European solidarity, the belief that it's bringing prosperity. [Juncker is] saying the only way we are going to keep the E.U. together is by the threat of what happens if you think about leaving." [15]

In For A Pound

When the United Kingdom joined the European Union, it refused to join the Eurozone. It refused to replace the British Pound currency with the Euro and the German control lurking behind it.

As noted in this book's Introduction, a nation's values are reflected in its currency. In the Eurozone, 19 nations have surrendered their uniqueness and dissolved their identities in an unproven currency that says "I am not French or Italian or Dutch. I am a European," whatever that may mean.

The United Kingdom never surrendered the British Pound, once the world's reserve currency, that even today helps the U.K. remain the fifth largest economy on the planet and remains a rich part of their heritage and values.

The Pound, reported the BBC in 2014, has "a credible claim to be the oldest living currency in the world." [16]

In the Eighth Century, this Roman and Frankish form of money was introduced in central and southern England by the Anglo-Saxon King Offa. It consisted of 240 silver pennies that, when put together were supposed to weigh an English pound.

The main Roman coins were the *denarius*, the solidly-valued *solidus* used in military pay (and origin of our word "soldier"), and the silver pennies that added up to a pound called *libra*, Latin for "weight or balance" (which we know as a Zodiac sign used by astrologers, Libra the scales).

This *libra pondo, "a pound by weight,"* name for this coinage lives on in the ornate "L" symbol with one line through it used today for the British Pound, £. It also lives on in our abbreviation for libra that stands for pounds of weight, lb.

A Pound was a very substantial unit of money. In the year 980 it could purchase 15 head of cattle. But its debasement began in the 15th Century, and money historian David Sinclair estimates that by Year 2000 its purchasing power had fallen "four-hundred fold." [17]

Since Great Britain abandoned its own gold standard less than 100 years ago, the Pound has become just another fiat currency like the U.S. Dollar. Soon it will no longer even be paper, but durable plastic, and soon after that the advanced world will go cashless.

Currently the Bank of England and Bank of Canada are studying adoption of DLT, Digital Legal Tender — an official sort of Bitcoin. The Canadian idea — one being considered under the bank's "Project Jasper" — has already been nicknamed the "Can Coin." Given the nanny statist nature of government officials, critics already speculate that such a coin could be programmed to control what you are permitted to purchase in a vending machine, e.g., no candy bars or soda pop.

Older United Kingdom voters can remember when the Pound was truly "sterling." In previous centuries it surpassed the dollar as the world's most respected major currency. For many such Brits, the Pound was like carrying a Union Jack flag in their wallet.

The Pound, with its images of the nation's symbols and great achievers, is a vivid reminder of how great Great Britain has been — and remains.

For a patriotic Briton, the mere sight of this historic currency must evoke feelings of heritage and pride.

Sometimes the currency, or even the ghost of the true money, of a nation can save it. By helping remind Britons of all they have achieved, the British Pound might well have tipped the balance in the Brexit vote. What patriotic U.K. citizen would want to see his or her nation dissolved into a new and undemocratic European Union empire?

Britons were overtaken in 1066 in the Norman Conquest by French-speaking Vikings from across the channel in Normandy. But they have stood triumphant for almost a thousand years since then against the Spanish Armada, Napoleon, and the Battle of Britain. They have remained unconquered for longer than any other major nation.

As Prime Minister Winston Churchill, descended from the Dukes of Marlborough and an American mother, said in 1939:

> *"If the British Empire is fated to pass from life*
> *into history, we must hope it will not be*
> *by the slow process of dispersion and decay,*
> *but in some supreme exertion for freedom,*
> *for right, and for truth."*

If investors had heeded the advice and warnings we set forth in six previous books [18], they might have profited handsomely while this giant Brexit Money-Quake shook the planet and set assets tumbling. [19]

A word to the wise: this Brexit vote is the first of many more soon to come. Read our books and quickly pick up the broken pieces of your investment portfolio. You will want to move quickly at least a portion of what remains before the falling dominoes and other pains of aftershocks hit.

Do not just hunker down like those Romans 2,000 years ago in Pompeii when they felt the shaking. They hunkered down because of their false assumption that the ancient volcano Vesuvius would not erupt in their lifetimes. Those who did not flee can be seen today, overtaken by the tremors, gas and hot ash that killed them.

*"The man of system...is apt to be very wise
in his own conceit, and is often so enamoured with
the supposed beauty of his own ideal plan of
government that he cannot suffer the smallest deviation
from any part of it....*

*He seems to imagine that he can arrange the different members
of a great society with as much ease as the hand arranges
the different pieces upon a chess-board.*

*He does not consider that in the great chess-board
of human society, every single piece has
a principle of motion of its own,
altogether different from that which
the legislature might choose to impress upon it."*

– **Adam Smith**
The Theory of Moral Sentiments
(1759)

Chapter Two

The Accidental Empire

"America has never been an empire.
We may be the only great power in history
that had the chance, and refused —
preferring greatness to power
and justice to glory."

– George W. Bush
November 19, 1999 [1]

In America, millions celebrated the United Kingdom's June 2016 Brexit vote, widely seen as the U.K.'s own Declaration of Independence from an increasingly oppressive and authoritarian European Union.

This act of secession from the European Union's emerging empire carried echoes of America's own 1776 assertion of independence from the world's then-greatest military power, the British Empire.

In their 18th Century world of rising empires and conflict, America's Framers wanted our new nation to follow a different path in international relations.

"Why, by interweaving our destiny with that of any part of Europe, entangle our peace and prosperity in the toils of European ambition, rivalship, interest, humor or caprice?" asked President George Washington in his 1796 Farewell Address. "It is our true policy to steer clear of permanent alliances with any portion of the foreign world."

"The great rule of conduct in regard to foreign nations is in extending our commercial relations, to have with them as little political connection as possible" while keeping "perfect good faith" with existing agreements, said Washington. [2]

One of the "essential principles of our government," said President Thomas Jefferson in his 1801 First Inaugural Address, was "peace, commerce, and honest friendship with all nations, entangling alliances with none." [3]

Yet Jefferson called our new country the "Empire of Liberty."

His protégé President James Madison in *Federalist Paper* Ten argued for "extend[ing] the sphere" to enlarge our Republic.

Madison shared Jefferson's optimistic belief that, contrary to the political philosopher Montesquieu, a republic need not be small to survive. "The reverse is true," said Jefferson, as he believed the United States had already proven. [4]

Alexander Hamilton in *Federalist Paper* One described the young United States as "in many respects the most interesting...empire...in the world." [5]

A Republic Transformed

Benjamin Franklin famously said that he and the other Framers had made the United States "a Republic...if you can keep it."

Have we kept our Republic? Or, like the ancient Roman Republic, have we instead turned into an empire?

The good news, as George W. Bush seems to believe, is that America never turned into an empire.

No, we are just a Republic, free from foreign entanglements, as Washington and Jefferson wanted.

However, somehow we have acquired more than 650 military bases outside the United States, manned at any moment by at least 150,000 soldiers, sailors, fliers or Marines.

"Who can doubt that there is an American empire?" wrote historian Arthur Schlesinger, Jr. It is "an informal empire, not colonial in polity, but still richly equipped with imperial paraphernalia: troops, ships, planes, bases, proconsuls, local collaborators, all spread around the luckless planet."

The Department of Defense also employs what used to be called "mercenaries," not entirely unlike the British-hired German Hessians in our revolution. Ours are private contractors whose injuries or deaths in theory do not have the same political consequences of such things happening to our soldiers.

Two of the heroes who died while fighting to save America's ambassador in Benghazi, Libya, were U.S. citizens and private contractors.

"The United States probably has more foreign military bases than any other people, nation, or empire in history, and it's doing us more harm than good," writes liberal investigative reporter David Vine. [6]

The entangling complications of such overseas forces can be hard to anticipate. In July 2016, for example, the government of Turkey, America's longtime NATO ally, fought off a *coup d'etat*. One of the surviving government's responses was to send legal prosecutors into the main military airbase the United States built there, Incirlik.

It is not publicly known how many American B-61 atomic bombs were stored at this one airbase in Turkey — by one report, 50 — each with the potential explosive power of more than 11 Hiroshima-sized nukes.

This is part of the U.S. nuclear arsenal kept abroad to deter Russia from attacking Turkey or our other allies. B-61 bombs are stored at U.S. bases in

Germany, the Netherlands, Belgium and Italy that may be secured primarily by soldiers of the host nations, not U.S. forces. [7]

Making an Empire

How did America begin its fundamental transformation into today's empire?

We were a trading nation, and this involved us with other nations and powers. In what history remembers as the XYZ Affair, French government officials secretly demanded bribes from our second president, John Adams, to halt French harassment and seizures of American merchant vessels. When Adams made this public, our people responded with the chant: "Millions for defense, but not one penny for tribute!"

Adams, alas, gave the notorious Barbary pirates a fully-outfitted warship as ransom for American hostages who would have been sold into slavery.

(In August 2016 the *Wall Street Journal* reported that President Barack Obama, on the same day Iran released four American hostages, secretly delivered to Tehran in an unmarked cargo airplane Euros and Swiss Francs worth $400 Million. Mr. Obama's press secretary denied that this was ransom. But if this arrangement was legal and ethical, why did the President go to such lengths to conceal it? Has he made other secret payoffs? He has raised the value (and risk) of each of us by $100 Million — for taxpayers.

As columnist Charles Krauthammer noted, it is illegal to conduct such a transaction with U.S. Dollars, hence the huge pallets of Euros and Swiss Francs. Some legal scholars call President Obama's transaction illegal regardless of currency. If a private company had done this, said Krauthammer, those involved could be criminally prosecuted for money-laundering. And as we have documented in past books, if an ordinary citizen were caught in possession of such a pile of cash, our government would have confiscated this money under civil asset-forfeiture laws.)

Thomas Jefferson was made of sterner stuff, as Fox News journalist Brian Kilmeade and Don Yaeger explain in their fine 2015 history *Thomas Jefferson and the Tripoli Pirates: The Forgotten War That Changed American History.* [8]

As America's third president, Jefferson sent U.S. Marines to destroy one center of this "scourge of the Mediterranean" who had declared it their duty to plunder, enslave or kill non-Muslims. Jefferson's successful attack echoes today in the Marines' Hymn lyric "to the shores of Tripoli," the pirate base only 404 miles west of today's Benghazi, Libya.

Jefferson tried to find an alternative to either war or surrender during his second term as President. His idea: economic embargo. Sadly, he was too far ahead of his time. The infant United States was not yet strong enough to have sufficient economic clout for this. Jefferson's embargo mostly crippled America's free market and harmed American merchants.

Today America's economic might is a much more powerful tool, as former U.S. Ambassador to India Robert Blackwill and co-author Jennifer Harris explore in their 2016 book *War by Other Means: Geoeconomics and Statecraft.* [9]

Texas and Mexico

Early in our history, Americans quested for opportunity more than for empire. As adventurous individuals, many responded to the advice of newspaper editor Horace Greeley, who wrote "Go West, young man."

As for our military, "Between 1816 and 1860 the American army numbered on average less than 20,000 men, little more than one tenth of 1 percent of the population," writes Harvard economic historian Niall Ferguson in his book *Colossus: The Price of America's Empire.* He notes that this was "a tiny ratio of military participation by European standards." [10]

This brought Americans, mostly from our Southern states, to settle in the Mexican region known as Texas. They brought slaves into Mexico, where slavery was illegal. They clashed with and defeated the Mexican government after a contingent of Americans — including Davy Crockett — were martyred at the Alamo.

These settlers declared Texas a country, and it soon won diplomatic recognition from Belgium and several other nations. Texas remained independent from 1836 until 1846, when it was made a state of the United States.

The U.S.-Mexican War that erupted in 1848 led to America's conquest of what had been Mexican lands all the way to the Pacific Ocean, and from these were carved the new U.S. states of California, Nevada, Arizona, Utah, New Mexico and parts of Colorado, Wyoming, Oklahoma and Kansas.

This war apparently had been planned with care by Democratic President James Polk of Tennessee, who made California a prime target of American territorial ambitions. It was seized almost the instant the war began.

Spain had long ruled Mexico, but in 1810 the people of Mexico were inspired by America's successful revolution to overthrow their imperial Spanish colonial rulers.

Californios

However, Mexico's revolution was not welcomed everywhere. The ruling class in California were not Mexicans. These Californios were Spaniards whose loyalty remained with Spain.

Before the Americans arrived, Mexico had three times sent military units into California to put down rebellions by its Spanish-speaking residents. The Mexican government had also confiscated the missions and their very large land holdings from the Roman Catholic Church.

(Abraham Lincoln would later return these California missions to the church…but not the huge landed estates previously owned by them.)

When famed "Pathfinder" John C. Fremont arrived at a pass near today's downtown Los Angeles, many of the Californio owners of ranchos greeted him as a liberator who had freed them from Mexico. Their enthusiasm may have been enhanced by his promise that the United States would honor their vast land grants from Spain.

Fremont would go on to become the first U.S. Senator from California and in 1856 he became the first presidential candidate of the newly-formed anti-slavery Republican Party.

In Northern California, a group of visiting Americans near what today is the wine country of Sonoma captured a few Mexican soldiers and declared themselves rulers of a new government, the Bear Flag Republic.

The banner they raised for this new republic is essentially the flag of the State of California today, complete with Grizzly Bear, although its red star has taken on new meaning in recent decades with monolithic Democratic Party rule over the state thanks to Mexican-American voters.

The Bear Flag Republic lasted for less than two weeks before its citizens turned their government over to the United States for annexation. This gave President Polk the option of saying that he had taken California not from Mexico but from revolutionaries who had already defeated and evicted Mexican rule.

By lucky coincidence, within months of America's conquest, gold was discovered in Northern California. It touched off a worldwide gold rush of 1849ers that brought instant prosperity to California and the nation.

The resulting flood of hundreds of thousands of new arrivals from the eastern United States and abroad destroyed any hope by Mexico of reconquering its lost Golden State — named by Spanish explorers for a mythical magical island of enchantment and talking animals.

Spain, of course, after eight centuries of Moorish Muslim rule reconquered its land in 1492 in what Spaniards call *La Reconquista.*

Today, in what some call the second *Reconquista*, Mexicans have been flooding into the United States.

A similar flood of immigrant settlers helped bring down the Roman Empire in the fifth century A.D. The British, French and other former imperial powers are now finding the chickens of their own past empires coming home to roost in floods of colonial immigrants.

Homegrown Colonies

The race between Northerners and Southerners to admit new states as either free or slave states would define the future of the United States. That race effectively came to an end with the admission of California to the union as a free state. The South had lost, making war or secession from the union practically inevitable.

The South had almost seceded in 1850. Had it done so, it might have won. The economies in Great Britain and France were dependent on Southern cotton for their factories. Both might have felt it necessary to enter the situation on the side of the South in order to maintain their supply of cotton.

Imagine secession in 1850 and a war in which we saw not Northern ships blockading Southern ports — but British and French warships blockading Northern ports and securing for the South all the weapons, gunpowder and other military supplies it needed.

Instead, the South agreed to the Compromise of 1850 to avoid either secession or war. The British Empire's strategic planners saw that war would still come, so they raced to plant the Nile Valley of Egypt and other lands under their control with long-staple cotton.

By the time war came in the United States, the British and French had developed alternative cotton supplies and no longer needed to side with the American South.

Slavery was a powerful issue dividing the South and North, but it was not the initial cause of the Civil War. Taxes were.

In 1860 the Southern slave states were paying 80 percent of federal taxes, mostly in the form of tariffs and imposts on their imports and exports. They were also required to ship their cotton on American flag vessels, most of which were owned in New England, New York, and elsewhere in the North.

Because of this quasi-monopoly on shipping, Southerners had no choice but to pay exorbitant shipping rates. Much of the profit from slavery, a monstrous way of producing goods, went into the pockets of Northerners who prided themselves on not owning slaves while they indirectly exploited the slaves' forced labor.

Imperial Patterns

One of the defining traits of an empire can be that it forces its colonies to do their shipping only in the empire's vessels. (Today we require something similar of Puerto Rico, thereby treating it like a colony.)

In the imperial pattern of European nations, the ruling country was in a temperate climate and the colony was often in a desert or tropical climate that limited its choices of crops or enterprises.

Under the old politics of mercantilism, which aims to create a profitable flow from colony to colonizer, the colony usually supplied cheap raw materials, usually crops, lumber or oil.

The imperial colonizer fabricated these materials into more expensive finished products such as machine-woven cloth and then sold them back to its colony at a handsome profit.

With its raw cotton, tobacco and sugar cane, the South was in the traditional position of a colony.

In the notorious slave triangle of centuries ago, the colony would produce sugar; the empire would process this into the alcoholic drink rum; and the rum would be traded in Africa for more slaves — Africans who had already been enslaved by other Africans, usually Muslim slave traders.

The South, in other words, had black slaves — but the North had enslaved the South by turning it into a *de facto* colony. The North, through its superior political position, had colonized the South.

The admission of California and other Western territories to the Union as free states meant that this political position of Northern colonial rule over the South would be permanent. And the massive tax burden caused by the flow of its earnings to Northern pockets would keep increasing the North's dominance.

The only way out of this for the South would be another American Revolution, a secession, or as we might say today, a "Confedexit."

The Southern states did not call themselves The Confederacy by accident. America for years had a different, states' rights-oriented government after the American Revolution, but prior to today's Constitution. That earlier, less-centralized government was called the Articles of Confederation. This is what the South was apparently trying to restore.

The Confederacy would lose its revolution in a bloody fight that cost both sides, combined, between 620,000 and 750,000 lives, because the North would not let its lucrative Southern colonies depart.

The British and French had found a relatively bloodless way to end slavery in their colonies. They effectively took ownership of slaves by eminent domain and a payment to owners, then emancipated their slaves.

Cinco de Mayo

Early in our Republic, President James Monroe set forth a doctrine devised by his mentors Thomas Jefferson and James Madison. This doctrine held that the nations of Latin America should be independent of any rule by Europeans.

This Monroe Doctrine laid the basis in our international relations for using American military and diplomatic power to deter and repel any European colonial activity in the Western Hemisphere. America said to Europe: "This is our hemisphere. Keep out."

One by one, the nations of Latin America rebelled against Spanish and, in the case of Brazil, Portuguese rule and won their independence. Several then fell into internal bickering, power struggles, corruption and the rule of home-grown military and strong-man rulers.

As the United States became enmeshed in our War Between the States, the French ruler Napoleon III decided that we were too distracted to deal with a European incursion into Mexico.

Louis Napoleon hastened to install a Habsburg imperial ruler of his liking, Maximilian and his wife Carlota as the Emperor and Empress of Mexico.

When America's Civil War ended, the American president had a simple message for Napoleon III. His French troops initially had difficulty suppressing poorly-armed, poorly-trained Mexicans who defeated the French in the Battle of Puebla on May 5, 1861 — the basis for the modern celebration Cinco de Mayo.

The famed Mexican historian Justo Sierra Mendes argued that Americans, too, should celebrate Cinco de Mayo. If the French had won that battle, he wrote, France was considering using its navy to aid the Confederacy, which might have tipped the outcome of America's Civil War to a different winner. [11]

Would Napoleon's legionnaires like to take on a few thousand battle-tested American troops armed with the most advanced weapons of that time?

If not, Your Excellency, you are in violation of America's Monroe Doctrine. Unless you wish to be at war with us, remove all French forces and your silly Emperor immediately from the country on our southern border.

France withdrew its forces, leaving the Emperor Maximilian to be shot by the Mexicans who he thought were happy to be ruled by him. He lives on, however, in Mexico's culture — in the distinctive Germanic Oom-pah sounds that set Mexican music apart from the rest of Latin America.

Greenbacks

"Oh, I don't give a damn about a greenback-a dollar…spend it fast as I can," sang musician-songwriter Hoyt Axton in his first hit song.

Most people think of "greenback" as slang for a dollar, and so it has become.

But greenbacks were in fact a special currency issued by the Union during the Civil War. Unlike the U.S. Dollar, the greenback was fiat money, paper unbacked by precious metal as the Constitution required.

This money printed out of thin air was a cheap way for a cash-short nation to pay for weapons and soldiers. The soldiers had to accept it, but ironically the government did not. It refused to accept its own greenbacks as payment for tariffs and certain other taxes.

Think about that — money so debased that the government that issued it refused to accept it as payment for taxes. Only years later did the government reimburse some greenbacks for a fraction of the gold value they would have had as U.S. Dollars.

Greenbacks, however, whetted an appetite among farmers and others, especially populists. What they wanted was a currency like greenbacks that had depreciating value. Why? Because it let people borrow money that would have had a fixed value if measured in gold.

Since the government kept printing more and more greenbacks, the borrowers could then acquire greenbacks and repay their loans with the cheaper currency.

If you could borrow $1,000 but, because of currency debasement, you only had to repay $500, would you?

Many borrowers were tempted to do this, even though it had become a legal but unethical way to cheat those who trusted them to repay debts with money of the same value.

The movement to make greenbacks our national currency — which in our time, in effect, has happened — fed into the populist movement to replace the gold standard with silver, a much cheaper and more available kind of money.

Farmers and other such borrowers generally hated the gold standard because it meant that dollars backed by gold held or even increased their value. Silver, just like greenbacks, allowed borrowers to repay their debt in money worth less than what they had borrowed.

This is why Democratic presidential candidate William Jennings Bryan gave his famous speech about not crucifying mankind upon a "cross of gold." It was an appeal to those who wanted to shortchange lenders.

War Wizards

As we have explained in an earlier book, L. Frank Baum's *The Wizard of Oz* story was almost certainly a metaphor for the struggle between gold advocates and silverites. In his original story Dorothy's slippers were not ruby, but silver. They travelled on the yellow brick road. And Oz, of course, is the abbreviation for ounce, as in an ounce of gold.

Our currency from the founding to 1913 had been as good as gold, and actually increased in purchasing power during those years. The dollar was a sound investment, like a golden bond that paid dividends, and this honest money made America prosperous and free.

It also helped that a Jeffersonian Democrat named Andrew Jackson had blocked the schemes of America's elite to establish a national central bank like those in England and Europe to control and manipulate our currency.

The Founders had seen the conjuring tricks — as Thomas Jefferson called them — that bankers could do with paper money and debt.

America's Revolution had to be fought with debt and paper money because our access to British Pounds had been cut off.

Our British foes, who knew how to fight like an empire in many ways, also crippled our Continental paper currency's value and acceptability by counterfeiting vast quantities of them. Things of no reliable value, it was said, were "not worth a Continental."

Our Framers therefore specified hard, honest money in our Constitution, and President Jackson helped protect our economy by preventing the machinations and money-corrupting ways of central bankers.

But these hard-won safeguards that protected our money and built our prosperity honestly were about to be changed by the coming of The Machine.

One turning point came with a young Progressive named Teddy Roosevelt. He would win fame as a media-promoted war hero on San Juan Hill in Cuba during a war with Spain that won the United States the colonies of the Philippines, Puerto Rico and Cuba.

The U.S. was a rising great power among the empires. So was Japan, and Roosevelt was the first president to win a Nobel Peace Prize after he helped negotiate the aftermath of a Japanese naval surprise attack that smashed the Imperial Russian fleet.

Chinese leader Dr. Sun Yat-sen's Denver-born American geostrategic advisor, Homer Lea, warned in his 1909 book *The Valor of Ignorance* that a major clash of empires was coming in the Pacific, and that it would begin with a Japanese attack on the American fleet at Pearl Harbor, Hawaii. Precisely such an attack happened 32 years later. [12]

Like most Progressives, Teddy Roosevelt loved wielding power. He asked Congress for funds to sail his shiny new Great White Fleet of 16 warships around the world in a global display of our growing military might.

"Congress did not think it was a good idea to send the fleet around the world, so they didn't appropriate the money to do it," recounted Secretary of the Navy Ray Mabus in 2009.

"Roosevelt assumed there was enough money to get about halfway. He said, I assumed Congress wants the fleet back, and I assume the money will be coming, as it was." [13]

Uncle Sam's Unusual Empire

While European nations watched our rising power and wealth with envy and fear, neither they nor we knew what a peculiar empire we would build.

"The United States hasn't annexed anyone's soil since the Spanish-American War," wrote famed historian Victor Davis Hanson.

"We do not send out proconsuls to preside over client states, which in turn impose taxes on coerced subjects to pay for the legions," Hanson continued.

"Instead, American bases are predicated on contractual obligations — costly to us and profitable to their hosts."

"We do not see any profits in Korea," writes Hanson, "but instead accept the risk of losing almost 40,000 of our youth [stationed there to deter Communist North Korea from attacking] to ensure that Kias can flood our shores and that shaggy students can protest outside our embassy in Seoul." [14]

During World War II and before, the United States established and retains *de facto* control over a variety of South Pacific islands such as American Samoa.

Travel to the Bahamas, a former British colony east of Florida, and chances are you will see — purely coincidentally — small U.S. Navy warships such as mine sweepers at anchor in its largest ports.

But although more powerful in sheer military might than any past empire, the United States is usually mild to the point of apology for all this might.

"The desire of a young Roman *quaestor* or the British Victorians was to go abroad, shine in battle, and come home laden with spoils. They wanted to be feared, not liked," writes Hanson.

Coca-Colonialization

And the British certainly intended that their empire would be profitable, even though trying to maintain the Raj in India drained them. Where others invested in companies, the British through its East India Company and other enterprises invested its treasure in modernizing and developing resources and infrastructure in its colonies.

Today, America's "bases dot the globe to keep the sea-lanes open, thugs and murderers under wraps, and terrorists away from European, Japanese, and American globalists who profit mightily by blanketing the world with everything from antibiotics and contact lenses to BMWs and Jennifer Lopez — in other words, to keep the world safe and prosperous...." even for America's Leftist critics and other envious foes, writes Hanson.

Britain's imperial heritage remains enormous. As noted earlier, as former colonies we speak English, the world language of business, science, diplomacy, and the Beatles.

In India the national legislature for decades after independence has carried on in English. In this huge, populous land with 14 diverse native tongues, English has been the only language all speak in common.

As Great Britain's English-speaking successor empire, America's ascent was made easier by Britain's established footprints. Two of our objectives were to have commercial and cultural success beyond our borders selling products from soda pop to Hollywood movies. Our success in doing this has been called America's "Coca-Colonialization" of other cultures. (It is coincidental that we are also the world's largest military arms seller.)

The United States simply seems to have little appetite for building an old-fashioned kind of empire. Although we have maintained bases in Germany,

Japan, and South Korea several decades after fighting wars there, America generally does not have the British Empire's appetite for expending generations of its families and huge investments in foreign lands.

"In the heyday of the European empires," writes Harvard's Niall Ferguson, "the dominant power was supposed to be a creditor, investing a large proportion of its own savings in the economic development of its colonies. Hegemony, in short, also meant hegemoney." [15]

Ferguson, a Scot, in his book *Colossus: The Price of America's Empire*, embraces the reality that the United States is already an empire. He urges us to fill the vacuum left by the waning of the British Empire, because the world needs the global security and economic stability that only an American Empire could bring.

Following World War II, as we have noted, the *Pax Americana* produced the longest period of relative peace in Europe since the *Pax Romana* under the Emperor Augustus 2,000 years ago. Neither the United Nations nor the rising imperial European Union likely could achieve the positive results Ferguson sees for an American Empire.

"Demilitarizing" the Military

The politicizing of American culture has taken some odd twists and turns. After World War II what President Dwight Eisenhower called the "Military-Industrial Complex" created a deep crony relationship between arms suppliers and Washington politicians in which fat campaign contributions led to fat military contracts, which led to yet more campaign contributions.

After the fall of the Berlin Wall and Soviet Union, and the fading of the global Cold War against Soviet Communism, liberal politicians turned to giant banks and other financial institutions and eased regulatory restrictions on them in exchange for huge campaign contributions and other goodies.

Today the Department of Defense receives less than 16 percent of the total federal budget.

One reason is that the Department of Defense is no longer the old war machine it used to be.

Instead, as Georgetown Law Professor and civilian advisor in the Pentagon Rosa Brooks explores in her 2016 book *How Everything Became War and the Military Became Everything: Tales from the Pentagon*, America's military has moved beyond fighting to kill people and break things. [16]

More than two millennia ago in China, its great military strategist Sun Tzu in his treatise *The Art of War* recognized that wars are won by using every facet of your own and an opponent's culture. Wars are won by knowing and exploiting a foe's weaknesses in every dimension.

Wars are won by what we now call propaganda, deception, attacks, methods used to break an enemy's will, and many other tactics and strategies. Sun Tzu's view of war is what today we might call holistic and all-pervading. War is to be fought using all means available.

Today's Pentagon would agree, especially in our time when terrorism and other factors have, in Brooks' words, blurred the line between "war and non-war."

Today's American military does more than talk about "winning hearts and minds," as we did in Vietnam. A significant portion of today's Pentagon is meals-on-wheels, road and other infrastructure building in foreign lands, responding to the Ebola virus in Liberia, reforming agriculture in Afghanistan, working against climate change, boosting the economies of other lands, and doing a thousand other things that have nothing to do with shooting or killing.

The Pentagon today has become "like a Super Walmart with everything under one roof," a retired general told Brooks.

"Like Walmart," Brooks writes, "the military can marshal vast resources and exploit economies of scale...." that provide "tempting one-stop-shopping" for thousands of things to assist foreign nations and other government departments.

If this seems vaguely familiar, this is because the ancient Roman legions spent most of their time not fighting but building aqueducts and roads so skillfully that some remain in use 2,000 years later.

Progressive lawmakers are often willing to fund a Pentagon that in some ways seems more like a social services and welfare agency than a fighting military.

With a significant portion of the Pentagon's budget now spent on non-war activities, the fighting edge of America's military may be losing a bit of its sharpness. President Obama reportedly has fired more than 100 of the military's most experienced and patriotic officers. A major news story in 2016 was how our forces in the Middle East had to cannibalize parts from some military aircraft to keep other aircraft flying.

"Militarizing" the Police

But while we "demilitarize" America's military, in recent years we have seen the militarization of local police departments. The Federal Government has been providing many with armored personnel carriers, military-style weapons, and other items used by our warriors overseas. [17]

Military weapons, say critics, may tempt local police to act more like soldiers than law enforcement officers whose job is to protect and serve. Some protestors have complained that this makes them feel like militarily-occupied people. But when protestors come armed with high-tech weapons, should the police be required to fight with inferior arms?

Less explicable is evidence from Senator Rand Paul (R.-Kentucky) and others that some surprising government agencies have created their own commando units armed like police SWAT (Special Weapons and Tactics) police squads. [18]

Thus we in recent years have discovered high tech military-like weapons and abundant ammunition in trained units of the Department of Education, NASA, the Food & Drug Administration, the U.S. Fish and Wildlife Services, the U.S. National Park Service, the Department of Agriculture, the Tennessee Valley Authority, the Railroad Retirement Board, and even the Consumer Product Safety Commission.

Why do such government agencies have their own mini-military commando units armed with automatic weapons?

It has been reported that the Clinton Administration purchased more than 65,000 Heckler & Koch MP-5 submachine guns. As small as an Uzi, these weapons are capable of firing 800 rounds of 9mm ammo per minute. When asked why such weapons were needed by the more than 10 percent of American law-enforcement people who are now Federal "police" — from armed Forest Rangers to IRS agents — a Clinton underling reportedly replied that such weapons were needed for "crowd control." [19]

Progressives such as Hillary Clinton and President Barack Obama are obsessed with taking firearms away from law-abiding Americans. Will they attempt to do so by enforcing the United Nations Small Arms Treaty as if it were superior to the U.S. Constitution's Second Amendment right to keep and bear arms?

Long ago in the 20th Century, both major political parties made it easy for Americans to acquire military surplus rifles and ammunition. Our government's priorities have changed drastically.

Too few realized that we were entering our current era in which power, money, immorality, and never-ending violations of the spirit of our Constitution's Framers have taken control of America.

At another crucial turning point in 1961, after being the five-star general who commanded the Allied Forces in World War II, then serving for eight years as President, in his Farewell Address Dwight David Eisenhower offered what for many seemed a surprising warning about what threatened America's future:

In the councils of government, we must guard against the acquisition of unwarranted influence, whether sought or unsought, by the military-industrial complex. The potential for the disastrous rise of misplaced power exists and will persist. [20]

"The national budget must be balanced.
The public debt must be reduced;
the arrogance of the authorities
must be moderated and controlled.

Payments to foreign governments
must be reduced.

If the nation doesn't want to go bankrupt,
people must again learn to work,
instead of living on public assistance."

– Cicero
Roman Senator, 55 B.C.

Part Two

The Machine

Chapter Three

Welcome to The Machine

"War is a racket....
It is the only one in which
the profits are reckoned in dollars
and the losses in lives."

– Smedley D. Butler
Major General, U.S. Marine Corps
Awarded two Medals of Honor [1]

In ancient Athens the playwright Euripides developed a gimmick that his theater-going audience loved. He wrote plays that brought his characters to a perilous situation, a cliffhanger with no escape possible. A giant crane then swung out over the stage and lowered a large basket with a new character standing inside.

This actor depicted one of Greece's pagan gods such as Zeus, who would wave a magic wand and resolve the story's cliffhanger problem by "divine" intervention. The hero could now escape, triumph, or be reunited with his true love, so the story ended happily.

This plot gimmick was called *Deus ex machina*, literally "God from the machine," and as a metaphor has been used by storytellers ever since Euripides to resolve stories by what appears to be an unexpected intervention.

Today a variant of this is used even by the President's economic advisors.

"Since the end of the second World War, economics professors…have been telling us that the economy is one big machine," says former Federal Reserve economist Arnold Kling, "that can be effectively regulated by economic experts and tuned by government agencies and the Federal Reserve Boards."

"It turns out they were wrong," says Kling in the descriptor of his 2016 book *Specialization and Trade: A Re-Introduction to Economics*. "Their equations do not hold up. Their policies have not produced the promised results. Their interpretations of economic events — as reported by the media — are often off-the-mark and unconvincing."

And yet these economists, usually followers of the late British economist John Maynard Keynes, continue to act and speak as if they had a miraculous *Deus ex machina* power to level out the downs of the business cycle, to stimulate growth by their mere pronouncements, and to hypnotize people with a "wealth effect" illusion that makes our stagnant economy appear prosperous so that investors go on investing and consumers keep on buying.

As Kling reminds us, the economy is a living thing influenced by the feelings of billions of people and variations in millions of factors. These are far beyond the simple-minded economy-as-machine metaphor calculations these economists use in making policy decisions….beginning with how much buyers and sellers think their money and credit are really worth.

The Money Machine

What is The Machine, and who gave birth to it?

In the 1912 Republican National Convention, Teddy Roosevelt's attempt to reclaim the presidency that he had handed over to friend William Howard Taft was rebuffed. Teddy's followers marched out, chanting "Thou Shalt Not Steal!"

The Grand Old Party's presidents won 50.6 percent of the vote — 27.4 percent for Roosevelt's new Progressive Bull Moose Party and 23.2 percent for the incumbent Taft — but this was split in two. Socialist candidate Eugene V. Debs won 6 percent. Progressive Democrat Woodrow Wilson became president with only 41.6 percent of the votes.

Thomas Jefferson had said that "great issues should never be forced on slender majorities." Wilson had nowhere near a popular vote majority mandate, yet in his first year in office signed huge changes into law.

In 1913 Wilson imposed a Progressive income tax. The Framers had made such a tax unconstitutional, as the Supreme Court upheld four times. So our founding document was amended to let government tax individuals at different tax rates. Politicians craved this because it allowed them to collect the majority of government revenue from a minority of voters.

Also in 1913, Wilson signed the repeal of how the Framers wanted senators to be elected — by the legislatures of their states so that in Washington they would represent their state's rights and interests. Since 1913, senators have been directly elected by voters, not state lawmakers.

In 1913 Wilson signed into law the Federal Reserve System, a quasi-public American Central Bank similar to those that controlled the currencies and interest rates in Europe. The Fed was heralded as a protector of the dollar's value.

In reality, as its charter says, the Fed was created to "furnish an elastic currency." It almost certainly was intended eventually to replace the solid gold-backed dollar that restricted how much the government could spend or grow. This set the stage for an ever-expanding Leviathan government, a money and power Machine that our Framers tried to prevent.

As World War I got underway, British propagandists were busy in American cities putting up posters depicting Germany's soldiers as atrocity-committing "Huns."

Although more than a quarter of European-Americans had German ancestry, and despite the fact that even the British royal family was German — Queen Victoria was the German Kaiser's grandmother — this British propaganda in a more trusting, less cynical age swayed American popular opinion to the British side.

In 1916 Wilson won re-election on the slogan "He kept us out of war." Six weeks after his inauguration, Wilson plunged the U.S. into World War I on the British side.

The Credit Card War

Many of the countries fighting in World War I assumed that they would win quickly, and that as victors they would then compel the defeated foe to reimburse the winners' costs, as we explored deeply in our 2010 book *Crashing the Dollar: How to Survive a Global Currency Collapse.*

"Scarcely an eighth of Germany's wartime expenses were covered by taxes," wrote Jens O. Parsson in *Dying of Money: Lessons of the Great German and American Inflations.* Instead, Germany "covered its deficits with war loans and issues of new paper Reichsmarks." [2]

In other words, Germany fought World War I by borrowing and then running its printing presses, as did most of the other combatants on both sides. This is tantamount to paying for a war with a credit card. It provided immediate currency and, writes Parsson, avoided the political risk that overburdened taxpayers might turn against the war.

The only reason Germany could risk printing millions of Reichsmarks was that "a day or two before World War I opened…Germany abandoned its gold standard," wrote Parsson, "and began to spend more than it had, run up debt, and expand its money supply."

Great Britain, France, Italy and the other combatants also found ways to avoid honoring their own gold standards, which prior to the war would have given their citizens the power to exchange their national currencies for a fixed amount of gold.

A gold standard thus constrains those in government from printing money that the government lacks sufficient gold to redeem.

As Europe's War Machines geared up and began grinding soldiers into red mud, the world was sending its gold to the United States — to buy reliable, still-gold-backed U.S. Dollars, or American weapons, or for safekeeping.

Five months after the United States entered the war in 1917, President Woodrow Wilson issued a proclamation requiring all who wished to export gold from the United States to obtain permission from the Secretary of the Treasury and the new Federal Reserve Board. Almost all such applications were turned down.

The Health of the State

"War is the health of the state," wrote American social philosopher Randolph Bourne, who died of the Spanish influenza that swept the world killing an estimated 50 million people around the planet during World War I. This plague killed more soldiers than did all the battlefield bullets and bombs.

What Bourne meant is that a government in wartime can throw off many legal constraints on its power. It can impose martial law, conscript labor and soldiers, silence critics, confiscate property, and set aside a gold standard designed to prevent politicians from printing as much unbacked money as they wish.

(The modern version of this is President Barack Obama's former Chief of Staff, and later Chicago Mayor, Rahm Emanuel's mode of governing: "Never let a serious crisis go to waste…it's an opportunity to do things you couldn't do before.")

The Old Europe, knit together by an inbred aristocracy, proved deficient. A widely-repeated saying among British soldiers was that they had been "lions led by jackasses."

Many of these officers thought nothing of ordering their men to charge across open landscape into machine gun fire. The Grim Reaper now had a Machine to mow men down not one by one in skilled individual combat, but by the hundreds of thousands like naked stalks of wheat being reaped by a mechanical harvester.

Machines had made the old ways of battlefield fighting not only obsolete, but also suicidal. In our time "The Machine" has also made it unsafe to depend on our government's fiat currency.

The gold standard for the most part had created prosperity and stability for decades prior to the Great War.

When all major currencies were pegged to gold, their value relative to one another was fixed and secure. And when wars had to be paid for with hard cash on the gun barrel, not credit or inflated fiat paper money, the gold standard was a powerful deterrent to war and global incentive for peace.

When today's liberals say they want a universal world currency and peace, these are what was lost when the World War I powers abandoned the gold standard so they could use credit cards to pay for war.

What Mark Twain had called the "Gilded Age" had in many ways been an uplifting era, despite the difficult cultural transition from a civilization where most worked on farms to one where most worked in cities and factories.

Making Others Pay

The Great War was devastatingly costly for Great Britain, France and the other Allies. But their politicians, as well as the families of those killed and maimed, at least had the consolation of being the winners.

These victors imposed a huge bill for reparations on the losers. As specified by the Treaty of Versailles, the Inter-Allied Reparations Commission in May 1921 decided that reparations owed by Germany were 132 Billion gold Reichsmarks, then equivalent to roughly $31.4 Billion 1921-valued U.S. Dollars.

"This was about four times Germany's maximum annual national product and greater than Germany's entire national wealth," wrote Parsson. "It was like asking the United States in 1973 to pay more than four trillion dollars in gold over a period of years."

One analysis found that paying off this staggering sum would have taken Germany until 1988, while another calculated that Germany would not have been free and clear of its reparations debt until year 2020.

(What actually happened was that reparations were suspended during the Great Depression and World War II, then payments resumed in 1959, and the reparations were officially paid off during a German reunification anniversary celebration on October 2, 2010.)

The victors at Versailles also stripped Germany of its extensive colonies and concessions in Africa and the Pacific. The colonies were neither offered nor granted independence; they were merely redistributed like the other booty among the victorious colonial powers.

Germany was required to surrender German-speaking Alsace and much of Lorraine to France as well, and, for a time, its coal-rich mines in the Saar.

Germany was required to pay reparations not only in money but also in millions of tons of coal and steel, foodstuffs, and even intellectual property such as the trademark for Aspirin.

Moral Devastation

As Germans saw matters, they had been forced into the war by Russia mobilizing a million troops on their ally Austria-Hungary's border. France, Russia's ally, then refused to promise not to attack Germany's back if Germany went to war with Russia.

By 1918, Germany had made a separate and advantageous peace with newly-Bolshevik Russia and had ended the war with France and Belgium while German troops were still on their soil.

Germans found it difficult to understand why their leaders had surrendered.

The massive reparations on Germany caused its Leftist Weimar Republic to return to the printing press for operating money. By 1923 this begat the famous hyperinflation that forced workers to take their pay — sometimes as a wheelbarrow full of almost-worthless paper — and rush to the grocery store because the currency was literally losing value by the hour. We have described this horror in *Crashing the Dollar*.

This hyperinflation benefited some people, especially profligate speculators who could pay off their debts with worthless money, and those who could snap up amazing bargains with solid currency like gold-backed dollars.

But the Weimar inflation devastated Germans who had believed in traditional values such as hard work and thrift. They saw their savings from a lifetime of work, held in German paper currency, vanish overnight.

The frustration and anger of these cheated Germans would soon lead to the second half of World War I, which we call World War II, a nightmare in which many millions paid a terrible price.

The Weimar hyperinflation caused many whose faith and morals had been shattered to follow an insane leader. As the old saying goes, when you lose your faith this does not mean you believe in nothing; it means you can be talked into believing anything.

Building a New World (Order)

Shortly after losing 405,399 of our fighting men and women in World War II, Americans found their nation plunging into a new conflict — this time a United Nations "police action" in Korea. This struggle would claim another 36,516 warrior lives because a newly-Communist China sent troops to support Communist North Korea.

America's top military commander during World War II was General Dwight Eisenhower, who was elected President in 1952. Eisenhower told China and the north that if the war did not end within weeks, the United States would use nuclear weapons. The war promptly ended, but with a partition that leaves Korea split into two parts to this day.

Eisenhower's strategic dilemma was that our former World War II ally, the Soviet Union, had not withdrawn more than one million Red Army troops from occupied Eastern European countries. Instead, the U.S.S.R. had turned these nations into exploited colonies in its expanding empire.

A permanent million-soldier army in Western Europe to deter Soviet invasion would be painfully expensive, Eisenhower knew.

Instead, he decided to deter aggression with nuclear weapons rather than tanks and troops. In Europe, Eisenhower's strategy of turning war into suicide for both sides succeeded.

Under the new North Atlantic Treaty Organization (NATO), we pledged that an attack on any member nation would be responded to like an attack on the United States itself. We posted hundreds of thousands of American troops across Western Europe as a "tripwire" that would ensure American response if the Soviets invaded.

Perhaps the only good thing about Soviet Communists was that they were atheists. They had no expectation of going to heaven when they died. This life was all they had, and most preferred to keep it.

Sledgehammer

An ancient Asian saying is that to the man with a hammer, everything looks like a nail.

Nuclear weapons may be a 10-megaton hammer, ideal for stopping a mass Soviet invasion across the plains of Europe.

But what if the enemy is a terrorist hidden in a crowd? What if the enemy is a handful of guerrilla fighters lurking in a tropical jungle? Using a thermonuclear weapon here would be like using a sledgehammer to kill a mosquito, an absurd example of overkill.

Soon the world was ablaze, and brushfire wars using guerrilla tactics seemed to be breaking out in many places at once, fires fanned by Communist propaganda and Soviet-supplied AK-47s.

This was the start of a five-decade-long confrontation we called the Cold War. We "won" this war, but was it what the ancient Greeks called a "Pyrrhic victory," one almost as costly and damaging as a defeat?

War became permanent, and grade school children were drilled in "duck and cover," getting under their desks and not looking at the flash if a nuclear weapon exploded nearby. Many families invested in backyard bomb shelters.

In our once-free nation, military conscription was routine and nearly universal. The government disrupted what could have been the peak of singer Elvis Presley's career, cut his long hair, and sent him off to serve in West Germany, another country partitioned between capitalist and communist worlds.

A devout patriot, Elvis like most other young American men served proudly and honorably. Few questioned the need for such service in a time of peace, or how the government's power to enslave people squared with the Framers' understanding of individual liberty. Few asked if our methods of fighting communists were destroying the ideals of America's Founders and making us a bit more like the communists.

The military draft was also unfair, said critics, because the poor were drafted to fight and die while middle-class kids became draft-exempt by staying in college. Many were eager to leave college and get a job, but doing so risked being in a rice paddy with leeches on your legs and bullets aimed at your head mere months after you left college.

As in most democratic republics in human history, Americans were willing to valiantly pay the price in blood and money of fighting one war, or even two wars, if our nation's vital interests or survival were at stake as during World War II.

But by the 1960s we seemed to be mired in perpetual war, in one war after another without time to heal or live a normal life. And this seemed to be turning America into something new, troubled, and increasingly unfree.

Conscription was how the old Great Powers like Great Britain got cheap cannon fodder for its wars of mass slaughter such as World War I. Surely, free human beings deserve more respect than this. Surely, each of us has a right to life and liberty greater than this.

Dominoes

When John F. Kennedy was elected president in 1960, approximately 52 cents — more than half — of every tax dollar was spent on national defense.

(Today, by contrast, two-thirds of every tax dollar goes for "transfer payments," moving the dollars government takes from your pocket into somebody else's pocket, with government of course taking a hefty cut of it for itself.)

Why had Kennedy committed the first 16,000 armed American troops into Vietnam after the French Empire lost its colonial grip on Indochina?

Was defeating Communism here really a vital interest of the United States? Would losing in Vietnam start a line of other nation-dominoes falling in Communism's direction, as politicians of both parties told us?

By the time it ended with our withdrawal, the Vietnam War had led to the deaths of another 58,209 heroic American soldiers. Helicopters and modern medicine kept alive many of the severely wounded who in earlier wars would have died.

Our consolation was that at least the North Vietnamese had won their own Pyrrhic victory.

The Communist leader Ho Chi Minh had studied Marxism while working in a restaurant in Paris, but, unlike the French, had also studied *The Art of War* by the ancient Chinese military strategist Sun Tzu. Ho defeated the United States, but at such enormous cost in blood and treasure that no other Leftist nation would be eager to pay the price the Communist Vietnamese paid.

Feeding The Machine

When analysts studied this protracted war, they discovered many things. One of the most powerful questions they asked was: Why, despite the cost and sophistication of our military, had America's overwhelming power not given us victory in a Third World country like Vietnam?

They could have found this answer by privately asking almost any honest lawmaker or staffer in Congress. The answer is that America's military is a politicized machine designed to serve far more than military needs.

Everyone has heard of the $600 hammer in the budget for one weapon system. But have you heard about the coffee maker?

In budgeting for a new strategic bomber, the U.S. Air Force specified that the aircraft include a custom-made coffee maker built so it could "survive an 8-G [eight times the force of gravity] crash" of the aircraft.

The taxpayer cost of a coffee maker built to these incredibly high standards? $7,622.00.

But surely, you could hear Congress members of both parties say, "our combat pilots deserve to have hot coffee after such a crash."

In fact, an 8-G crash would almost certainly kill everyone on board. The coffee maker might still work, but no living human would be left to wake up and smell the coffee.

Those who condemn such "wasteful" spending on the $600 hammer that could be bought at Walmart for $5, or the simple coffee maker available there for $10, do not understand what The Machine is really for.

What needs to be kept in mind is that America long ago ceased being a free enterprise, free market economy.

Helicopter Money

Our economy since at least the end of World War II has run on government stimulus and the conjuring of paper fiat money out of thin air.

Former Federal Reserve Chairman Ben Bernanke has said that America's economy can be stimulated just by flying a helicopter over a city and tossing out a sizeable quantity of money.

From the point of view of our economic policy makers, building a new $50 Million military aircraft, and equipping it with a $600 hammer and $7,622 custom coffee maker produces exactly the same kind of stimulus spending as throwing money out of a helicopter.

Even better, the congressional authorization for this new aircraft will specify where each nut and bolt and every other part for this aircraft will come from. Would it surprise you to learn that these subcontracts will go to companies in the states of every key senator and the districts of every House member whose vote is needed to pass this authorization?

In this money-redistributing Machine, weapon system makers donate to lawmakers or to the President's party to get contracts. The money from those contracts is spent creating jobs. For a few in key congressional districts, pork gets redistributed to help the member of Congress win re-election. A juicy slice of company profits then gets kicked back to the incumbent Congress member in campaign contributions and other goodies.

The lawmaker is also ensured against the risks of losing by knowing that a plush job awaits him or her either as a Washington lobbyist or in the defense industry after leaving Congress. So the money and contracts go round and round in a revolving door of greed in both coins of our realm, money and power, paid for mostly by taxpayers in other parts of the country.

In the Military-Industrial Complex, a weapon is not just — indeed, not even primarily — a weapon. It is a stimulus spending program designed to spread the wealth and create jobs in many key parts of the United States. Cutting the cost of such weapon systems merely slows down The Machine's ability to redistribute wealth.

Military spending has many advantages. If a company makes and sells a customer a new lamp or hammer, it may be decades before that customer needs a new one.

But military things, from munitions to jet fighters, need frequent replacement, retrofitting, and upkeep. Ammunition is shot and gone. Aircraft crash or require replacement parts. And most of all, because the contest among nations is a win-or-lose, life-or-death "arms race," nations ignore the next generation of weapons technology at their peril.

Those lawmakers who are reluctant to upgrade America's military with the latest weapons might be viewed as lacking in patriotism.

The Welfare-Warfare State

This is the side of ever-bigger government spending known as the Warfare State.

Flip it over and you will discover the arguments for big government spending on other things — free healthcare, free college education, free food, and so forth — that the politicians promise will always be paid for by somebody else, not you.

Object to any of this and you will be called heartless, uncaring, and insensitive.

The rationale for this flavor of ever-bigger government spending is the "Welfare State."

Military spending has the advantage of being one of the few truly legitimate things government does, according to Article I Section 8 of the U.S. Constitution, the enumerated powers clause. Most of what our government does today, according to this clause, is unauthorized.

The Constitution lets government provide for the "general welfare," for example, but as James Madison clarified at the time, the "general welfare" is to make things we all use together, like a new road, not that give goodies to some of us.

Which reminds us, when Dwight David Eisenhower was President, he built the entire Interstate Highway System for only about 60 percent (in inflation-adjusted dollars) of the $844 Billion President Obama has spent on infrastructure — on "shovel-ready" jobs that he later admitted "turned out not to be so shovel-ready." Approximately one-quarter of the miles the average American drives each year are on Eisenhower's Interstate Highways. Since his time, our politicians have become much more skilled at spreading and squandering the earnings our people have had taken from them and their families in taxes.

With War in Mind

Eisenhower won quick congressional approval for the Interstate Highway System not only because it could be larded with pork for lawmakers to show being spent at home, but also because the roads were designated not just for leisure or commerce; they were also largely designed for national defense. Had the Japanese attacked and occupied parts of the West Coast in 1941, the argument went, we had so few intercontinental roads that it might have been difficult to evict them. Its official name is "The Dwight D. Eisenhower National System of Interstate and Defense Highways."

In 1958, when the education lobby wanted massive new federal spending during Eisenhower's administration, their legislation was craftily named "The National Defense Education Act" and justified its slice of the budget as helping America win the Cold War against communism.

Successful military societies train young minds to think and play in military terms, from ancient Sparta to today. As the British like to say, Napoleon's defeat at Waterloo was won on the playing fields of Eaton, their most famous aristocratic school.

American football, as comic George Carlin reminded us, is a war-like game played in stadiums modeled on the ancient Roman Colosseum in which the most exciting play is to throw "the bomb." Gentler baseball used to be pre-Imperial America's game, but today our national game is football.

Our great challenges are usually metaphorically framed as wars — the war on cancer, drugs, crime, smoking, women, Christmas, terrorism, and so forth.

When trying to move money from the warfare state to the welfare state, President Lyndon Baines Johnson cunningly named his effort the "War on Poverty."

President Johnson really did not have sufficient funds for either the Vietnam War or a giant expansion of Franklin D. Roosevelt's New Deal. Funding both with printed dollars, he soon had to halt honoring "Silver Certificates" by ending their convertibility to silver.

By 1971 Richard Nixon likewise ended the dollar's convertibility to gold for European central bankers who had been the anchor of the Bretton-Woods global currency system agreed to after World War II. Under it, the dollar was to be pegged and convertible by central banks to gold, and other currencies were to peg their value to the dollar, to stabilize the currency values of the Western powers.

Bretton Woods also created the International Monetary Fund (IMF), usually to be run by a European, and the World Bank, usually run by an American, in this new global monetary order.

After Nixon cut off the dollar's gold anchor, our currency soon lost a third of its value. The Nixon Administration negotiated an agreement with Saudi

Arabia that the Muslim nation would sell its oil only in exchange for U.S. Dollars. This shored up the dollar's status as the global reserve currency, a tremendous boon to us because we manufacture U.S. Dollars.

Thus was born the "Petrodollar." This caused a steady flow of Saudi students into American universities and of Saudi donations that have altered American politics and caused our government to bend and bow increasingly toward Mecca and Riyadh.

Wag the Dog

But in exchange for this, we apparently made a deal to defend Saudi Arabia, the home of Mecca, Muslim orthodoxy, and funding for Madrassas, Muslim schools throughout the world that teach of the coming world conquest by Islam by fire and sword. Will this prove to be the worst of those "entangling alliances" that our Framers warned against?

President Bill Clinton plunged America and NATO into a war in Kosovo fighting on the Muslim side against Christian Serbs. As usual this war would be bolstered by accusations of atrocities. But as our troops fought alongside Sunni Jihadists from the Muslim world, Americans wondered if our Saudi allies had requested this fight. Or were American pilots risking their lives because of Clinton Muslim oil state campaign contributions?

Clinton showed up on the Hollywood set of a movie titled *Wag the Dog* (from the saying that it is the tail that wags the dog, not the other way around). In the film, a fictional U.S. President needs a phony war in Albania — next to Kosovo — to help himself politically by distracting voters from a sex scandal weeks before an election. When the propagandist says he will tell the media how successful his fake war has been, the President has him killed. When Clinton on the movie set asked the filmmakers what this film was about, they could not bring themselves to say. *Wag the Dog*, you see, was about *him*.

The Peace Dividend

After President Ronald Wilson Reagan's and George H.W. Bush's triumph in the Cold War and the cave-in of the Soviet Union, massive defense spending was becoming harder to justify.

Bill and Hillary Clinton seized the "peace dividend" from America's triumph and gutted our defense budget by up to $125 Billion per year. Instead of massively cutting taxes for hard-pressed taxpayers, they diverted this money to political cronies and social spending.

Cashing in this "peace dividend" produced the so-called "Clinton prosperity" of the late 1990s, but we would pay a terrible price for the damage these cuts caused in our military and security capabilities when 9-11 happened. Most of the terrorists attacking us that day were Saudis.

The Clintons also cranked up President Jimmy Carter's Community Reinvestment Act, through which ideologues in the government could pressure banks to give mortgages to millions of high-risk borrowers.

The fallout from this partisan political squeeze of regulatory threats on banks would lead to the economic devastation in 2008 from which we have yet to recover.

The Machine is also a bubble machine, and this vast flow of easy money malinvestment into a housing bubble burst, destroying nearly 40 percent of the net worth that millions had invested in homes. Saving through owning an ever-appreciating home was the post-World War II American Dream.

The Clintons blew up that dream, leaving the Baby Boomer generation's Millennial children afraid and unable to buy a decent home and start a family. The Clintons created ten lost years or more of what should have been American economic growth — if only the government had kept its partisan paws out of what should have been the free marketplace.

A New Dark Age

As we noted in our book *The Great Debasement*, in 1932 a reporter asked the British economist John Maynard Keynes if there had ever been anything like the Great Depression.

"Yes," replied Keynes. "It was called the Dark Ages and it lasted 400 years." As monetary journalist Ralph Benko noted in recalling Keynes' remark, we are already living in a kind of Little Dark Age. "America is entering its fifth decade of punk (less than 3% average annual GDP) growth and second decade of pure stagnancy — growth arguably averaging under 2%," wrote

Benko. "Less than 3% is bad, but less than 2% is slower than population growth. That implies a severe absence of opportunity to flourish: a 'Little Dark Age.' "

During the Second Quarter of 2016, the U.S. economy was growing at an adjusted 0.8 percent annually — less than the official, and far less than the real, rate of inflation. This is yet more evidence that the recession begun in 2008 is still here.

The late longshoreman philosopher and author Eric Hoffer once observed that if you ask a Leftist or Progressive intellectual what time in history he would like to live in, the answer you will most often get is the Middle Ages. One of us once posed Hoffer's question to the famed Marxist psychoanalyst Erich Fromm, and got exactly the response Hoffer predicted. Fromm would have chosen to live in Medieval times.

Why do Progressives love this pre-Renaissance, pre-Enlightenment age? Because, said Hoffer, this was the last time in Western history that intellectuals (in this case, theologians) were routinely part of the elite that ruled the state.

Perhaps Progressives subconsciously yearn to create a new Dark Age because this is what societies become when ruled by intellectuals. It is their natural environment. Progressives have already moved the world toward a Dark Age by undermining the Enlightenment philosophies of free enterprise, free speech and free thought that were embodied in the American Revolution.

Serfdom and Socialism

When Americans vacation in Europe, many think of themselves as transplanted Europeans. This is in one crucial way mistaken.

Europe's history is very different from ours. As Leftist scholars sadly acknowledge, the United States was "born bourgeois." America's heritage comes directly from the values of the European Enlightenment with its ideals of individualism, private property and free market economics.

America came into the world already immunized against the earlier collectivist ideas that ruled Europe prior to the Enlightenment…old ideas and values that continue to infect and poison European thinking today.

After the fall of the western half of the Roman Empire, the Eastern Empire, better known as the Byzantine Empire, would survive until 1453 A.D., less than 50 years before Columbus landed in the New World. Meanwhile, Western Europe in the early 400s A.D. fell into centuries of violence and chaos.

The horror, said historian Lord Kenneth Clark, was comparable to being repeatedly raided, robbed and killed by motorcycle gangs. The response to this was feudalism, a social contract in which the lords of castles offered protection to peasant farmers and craftspeople in exchange for their vow to give the lord each year roughly one-tenth of their crops or products.

These peasants thus became serfs under a Duke or other aristocratic ruler of a castle, and this social system of mutual vowed obligations was feudalism. The ruler of the castle had strong walls, knights in armor, and stored food to withstand sieges by marauding bands of Vandals and other invading tribes.

Feudalism, today's Leftist historians argue, deeply imprinted Europeans with the idea that the ruler had a duty to care for his serfs, to protect and in hard times to feed them. This was *noblesse oblige*, the obligation of the noble rulers to provide for their serfs.

"Feudalism was the historical template on which a communitarian ethos was built" in Europe, scholar Morris Berman writes in his book *Dark Ages America: The Final Phase of Empire*. This "communitarian ethos," a primitive form of socialism or communism, has never left European culture. Indeed, many of the towns that grew up around feudal castles are still called communes. [3]

Europeans came here seeking the Enlightenment ideals of freedom, opportunity, and individualism. In America, former serfs could acquire property and wealth, not be trapped for life in feudalism's peasant class.

License to Steal

To understand just how different the European mind and values are from our own, consider this: Feeling hungry? In one European country, this now entitles you to steal food from the local supermarket.

An Italian court on May 2, 2016 set a dangerous precedent by ruling that a person's "need" in the form of "hunger" gives him or her the right to steal the property of others.

Western civilization was built on property rights, but these and other rights are rapidly being destroyed by court rulings, government regulations, executive orders, political social engineering, Nanny statism, and the deliberate debasement of our money. Get ready for this Italian legal ruling to be echoed soon by American courts.

Americans have food in abundance, and more than 25 percent of our total population is obese — 20 percent or more above a healthy body weight. But, ironically, millions of the heaviest among us feel not only hunger but also starvation. By the Italian court's new standard, they too could steal supermarket food.

This paradox exists, many scientists say, because today's fat and sugar-laden foods stimulate the appetite and cause us to gain weight. Overweight then prompts us to diet. But as new scientific research confirms, our bodies seem to perceive dieting as famine and weight loss as starvation.

The *New York Times* reported in 2016 that dieting spurs our bodies to unleash many hormones that stoke our food cravings and binge eating so we regain and surpass our previous peak weight. This drives a vicious cycle of more dieting and even more weight gain. The latest research suggests that this is why only about one percent of dieters achieve permanent weight loss.

On May 2, Italy's Supreme Court of Cassation overturned a lower court theft conviction of Roman Ostriakov for stealing cheese and sausages worth approximately $4.50 from a supermarket.

"[H]e took possession of that small amount of food in the face of an immediate and essential need for nourishment, acting therefore in a state of necessity," the court ruled. Theft, in other words, is "not a crime" if the thief says he is "hungry."

But in Italy, food could almost certainly be had for the asking at the church or charity down the street, or from the supermarket itself if Mr. Ostriakov requested it. He could have gotten free food without stealing.

Italy is a Euro-socialist welfare state whose government would likely have been delighted to feed him. But this court's Progressive judges may have found it delicious to implicitly remind their countrymen that Karl Marx advocated taking "from each according to his ability" and giving "to each according to his need."

The founder of the Soviet Union, Vladimir Lenin, however, shared the Bible's view that those who do not work should not eat. Without such a rule, everyone would be happy to devour the food in a socialist state, but few might work to produce more. Mr. Ostriakov could have offered to wash dishes at a local restaurant in exchange for a meal.

In South America's Incan empire, people were assigned to a group of 10 workers under a manager, who would be one of 10 managers under a higher manager — an authoritarian hierarchy that extended to the Inca himself.

As historian Victor Von Hagen explains, if a worker stole a loaf of bread in Incan society he would be put to death — *unless* he could show that he stole out of "need," in which case the manager above him would be executed for failing to provide the worker with sufficient food.

If one person's subjective "need" gives him a right to steal the property of others, how long will it be before some future court uses a similar logic to rule that a sex-starved man is entitled to force himself upon women? Or that those hungry for power be allowed to enslave others? Or that a "needy" egomaniac denied his 15 minutes of fame has the right to shut down city streets to make himself a media celebrity?

We suspect that we are seeing deeper hungers here. Hungry for power, Progressive judges here and abroad are overturning thousands of years of tradition to engineer new rules they wish to see imposed in Western societies.

When humans unconsciously sense disaster approaching, one stress response is to put on weight. We, after all, are descended from the winners who survived ice age winters, food shortages and famines when thinner people around them died from not packing on enough calories stored in their bodies as fat.

A Warning Sign?

An unexpected, growing European-American death rate has coincided with the spreading epidemic of obesity. Up to 38 percent of Americans of several ethnicities are now overweight by at least 20 percent, the definition of obesity. This overweight is a source of physical stress, which can lead to heart attacks and many other ills, including diabetes.

Experts have speculated why this obesity epidemic is happening. Is it caused by those Low Fat foods made with more sugar? By high-fructose corn syrup? By a sedentary couch potato or computer-addicted lifestyle? By our meat that contains antibiotics and hormones used to fatten livestock? By our increasing use of food as a drug, especially "comfort food" rich in fat and sugar that elicit soothing brain neurotransmitter chemicals, endorphins? By diets that cut calories, make the body feel it is starving, and activate our body's lifelong programming to store every available calorie as fat?

Psychologists know that one of our deepest subconscious fears is scarcity, running out of food. For thousands of years people coped with impending shortages by eating more. Americans today idealize being thin, but in the ancient world where crop failures and famine were always possible, being a bit fat was considered more attractive than having "a lean and hungry look."

We still have our ancient survival instincts. What if today's widespread obesity is happening because millions of us unconsciously sense that a disaster *is* coming, that the welfare state has brought not security but the opposite, danger of an enormous social and economic breakdown? Today's obesity may be our body's unconscious way of storing food for a fast-approaching time of disaster and scarcity.

Some are preparing a survival shelter with their teeth, feeling an urge to put on weight without knowing why. Many are getting ready for the breakdown so many of us sense coming by filling a home stockpile with preserved food before the "hungry" strip supermarket shelves bare. The prudent are also exchanging a portion of the politician paper promissory notes we call dollars for the hard, real survival money of gold.

Millions of us feel hungry, even if we weigh hundreds of pounds. This might be from chronic dieting — or might be nature's way of telling us that something is very wrong.

Perhaps our deeper hunger is for security against an approaching social breakdown caused by government giving others a license to steal while taking away our fundamental rights to life, liberty, property, self-defense, and honest money.

A 2015 study by Oxford University researchers Ben Fell and Miles Hewstone lays out evidence that economic stress and scarcity can impact even the genetics of those affected by altering epigenetically how their DNA expresses itself, causing a variety of ills including elevated levels of damaging stress hormone and accelerated aging.

Importing a Proletariat

One reason that Marxism never gained wide support here is that we never had a proletariat, a class of workers without hope of advancement who could therefore be used in class warfare against the rich.

American immigrants did not hate the rich; they came hoping to become rich, too. And here, unlike Europe, they had the social mobility that made such dreams plausible.

In America you could succeed; your children would do better than you did; and anyone's child had a chance to become President. We were the definitive bourgeois nation.

"No feudalism, no socialism," is how University of Texas Austin Professor of History Emeritus Walter Dean Burnham crystallized this analysis. [4]

Because the seeds of feudalism never infected the soil of America with collectivist values, the seeds of socialism have found it difficult to take root in the United States — at least until now.

But after more than a century of socially re-engineering American values with The Machine — built largely with European and socialist blueprints — the Left here has begun to colonize young American minds.

By prying open our gates to uncontrolled immigration, Leftist Progressives have also been able to import from Latin America and elsewhere the kinds of class warfare proletarians they have never been able to grow in American soil. A similar invasion of foreign tribes led to the fall of ancient Rome and the grim 400 years of the Dark Ages that followed.

Seeing that this was starting to happen, the Nobel Laureate economist Friedrich Hayek titled his warning book *The Road to Serfdom*. A giant paternalistic nanny state has infantilized a large share of America's people, making them willing to trade America's Declaration of Independence for the security of dependency on government.

Growing social violence, division, and terrorism make them willing to exchange their freedom and self-reliance for the security of Big Government's castle.

Americans are literally, for the first time, being turned into medieval serfs, permanently subservient to the lords of Big Government.

Chained

At its height the Roman Empire was already a welfare state that offered more than a million dwellers in its capital city "bread and circuses," daily distracting entertainment in the Colosseum and elsewhere.

Rome also offered free food, a guaranteed amount of raw grain — roughly 30 pounds per month — to any legal resident who brought a container to the government welfare office and asked for it. The political stability of Rome depended on guaranteeing people their bread and circuses.

While the Roman Empire could squeeze such goodies out of foreign colonies to buy calm at home, things were good. Few riots. Even those who bothered to work could take off up to 147 holidays each year.

An ancient Roman could even buy pizza, not made with tomato sauce —
no European had yet been to Peru in South America where tomatoes come
from — but with an aged, flavored fish sauce called *garum*.

However, as the overextended empire contracted, the money was debased,
wage and price controls were imposed, and the grain for Rome's bread was
becoming hard to get in adequate amounts. The Emperor issued a decree.
All those working on the farms of the giant estates owned by the rich were
now required to stay there. It became a crime to leave. The serfs there were
suddenly, in effect, chained to their plows and were now permanent serfs
for life so the Emperor could continue to dispense free grain in Rome to
keep the mob fed. This is what happens, to paraphrase former British Prime
Minister Margaret Thatcher, when a socialist welfare state "runs out of other
people's money."

This is why, with food running out, the socialist dictatorship of Venezuela
in August 2016 issued a decree that all citizens could now be conscripted to
work for up to two months at a time without pay on farms growing food for
the government.

As Thomas Jefferson said, "Were we directed from Washington when to
sow, and when to reap, we should soon want bread." [5]

Government, by the very nature of the quality of people attracted to politics,
is the least competent of all institutions at doing things efficiently.

Keynesians

For most of a century the government has been exerting increasingly
more control over one sector of America's economy after another through
mandates, regulations, taxes, manipulation of our money's supply and
quality, and direct command. Politicians have justified these actions by
claiming superior wisdom, efficiency, the need to distribute wealth more
fairly, and a hundred other pretexts.

We, of course, are not a primitive survival economy as in feudal times. We
need to innovate and grow to drive prosperity forward and create enough
surplus to benefit all.

So is government control growing our economy? On the contrary, America's economic engine has been slowing for decades and now generates almost no growth whatsoever.

One reason for this, writes Manhattan Institute fellow James Piereson in his 2015 book *Shattered Consensus: The Rise and Decline of America's Postwar Political Order*, is that the political and monetary agreements we persuaded the advanced world to join at the end of World War II — America's benign "Empire" — have been unraveling.

Like history's Dark Ages, today's stagnant Progressive economy has its own plague, its own New Black Death, wrote *Forbes* Magazine columnist Louis Woodhill. This "plague is the result of Keynesianism," whose ideas have pushed Europe to the brink of economic collapse, and if Progressives get their way could do likewise here.

"In the 1300s, the Black Death killed about a third of Europe's population," wrote Woodhill. "If its spread is not checked, Keynesianism may wipe out a third of Europe's GDP (Gross Domestic Product)."

To be fair to Lord Keynes, he proposed that government stimulus be used occasionally, not constantly as America's presidents do today. Keynes proposed occasional injections of easy money into a down economy as a brief economic pain reliever. Today's politicians and central bankers have turned such stimulus into a full-time addictive drug that utterly distorts free markets and makes them unable to heal themselves.

The Quiet Coup

The Federal Reserve's Money Machine in 2008 and 2009 ran the printing presses and flooded a marketplace near collapse with trillions in liquidity. We now know it was also making or facilitating more than $20 Trillion in loans to keep foreign banks solvent.

The politicians had long used the War Machine and military spending to stimulate the American economy and line their own pockets with lavish campaign contributions, high-paying jobs, and speaking gigs from military contractors.

But by the 1980s another player was starting to rival the Warfare State as a source of political contributions and other money-making opportunities.

This new version, the Banking and Financial Machine, is why we proudly say that America has "the best government money can buy."

By 2009, a former chief economist at the International Monetary Fund, Simon Johnson, could write that "the finance industry has effectively captured our government" in what he called the "quiet *coup*" *d'etat*. [6]

In the 2008 crash a year earlier, the American government and Fed rushed to offer huge bailouts to our shaky banks, not the little mom and pop businesses and homeowners whose lives and savings were devastated.

Many of the giant banks, it turned out, apparently engaged in borderline-illegal—and certainly high-risk — behavior unbecoming America's old-fashioned image of sober, ethical bankers.

That image had come, in part, because of 1933 Depression-era regulations, known as Glass-Steagall, that separated commercial and investment banking. Under the Clinton Administration, which was eager to get huge campaign donations from the giant banks, this law had been modified and greatly weakened by the Gramm-Leach-Bliley Act of 1999.

Big political contributions, wrote Johnson, purchased "a river of deregulatory policies" that washed away old legal limits on moving capital internationally, on credit-default swaps, on how much leverage investment banks could use — and even allowed banks, not regulators, to measure their own riskiness. With the Glass-Steagall regulatory chains largely removed, some of the biggest banks began to act like casinos. After all, their new political connections gave certain banks the best of both possible worlds.

If big bankers made speculative investments and won, they could pocket the winnings. If they lost, on the other hand, because they were "too big to fail" the government would bail them out with taxpayer money.

So why follow the old standard of maintaining a balance between risk and prudence? Just throw the dice, which the banks' huge political contributions have loaded to let them win most of the time.

Under the emerging "bail-in" regulations, the government can now use both investor and depositor money to cover a bad bank's debts in a crisis, as we analyzed in detail in our book *Don't Bank On It! The Unsafe World of 21st Century Banking.*

As the 2008 crisis showed, the banks literally had a "heads I win, tails you lose" deal. Since then, the Obama Administration has found it useful not to seek criminal charges against most bankers — but to declare that they are "not too big to jail" and to use that threatening club to get bankers' approval to pay more than $200 Billion in a wide array of fines, penalties and purported reimbursements.

This has provided the Obama Administration with funds it has "spent" without congressional approval. A significant portion of some bank penalties has gone directly to left-wing community organizers and radical activists.

And speaking of money and morals, does anyone think it surprising that the potential next president, Hillary Clinton, was paid $675,000 by the banking giant Goldman Sachs to give three short speeches? Or that she refuses to release the three transcripts of what she said to them in exchange for all that money? Or that the Clintons pocketed more than $20 Million from this one industry? Or that so many politically-appointed Treasury Secretaries and Fed officials are Goldman Sachs alumni, as are Mark Carney, Governor of the Bank of England, and Mario Draghi, head of the European Central Bank? Are they manipulating the value of currency solely for our benefit — or also to further enrich Goldman Sachs and the "Deep State"?

The military side of The Machine continues to receive enormous government contracts and makes large political contributions. In early 2016 military contractors were among Hillary Clinton's biggest donors.

However, according to veteran IMF economist Simon Johnson, in the cozy relationship with the Federal Government and politicians, the financial industry is now on top in our "Deep State" ruling oligarchy we call The Machine. How much better things would be if too-big-to-fail banks were allowed to fail and were forced to find their way in a healthy free market!

Our dollar has no secure anchor or steady worth. It does not reliably serve as a unit of account, medium of exchange, or store of value. In truth, the dollar arguably is therefore not even really money.

In 1912, just before Woodrow Wilson started the deliberate long debasing slide that has cost the dollar 98 percent of its purchasing power, the financier J.P. Morgan explained to Congress what is the bottom line reality of economics, as true today as it was more than a century ago:

"Gold is money," said Morgan. "Everything else is credit."

The word "credit" comes from the Latin word *credo*, "belief." Paper money is "faith-based" currency; if, as always eventually happens, people cease to believe in its value because politicians go on conjuring more and more of it out of thin air, it collapses.

How much better it would be if we had separation of money and state so that, as Friedrich Hayek proposed, we all had the right to trade freely using whatever currency we wished, including the most ancient and universally accepted money, gold.

Until we are able to Dexit, to secede or exit from the U.S. Dollar — the only currency the government accepts as payment for its taxes — and affirm our God-given right to make currencies compete for our support, we should probably start calling The Machine that rules us the Financial-Military-Industrial Complex.

"Instead of funding issues of paper
on the hypothecation of specific taxes...
we are trusting to tricks of jugglers on the
cards, to the illusions of banking schemes
for the resources of the war [of 1812],
and for the cure of colic to
inflations of more wind."

– Thomas Jefferson
1814 Letter to M. Correa de Serra

*"This [Federal Reserve Act of 1913] establishes
the most gigantic trust on earth.*

*When the President signs this bill, The Invisible Government
by the Monetary Power will be legalized.*

*The People may not know it immediately, but
the day of reckoning is only a few years removed.
The trusts will soon realize that they have gone
too far even for their own good.*

*The People must make a declaration of independence
to relieve themselves from the Monetary Power.*

*This they will be able to do by taking control
of Congress. Wall Streeters could not cheat us if you Senators
and Representatives did not make a humbug of Congress....
The greatest crime of Congress is its currency system.*

*The worst legislative crime of the ages is
perpetrated by this banking bill.*

*The caucus and the party bosses have again
operated and prevented the People from getting the
benefit of their own government."*

– Rep. Charles A. Lindbergh, Sr.
December 22, 1913
Speech to Congress

Chapter Four

The Money Changers

*"Your kids will not know
what money is."*

– Tim Cook
Apple Computer CEO, 2015 [1]

Like character and reputation in an individual, its currency is the mirror in which a nation reveals and sees itself, its character and integrity.

What does it tell us, therefore, that America is planning to go cashless, to do away with the kinds of coins or bills that people have carried in their pockets for thousands of years?

How revealing it also is that on the cliff edge of this leap into cashlessness, our government is suddenly making all sorts of superficial changes in how our money looks.

Perhaps as with stamps, the aim here is to turn soon-to-be-gone new currency into collectors' items that will have a special value of their own.

The Euro has done this in much of Europe. In 2012 the *Wall Street Journal* reported that a German fad for post-World War II Deutsche Marks, beloved by older citizens, has led to their being accepted at an exchange rate of just under two D-Marks to one Euro by a growing number of merchants.

This old currency is cherished not only for its sturdy paper but also because it features German composers and other cultural heroes. Like the British Pound, it gives people far more sense of identity than do soulless, de-nationalized Euros.

The modifications proposed for the U.S. Dollar may enhance their feeling of history and value as learning tools.

The advocates of these image changes were, in some cases, activists seeking to promote other activists. But in some cases this attempt to put ideology into American currency has alienated many people.

Making Book on Our Money

This measure is by Democratic Senator Jeanne Shaheen of New Hampshire, the first woman in American history to serve as both a state governor and U.S. Senator. Her aim in re-facing our currency, Shaheen says, is "to point out the significant contributions women have made in U.S. history." [2]

Women have made enormous contributions on many sides of issues. So which women are to be put on our money — heroines of the Right, or of the Left? And why was Andrew Jackson — the only President who ever reduced America's national debt to Zero — targeted to be replaced by a woman?

Senator Shaheen is a longtime comrade of 2016 Democratic Presidential candidate Hillary Clinton, whose campaign thus far is targeted on female voters via an appeal to elect her as America's first woman President. Is the real purpose of Shaheen's legislation to help mobilize women and promote the Clinton campaign?

Money As Propaganda

Since ancient times, rulers have used money as propaganda, usually by putting their own face on a nation's coins. Old coins would be called in, and new debased coins containing less gold or silver in their metal would typically be struck to honor anniversaries and other events in a ruler's reign.

The image of a woman, Queen Elizabeth II of the United Kingdom, today appears on many Commonwealth currencies, coins and stamps around the world. Few object because today the Queen reigns but does not rule or stand for election.

Since the emergence of democracy, by contrast, elected politicians have faced disapproval if they attempt to put their own image on their country's money to promote themselves.

Since George Washington said "No" to attempts to put his own portrait on American currency, both tradition and law have come to require that a person be deceased for two years before being so honored.

In a democratic republic like ours, the nation's money should not be used as advertising, or like a taxpayer-funded campaign button, to promote any particular living politician, dynastic family, ideological cause or current political party.

For this reason, some questioned the 1964 minting of a John F. Kennedy half-dollar — not only because this came less than two years after his 1963 assassination, but also because his two brothers were considering their own runs for the presidency and might benefit politically from their family's last name on this new American coin.

Cashing In

Few doubt that putting the image of prominent Democrats and Republicans on our money enhances the public image of their political parties and the ideas they represent. We cannot tell the dancer from the dance, or the politician from his or her policies, beliefs and ideology. Our currency has become *de facto* advertising for giants of the two major political parties.

Republican Abraham Lincoln appears on every $5 bill and penny. The U.S. Mint issued a Dwight David Eisenhower dollar from 1971 until 1978. Other GOP Presidents: Ulysses S. Grant is shown on the $50 bill and William McKinley on the $500 bill.

The Democratic Party evolved out of the Democratic-Republican Party of Thomas Jefferson, who today is seen on the $2 bill and nickel, and his protégé James Madison is found today on the $5,000 bill.

America's Framers unaffiliated with any of today's political parties include George Washington, now on the $1 bill and the Quarter; Alexander Hamilton, today on the $10 bill; and Benjamin Franklin, whose wise face graces our $100 bills, also known as "Benjamins."

Democratic President Franklin Delano Roosevelt's profile is seen on our dime. Woodrow Wilson starred on the biggest currency, the $100,000 note that never circulated but during the Great Depression was used to transfer funds among Federal Reserve Banks. Grover Cleveland now appears on the $1,000 bill, having been replaced as the face on the $20 bill in 1928 by Andrew Jackson.

President Jackson on America's currency has always been controversial. He was both a slave owner and the Chief Executive who forced more than 46,000 Native Americans off their valuable property in the East and onto the brutal "Trail of Tears" to then-desolate Oklahoma.

The Democratic Party was the party of the slave owners, the Ku Klux Klan, Jim Crow and Bull Connor, but in recent years the embarrassment of its history of white divide-and-conquer racial politics has prompted many Progressive Democratic clubs to end their traditional annual Jefferson & Jackson dinners.

Jefferson, Washington and Madison were also slave owners, but each of these American giants had other redeeming qualities. Jefferson, for example, tried to end slavery and argued that Native Americans were the equal of Whites in every way.

Coining Women

Senator Shaheen somehow neglected to mention that women have already graced our currency. Many American coins — including our very first mint-issue coin, the famed Birch Cent — carried idealized images of women symbolizing Liberty and virtue. Much of America's early money portrayed women. [3]

Since 2007 the U.S. Mint has issued half-ounce gold coins honoring America's First Ladies, a series that perhaps with an eye to a possible first female President being elected in 2016, it now calls "First Spouses."

The Native American guide to Jefferson's Lewis and Clark Expedition to the Pacific was Shoshone Sacagawea, who is honored on a $1 coin. So, too, was women's suffrage pioneer Susan B. Anthony until 1981. (Helen Keller appears on the reverse side of the 2003 Alabama Quarter.)

Alas, some of these women also fall short of the ideal of Progressive Political Correctness. Sacagawea was married to a French fur trapper. She is depicted carrying his baby son on the $1 coin. As an adult, he would ride with the Mormon Battalion.

Susan B. Anthony in 1872 wrote to her feminist ally Elizabeth Cady Stanton: "I shall work for the Republican party and call on all women to join me…." She was also highly critical of abortion.

The organization that inspired Senator Shaheen's legislation calls itself "Women on 20s" and has proposed replacing Andrew Jackson with women who are almost all reliable heroines to the Left or to Left-aligned groups.

Their carefully narrowed list of women to adorn the $20 bill included FDR wife Eleanor Roosevelt, civil rights activist Rosa Parks, Cherokee chief Wilma Mankiller, and the apparent winner underground railroad conductor Harriet Tubman. Activists earlier also proposed radical feminist Betty Friedan, along with four Democratic — but zero Republican — officeholders. Another they proposed for the $20 bill was Margaret Sanger, an abortion and eugenics advocate and pioneer of Planned Parenthood who said her aim was to reduce America's African-American population.

Why are nearly all the figures proposed to replace small-government advocate Andrew Jackson the heroines of the liberal-left? Why are conservative and Republican heroines — e.g., Revolutionary War fighter Molly Pitcher, Annie Oakley, Dolly Madison, Betsy Ross, Clare Booth Luce, Republican and first elected Congresswoman Jeannette Rankin, actress and Republican activist Ginger Rogers, actress and ambassador Shirley Temple Black, to name but a few — excluded from consideration….unless we count Susan B. Anthony, abortion foe, or Tubman, gun rights advocate, both Republicans, although the media rarely mention this.

As noted earlier, Great Britain has long featured Queen Elizabeth II on its currency. The Bank of England plans in 2016 to replace the image of social reformer Elizabeth Fry with that of Sir Winston Churchill on its £5 note, and in 2017 to put the face of novelist Jane Austen on its £10 note. The Austen choice is particularly interesting because she will replace the face of evolutionary scientist Charles Darwin, a hero to many environmentalists and atheists.

Junking Jackson

The idea behind such currency changes, according to Shaheen, is to use our currency as a teaching tool about the contributions of women.

Such teaching cuts both ways, of course. Removing the long-familiar face of President Andrew Jackson implies that he is no longer Politically Correct, and the advocates of this change make no secret that erasing Jackson is also important to them.

These are the same Progressives who have just turned the once-free Internet into a government-controlled monopoly and who advocate much tighter control over what people may say in our media. As George Orwell foresaw, collectivists are eager to control our language and to rewrite history to impose their views.

So why are Andrew Jackson and his followers now being targeted for erasure?

"The Jacksonians were libertarians, plain and simple," wrote economist and historian Murray Rothbard, as we quote in our book *Don't Bank On It! The Unsafe World of 21st Century Banking.* "[T]hey strongly favored free enterprise and free markets, but they just as strongly opposed special subsidies and monopoly privileges by government to business or any other group."

"In the monetary sphere," Rothbard continued, "this meant the separation of government from the banking system, and a shift from inflationary paper money and fractional reserve banking to pure specie [gold and silver] and banks confined to 100 percent reserves."

President Jackson waged a successful political fight to prevent America's economy from being controlled by a European-style central bank in the hands of special interests. Despite his flaws, thanks to his efforts, we remained largely economically free until Progressive Democratic President Woodrow Wilson forced both the Federal Reserve central bank and the Progressive Income Tax onto our nation in 1913.

Jackson succeeded in drastically lowering taxes and, wrote Rothbard, "for the first and probably the last time in American history, paying off the federal debt."

Progressivism and our giant government would have been impossible if President Jackson's policies favoring independent small banks and honest, hard money, small government, low taxes and zero government debt were still in effect. No wonder today's Progressives want him erased and forgotten. No wonder they do not want young people looking at Jackson's image — he was brutal to slaves and Native Americans — on the $20 bill and asking who he was in our early history. They might even discover how far to the extreme Left today's Democratic Party has moved since Jefferson and Jackson helped found it.

As we observed in our earlier book *The Inflation Deception: Six Ways Government Tricks Us...And Seven Ways to Stop It!*, "The Federal Reserve and the government welfare state cynically took their revenge by putting paper-money-hating Andrew Jackson's face on the $20 bill and Jefferson's face on Food Stamps to lend their legitimacy to both pieces of fiat paper that Jefferson and Jackson would repudiate were they here today."

Graven Images

The currency we rely on has become debased and politicized, and is little more than the promises and platitudes of today's Progressive politicians. The U.S. Dollar has lost its once-solid value, and it is being turned into a propaganda vehicle for promoting their ideological values and political ambitions. Such are today's new money changers.

Do not be surprised to see Old Hickory, Andrew Jackson, replaced with Politically Correct faces, whether of women or of Democrat James

Buchanan, a lifelong bachelor now portrayed by some Progressive historians as America's first "gay" President [1857-1861].

The fast-approaching "cashless society" will give Progressives total control of our money and credit, and the future soon will be "de-faced" of all people they deem Politically Incorrect.

Jesus said: "whose image is on the coin?" "Caesar's," came the reply. At least this gave Caesar an incentive to mint coins people would see as valuable, even noble.

Face Value

Rulers have always understood the propaganda value of having their face on a nation's coins and bills. They saw this even before our modern age of "branding" products and celebrities.

But even more important than preserving their reputation for putting their face on honest money, rulers have loved and craved wealth and power. This for thousands of years led many to melt down their nations' coins and re-mint them with a lower percentage of precious metal content. This debasement of the currency instantly gave the ruler many more coins to spend.

As we explained in our book *The Great Debasement*, this term refers to England in the years 1542-1551. During the reigns of King Henry VIII — who had two of his six wives beheaded — and of his sickly, short-lived son and successor Edward VI, the English Crown within a decade gradually removed more than half the silver from the nation's coins.

In March 1542 fully 75 percent of the average English coin's value was the silver in it. This silver value in coins was reduced to only 50 percent by 1545, then to 33.33 percent by 1546.

By 1551, so much silver had been taken out of English coins and replaced with base metals that their silver content constituted only 25 percent of their face value.

This Great Debasement of their money so shook the English people that we can still hear its echo today in one of Elizabethan playwright William

Shakespeare's most popular masterpieces: "No, they cannot touch me for coining," the Bard's King Lear says. "I am the king himself."

After the 1559 coronation of Henry's second daughter as Queen Elizabeth I, she launched a plan to retire the debased coinage and replace it with more honest money. Her reign is remembered as England's Golden Age.

"As Fair to the Ignorant"

One of Queen Elizabeth's economic advisors was financier Sir Thomas Gresham, author of "Gresham's Law," the recognition that "bad money drives out good."

When people have a choice of trading in either a solid currency or a debased one, they will stash away the good money for themselves and use the debased money in trade, thereby taking good money out of circulation.

For this reason "good and bad coin cannot circulate together," wrote Gresham in a 1558 letter to Elizabeth. In it he explained to her that her father's and half-brother's "Great Debasements" were the reason that "all your fine gold was convayed out of this your realm."

"Brass shines as fair to the ignorant as gold to the goldsmiths," said Queen Elizabeth I.

Yet where money — the medium we earn in exchange for the precious hours of our lives and the sweat of our brow — is concerned, many people strive not to be ignorant. King Henry VIII had to impose legal tender laws to force sellers and buyers to accept his debased, devalued coins.

Smith's Law

More than 450 years after Gresham's stroke of genius, we noticed that Craig R. Smith in an inspired "Eureka" moment had discovered a corollary to Gresham's Law — that bad money drives out not only good money...but also a society's good values.

We modestly call this corollary that identifies a nexus between a nation's currency and its moral and ethical values "Smith's Law."

We see the workings of Smith's Law all around us. As Pat Boone says in this book's Foreword, "A nation's currency has consequences.... Bad, debased money drives good morals out of society, causing a downward money-and-morality spiral that goes on debasing our money and its users."

In 1913, the new Federal Reserve System began. Politicians told us it would protect the U.S. Dollar's value. Instead, it debased the value of the dollar, causing the very nature of our society to transform for the worse.

The Fed had actually been chartered to "furnish an elastic currency" that freed politicians from the constraints of the gold standard. These politicians no longer had to back each dollar they spent with a fixed amount of gold.

Almost overnight, our Progressive politicians began to have enough wealth to fulfill their collectivist dreams. They undertook the building of both a Warfare State and a Welfare State.

Progressives could now afford the trappings of military might and the kinds of entangling alliances that lured countries and their patriotic young soldiers into foreign wars. They could also make enough voters dependent on government welfare to buy easy re-elections, while harming families.

Democratic President Woodrow Wilson signed both the Fed and the Progressive income tax into law. Wilson hated America's Constitution and all its constraints on government power.

The Beehive

In 1912 Woodrow Wilson delivered a speech titled "What Is Progress?" that reveals much about the mindset and values of his ideological comrades then and now. [4]

He described how inside the "house" of America he and other Progressives were fashioning a new and superior structure that would replace it.

"[A] generation or two from now," said Wilson, "the scaffolding will be taken away, and there will be the family in a great building whose noble architecture will at last be disclosed, where men can live as a single community, co-operative as in a perfected, co-ordinated beehive...."

A beehive is the perfect embodiment of a collectivist society. We admire bees for their industriousness. However, in nature the hive is a place where almost all the workers are nominally female, yet only the Queen Bee has offspring.

It is a place with almost no males except a few drones, whose job it is to mate with the Queen once during her courting flight. Thereafter, these drones are prevented from re-entering the hive and, without honey, quickly die. Does this sound like the new American slacker society of unemployed males?

Bees have been around since the time of the dinosaurs, scientists tell us. Their society is durable.

Yet the bee has scarcely changed during all that time. Most bees are collectivist species that make no "progress," as we use the term. They are thus a fitting symbol for today's back-to-feudalism Progressives.

What Wilson called the "Beehive" that he and his Progressive comrades were building to replace the Constitution is a major part of what we call "The Machine."

America's Framers designed our Constitution to keep government small so that individual Americans could become large, self-reliant, strong and prosperous. They gave us a democratic republic in which government was to serve The People, not turn into an aristocratic ruling class.

Yet after roughly a century under The Machine — with our money debased and nearly everything around us now politically, ideologically controlled — we have been made into serfs under an imperial regime in some ways worse than that of King George III.

"Our Tools Shape Us"

This book's introduction began with the words of Canadian media philosopher Marshall McLuhan: "We shape our tools, and thereafter our tools shape us."

America's Founders shaped tools to protect our liberties — the Declaration of Independence that defined our rights as "unalienable" because they came not from government but God; a Constitution intended to put government in a strait jacket to restrain its growth and power; and hard, honest money to limit how much our politicians could spend.

Knowing that, as Thomas Jefferson wrote, "The natural progress of things is for the government to gain ground and for liberty to yield," he warned: "Put not your faith in men, but bind them down with the chains of the Constitution" and its tight limits on government expansion.

But under the Progressive movement a century ago, the Constitution and its safeguards were amended. The monstrous ambitions of politicians were unleashed.

Since the Federal Reserve was given European central bank-like control of our currency in 1913, and the last vestige of the gold standard was abandoned by Richard Nixon in 1971, the value of the U.S. Dollar has fallen to only around two cents of the purchasing power it had in 1913. And government has increased income taxes because we make "more" dollars!

We have calculated that manipulation of the dollar and deliberate use of inflation as a *de facto* tax has robbed the American people over the past 100 years of at least $220 Trillion Dollars.

Ninety-four million Americans cannot, or will not, find needed full-time jobs. The claim that we have approximately five percent unemployment, like most of the massaged, self-serving data issued by our government, is at best misleading and at worst downright dishonest. Those who stop looking for work are no longer counted in the unemployment statistics.

Many avoid taking jobs because this might put their welfare payments at risk. So the welfare state gives people an incentive *not* to work. And welfare payments nowadays can turn the social safety net into the proverbial hammock.

Sixty percent of the American people now receive more in government benefits than they pay in taxes.

More than 40 percent of babies in America are now born to single mothers in homes where Uncle Sam has taken over the provider role of a husband. And these numbers reflect a widespread decline in marriage and the personal maturity that providing for a family produces.

The national debt is fast approaching $20 Trillion, growing at between $15,000 and $58,000 per second. Economic growth has slowed to near-zero, a state verging on permanent recession.

The Party of Loot

One of our two major political parties came close to nominating a self-described socialist, Vermont Senator Bernie Sanders, as its presidential standard-bearer. It instead nominated former Secretary of State Hillary Clinton, who moved to the left of Sanders on many issues in order to defeat him. She now promises to revive an almost moribund economy by raising taxes and increasing regulations.

If you were an investor, how much would you spend to start or expand a business or hire employees in a country where every next election threatens you with socialist expropriation of what you have built?

In today's land of class warfare, divide-and-conquer Balkanizing politics, envy and covetousness, some of our most powerful politicians now proclaim: "You didn't build that!" They argue that the government did, by paving a public road near your company or educating your employees.

The implication of this emotional Progressive rhetoric is clear. If the government built your company, it owns and can confiscate your company. So say today's Leftist politicians to win votes, and to justify confiscatory taxes on businesses and the successful. "Let us take their money and give it to you," Progressives tell their voters.

But when free enterprise capitalists are demonized, and accused of stealing what they have by self-serving politicians, then the mob will soon decide it no longer needs welfare-state politicians as its middleman. It will just rob the rich and loot their businesses itself, and pocket what the Leftist politicians would have taken as their "cut."

With their polarizing, rabble-rousing and uncompromising behavior, today's Progressive lawmakers are undermining the very rule of law itself. No wonder we recently have seen mob violence from Baltimore to Milwaukee.

A Perpetual Wealth Machine

Today's Progressives have built and operated their European central bank Machine not on socialist blueprints, but on the economics of British economist John Maynard Keynes, who in his early life was sympathetic to Marxism but ultimately repudiated the Soviet Union. He also had the virtue of being that rare economist who also invested — and who made, lost, and then remade a fortune by doing so.

Keynes believed that the ups and downs of the business cycle could be leveled out by collecting more taxes when times were good and then having government inject that saved revenue back into the economy as stimulus when things were slow.

Savings are bad, Keynes thought, because saving money keeps it out of the economy. If stimulus is given to those who need to spend it, such as the poor who need all they have to buy food, this will move the money more rapidly from hand to hand in the economy.

This increase in money's "velocity," Keynes thought, created a "multiplier effect" that gave $1 of stimulus money the impact of $1.50 in the economy.

We know a lot more today than when Keynes was putting forth such innovative theories in the 1930s. We know, for example, that the Keynesian multiplier effect works — but mostly in poor, backward societies with limited money supplies. In advanced societies with computers that can discount such government stimulus within seconds, the effect of $1 in stimulus can be as small as 29 cents, a loss of 71 cents per stimulus dollar spent, according to an Independent Institute study we analyzed in *The Great Debasement*.

After nearly $8 Trillion in Federal Government spending since 2008, the "velocity of money" is nearly the slowest it has been in 50 years. The St. Louis Fed calculated that much of this Keynesian spending acted as an "anti-stimulus," frightening businesses out of new growth or hiring because of the growing risk of inflation.

Most of this money had not come from government saving it — which in any event would have violated Keynes' "paradox of thrift," that saving is bad.

Most came from government and the Federal Reserve conjuring it out of thin air merely by printing pieces of paper marked as "legal tender." This tool shaped us, but not as we had intended.

"The reality is that deficit spending does not produce economic growth when the money is borrowed, only when it comes from previous surpluses," writes *Forbes* Magazine columnist Jeffrey Dorfman. "Keynes himself was clear that a government should run surpluses in good times and save that money." [5]

"Modern Keynesian economists…would have you believe that deficits and debt do no harm to an economy and that government deficit spending can boost the economy, lower unemployment, raise average incomes, and generally make life better all the way around," writes Dorfman.

"[I]f you believe both parts of this theory," he concludes, "then Keynesians have found a perpetual wealth machine."

"There really is a free lunch."

The Hard Truth of TANSTAAFL

Both Nobel Laureate economist Milton Friedman and science fiction writer Robert Heinlein used TANSTAAFL, the acronym for "There Ain't No Such Thing As A Free Lunch."

You might be given a free ham sandwich at a party, but somebody had to pay the cost of raising the pig, growing the wheat, baking the bread, and producing everything else, as well as the delivery cost, that went into providing you that sandwich.

Since government produces almost nothing and is ultimately just a legal monopoly on the use of force, it uses a variety of techniques — taxes, fines, mandates, regulations, and so forth — to make other people pay the real world costs of everything government spends or gives away.

If the Keynesians really have created a perpetual wealth machine, says Dorfman, then we all can quit our jobs and stop paying taxes — because the government can magically and without effort produce all the wealth everybody needs for free.

All we need to do is run deficits forever, if the Keynesians are right. So why, Dorfman asks tongue-in-cheek, is no prominent Keynesian government economist calling for an end to taxes?

The commonsense reality is that no free lunch exists in the real world. Somebody has to produce real goods and services. If not, then the government can give you mountains of fiat paper currency that it claims is "money," but there will be little this worthless monopoly money can buy.

This is what happened in 1923 in Weimar, Germany, when the government decided it could fund everything with mere paper, not gold or currency backed by something real. The economy melted down. Speculators got rich, but those who had worked and saved all their lives saw the entire value of their savings go up in a blaze of hyperinflation.

We are actually doing something similar today, only in slow motion. Our Keynesian-guided government and Federal Reserve have provided enough stimulus to take the stock market to record highs, but the companies behind those stocks are doing little actual business.

The share price rise is coming mostly from near-zero Fed lending rates that make it easy for big companies to buy back their own stock and thereby juice its value. Our economy is a grand illusion, a mirage produced by sleight of hand.

Such monetary magic did not begin with John Maynard Keynes, nor even with socialism and Progressivism. It began in the United States with one of America's Founding Fathers — widely disliked back then, but surprisingly glorified by today's Left-slanted media. His name: Alexander Hamilton.

Alexander the Great

On Sunday, June 12, 2016 the Broadway stage play "Hamilton" won 11 Tony Awards, including those for Best Musical and Best Book and Original Score for its creator Lin-Manuel Miranda. [6]

How odd that liberals are paying $1,000 per seat to see a Hip Hop and Rap glorification of this least-liberal of America's Founding Fathers.

The blockbuster musical focuses on the immigrant energy and genius of Alexander Hamilton, who rose from an out-of-wedlock birth in the Caribbean to become aide to General George Washington and America's first Secretary of the Treasury.

Miranda deserves credit for seeing the dramatic potential in Hamilton, from his battlefield courage at Yorktown to his adulterous, scandalous affair, to his quarrels with Thomas Jefferson, to his death in a pistol duel with Jefferson's "Progressive" Vice President Aaron Burr.

Hamilton's vision of an urban, industrial America has in our time triumphed over Thomas Jefferson's ideal of a rural republic of farmers.

We admire Jefferson, but as George Will wrote, we live today in "Alexander Hamilton's America." So why should liberals love Hamilton? Consider:

(1) Alexander Hamilton fought patriotically for America's independence from King George III, but he then urged George Washington to become ruler for life. Hamilton favored lifetime appointments for future presidents and senators as well, and argued that the president should appoint the governor of each state.

(2) Hamilton supported the Alien & Sedition Acts of 1798, which put tight controls on immigration. These laws also made it a crime to criticize the government and its high officials, which our second president, John Adams, used to imprison several members of Congress and dozens of journalists.

Had Thomas Jefferson not won the presidency in 1800 and halted enforcement of these Hamilton-backed laws, the United States might have slid into permanent dictatorship like the Soviet Union.

(3) Hamilton was an elitist who looked down his nose at working people and merchants. He devised government policies designed to favor the rich while denying the same subsidies and tax breaks to middle-class business people and small farmers.

Hamilton saw democracy as mob rule. When asked if, like Jefferson, he wanted government by the people, Hamilton snapped, "Your People, Sir, is a great beast." He favored rule by an unchanging aristocratic elite...an odd position for someone who rose solely by talent and the luck of gaining Washington's personal favor.

(4) Hamilton favored high taxes and heavy-handed enforcement. When small farmers west of the Appalachians distilled their crops into easier-to-ship whisky to sell in the East, the Federal Government imposed heavy taxes on distilled spirits. When farmers rose against this tax in the "Whisky Rebellion," Hamilton helped lead a crushing military show of force to compel their submission. He also advocated an armada of government cutters off the coast to crack down on tax evaders.

(5) Hamilton favored a large standing military with himself as one of its leaders. Most Founders distrusted this because such militaries in Europe were used to put down and keep down the People.

(6) Hamilton strongly supported a European-style central bank to manipulate money and credit, which thanks to Democratic President Andrew Jackson was prevented from taking full control of America's economy until 1913, when Democrat Progressive Woodrow Wilson gained the power to create the Federal Reserve because of a Republican Party split between President William Howard Taft and former President Teddy Roosevelt.

If Hamilton's plans for a central bank had prevailed, corrupt government interference with our economy might have doomed our young Republic from the start. On the other hand, Hamilton's tax and credit policies gave Jefferson's Administration enough credit to make the Louisiana Purchase from Napoleon.

Perhaps, however, his most wicked belief was this:

(7) Alexander Hamilton loved our national debt. "A national debt, if it is not excessive, will be to us a national blessing," he wrote in 1781. Nine years later he wrote that "public debts are public benefits."

Our Debt to Hamilton

Hamilton embraced his time's new ideas about "political economy" — the word "economics" had not yet been invented. One of the foremost among these was an idea first adopted in the Netherlands and then in England —

the innovation of treating the nation's debt not as a negative to be paid off as quickly as possible — but as an asset.

A nation's debt, Hamilton realized, could be converted into government bonds that paid a rate of interest and then sold to investors inside or outside the United States.

These bonds give the government immediate money to spend, and at the same time built a nation's international credit so it could borrow even more as it reliably paid on prior debts, as John Steele Gordon writes in *Hamilton's Blessing: The Extraordinary Life and Times of Our National Debt.* [7]

Hamilton, the "Father of Our National Debt," favored spending such borrowed revenues on "investments" to encourage industrial development around places such as Paterson, New Jersey. He developed bright young acolytes such as Samuel Colt to help rapidly industrialize the young nation.

When war finally came between North and South, the Hamiltonian North had gun and cannon factories. The rural agricultural Jeffersonian Confederacy had none.

Some regarded Hamilton's achievements as almost miraculous. Daniel Webster wrote: "The whole country perceived with delight, and the world saw with admiration. [Hamilton] smote the rock of the national resources, and abundant streams gushed forth. He touched the dead corpse of the public credit, and it sprung to its feet. The fabled birth of Minerva from the brain of Jove was hardly more sudden or more perfect than the financial system of the United States as it burst forth from the conception of Alexander Hamilton."

Hamilton said he condemned "the practice of accumulating debts" and that ideally "the creation of debt should always be accompanied with the means of extinguishment. This [is…] the true secret for rendering public credit immortal."

Hamilton understood what profligate politicians could do with this easy way to bring in huge revenues.

"The debt, too, may be swelled to such a size, as that the greatest part of it may cease to be useful as a Capital, serving only to pamper the dissipation of idle and dissolute individuals, as that the sums required to pay the interest upon it may become oppressive, and beyond the means, which a government can employ, consistently with its tranquility, to raise them, as that the resources of taxation, to face the debt, may have been strained too far to admit of extensions adequate to exigencies, which regard the public safety," Hamilton wrote in 1791.

Heavy enough debt, in other words, might drive taxpayers to revolution. We wonder what Hamilton would think of today's $19.5 Trillion debt and how supinely Americans have accepted a burden of debt that will continue to crush their children and grandchildren.

Why They Call It "Bondage"

Hamilton's critics, then and now, are horrified at Hamilton's desire to have a national debt that would never be paid off — that would be used to turn America's taxpayers into perpetual collateral for government debt by indenturing them like a donkey chained to spend its life pulling the burden of a millstone to enrich an elite of American and foreign bond buyers.

Why did you think they call it "bondage" and its victims "bond servants"— from the root word bound?

Soon enough our government would begin funding wars with "war bonds." And critics of Hamilton, when they looked at the skyscrapers of New York City, would see them as giant unmarked tombstones for all those whose life work continues to be stolen to enrich wealthy Hamiltonians in New York City and London. Whether Southern slaves or Northern taxpayers, they have given their lives working to pay the interest on never-ending government borrowing and debt.

The musical "Hamilton" reportedly persuaded Jack Lew, our current Secretary of the Treasury, to keep Hamilton's image on America's $10 bill…. and instead to remove President Andrew Jackson's image from the $20 bill. America has not been free from debt since Jackson's presidency; now you know why.

Perhaps liberals love the musical "Hamilton" because it depicts this Founding Father opposed to slave owners such as Jefferson. Truth be told, however, Hamilton did little to end slavery — and in real life may have helped his relatives buy and sell a few slaves.

When you think about his policy of unending government debt, Hamilton in fact has enslaved all of us.

Debt and taxes are how the government turns our human blood, our lives, into fuel for The Machine.

Liberals applaud Hamilton as an advocate of a powerful central government who worked to become part of the ruling elite. They do not even know that Hamilton was eager to restrict immigration and impose trade restrictions.

Too bad "Hamilton" does not tell the whole truth. It might have created an even better teachable moment.

Thomas Jefferson was in many ways Hamilton's opposite. "I wish it were possible to obtain a single amendment to our Constitution," Jefferson wrote in 1789. "I would be willing to depend on that alone for the reduction of the administration of our government to the genuine principles of its Constitution; I mean an additional article, taking from the federal government the power of borrowing."

The Constitution (Article I Section 10 Clause 1) did attempt to prevent government borrowing via mere pieces of paper, at least by the states. "No state shall...emit bills of credit," the Framers wrote, [or] "make any Thing but gold or silver Coin a Tender in Payment of Debts."

The antidote to today's growing cashless system and addiction to the drug of debt is honest money, which America functioned on successfully for more than 124 years in harmony with other honest money nations. This was known as the Gold Standard.

"With the exception only of the period of the gold standard, practically all governments of history have used their exclusive power to issue money to defraud and plunder the people."

– Friedrich A. Hayek
Nobel Laureate Economist

Part Three

"Like a Conquered Province"

Chapter Five

The Trap

*"For he is cast into a net by his own feet,
and he walketh upon a snare...
and the robber shall prevail against him.*

*"The snare is laid for him in the ground,
and a trap for him in the way.
Terrors shall make him afraid on every side...."*

– Job 18: 8-11 [1]

The escape hatches are slamming shut and being locked all around us. Our financial freedom is suddenly vanishing. What is behind these ominous actions? How can we protect and free ourselves? Why is The Machine turning into The Trap?

What if our ancestors who came here seeking the American Dream's freedom and opportunities had instead been trapped and prohibited from leaving their native land? History for America and the world would have been very different.

After a century of statists "fundamentally transforming" America's politics, economics and values, we are becoming the kind of high-tax, low-liberty, Big Government land our ancestors escaped to come here in search of something better. Welfare policies intended to produce security are now making us fearfully insecure.

Even more frightening, the kinds of exits through which our ancestors fled their native lands are being locked to limit your ability to escape.

As The Trap closes, we are losing not only what we earn and own, but also the ultimate survival right in any genuine democratic republic — the right to "vote with our feet" by freely departing with our earnings for some place more free.

Few are consciously aware that The Trap is closing around us, but because we carry the freedom-loving genes of pioneer ancestors we can sense the danger. We feel a restless urge to change and move. We feel growing stress that is literally hazardous to our health, stress that can trigger anxiety, insecurity, heart attacks and cancers. The current obesity epidemic may be our genetic survival instinct's response to the crisis we sense coming.

The Statists' Trap is already becoming a death trap if we do not soon wake up and take some simple steps to protect ourselves.

The fear we now feel about our economy and society is understandable, but its roots go far deeper than most of us know.

This ominous anxiety comes from hard facts, but even more from survival instincts that kept our ancestors alive, a sense of impending danger hard-wired into the survival code of our genetic blueprint.

Most of us now feel that something has gone very wrong and threatens our future, both as families and as a nation.

Millions of Americans now ask friends and relatives: "Where in the world can we move to escape what's happening here?"

In other lands this has long been a question people asked one another — but fewer now answer with one word of hope: "America!"

(Millions of poor people still come, often illegally and with the encouragement of statists such as President Barack Obama, but the promise offered to them is welfare and government dependency, not work and independence.)

We cannot recall any American when we were growing up asking what other country we should move to. Back then the world still dreamed of America as the shining city on a hill, the pot of gold at the end of the rainbow, the land to go to where dreams come true.

President Ronald Reagan reawakened that spirit of morning in America, that we were still the last, best hope of humankind. But today millions feel almost a sense of mourning for an American Dream that the advocates of Big Government are systematically killing.

Dream Wars

The American Dream for more than 100 years has contended with a collectivist alien ideology, which has now taken control of one of America's two major political parties as well as most of our universities and media.

The American Dream, which succeeded in making ours the freest, most prosperous nation in history, is based on personal liberty and responsibility, small government and large individuals, free markets and capitalism, private property and meritocracy.

The Progressive Dream — which began in the French Revolution and Romantic Movement two centuries ago and metastasized into socialism, national socialism, communism, fascism, and today's European-style welfare states — replaces God with the ultimate authority of science and a ruling Big Government elite.

Give science and government unlimited power and wealth, they promise, and they will produce a new Eden, a utopian Heaven on Earth created not by God but by Man.

In this human-made Eden, however, government is paternalistic, and therefore people are infantilized and permitted little more freedom than children. People are defined not as unique individuals created by God, but merely as members of groups based on Politically Correct or Incorrect class, racial, ethnic or whichever of 26 different gender identities they arbitrarily fit into.

These statists rule by the divide-and-conquer tactics of polarizing people into collectivized groups, then pitting these artificial groups against one another like little nations — black against white, poor against rich, male against female, and so forth.

The aim of such warfare is to secure perpetual political and social control by redistributing to government the wealth and power of the losing side in each of these struggles. Government is to be run by a narrow, superior Progressive elite that rules everyone else in the name of imposing "Equality."

The first priority of Progressives has been to gain and hold political power, which they have achieved by using tax money and government favors to buy votes. Today 49.5 percent of households in the United States have someone living there who receives a government payment of some sort.

Such ever-expanding government social programs, plus service on more than $19 Trillion in debt, already devour 71 percent of the entire federal budget — and will likely swallow it all by 2050, leaving no revenue to spend on anything else such as roads or national defense.

Social Insecurity

Progressives, often with the best of intentions, keep creating programs such as Social Security to make one or another group they favor feel more secure.

The price of this economic security, however, is that millions who are taxed more to pay for such expanding programs are made *less* secure.

Social Security could be renamed "Social Insecurity." Such programs redistribute the life blood of capitalism — capital — away from efficient private sector investment and jobs, and into the inefficient public sector that actually produces little or nothing.

Even Karl Marx understood that socialism may be a powerful system of wealth redistribution, but socialism is a very inefficient system for producing goods and services. This is why Marx wrote that a period of capitalism needed to come before communism to produce enough wealth to redistribute.

Profligate politicians for over 100 years have been redistributing America's accumulated wealth as if the free goody-making machine would never go empty. They looted America's economic engine via sky-high taxation, debasement of the dollar, mandates requiring businesses to fund collectivist ideas, and more.

These statists replaced the self-regulating efficiency of the free marketplace with politicized regulations and a crony pseudo-capitalism that enriched the ruling party's friends and punished its foes.

Wealth soon came not from serving ordinary customers, but from political favors handed out to his favorites by a king's whim. This is how things were — and in much of today's Europe, Africa and Asia still are — in the corrupt lands from which our ancestors fled.

Our Statist-Strangled Banner

After a century of choking the lifeblood out of capitalism, and the freedom out of the free market, the statists have killed a large part of the incentive and optimistic "animal spirits" (as economist John Maynard Keynes called them) that made the original American Dream work.

Anyone who looks can now see the cracks spreading across the edifice of America's economy as political pressure pushes it to the edge of catastrophic economic and social rupture.

Honest businesses have been pushed to the breaking point by the highest business taxes in the world — federal, state and local combined taxes that take on average 46 percent — and by crushing, often capricious regulations that terrify investors.

Millions of workers have not had a real wage increase in inflation-adjusted dollars for decades. We earn more, but everything costs more.

Consumers — feeling insecure about their jobs and income and tax burden — see Progressives demanding more money. We are increasingly afraid to spend, even though spending in the past produced 71 percent of America's Gross Domestic Product, because we are unsure whether we will earn more tomorrow to replace what we spend today.

We clearly are now standing in economic quicksand in an unreal, government-manipulated, politically-manipulated economy. The opening 11 market sessions of 2016 saw the sharpest year-opening percentage plunge in stock value ever recorded. By one estimate, investors lost $2.2 Trillion, equivalent to almost half of total annual federal budget outlays.

Only treasuries and gold held and gained value while other investments showed their fragility, slipping toward the brink of another Great Recession or worse.

The stock market by August 2016 was hitting record highs, but this clearly was not because of rising prosperity. An economy growing at less than 2 percent cannot sustain a stock market growing at 12 percent per year. We know intuitively that such tricks done with magic money cannot last.

"Investors have started the new year in panic mode," said veteran investment advisor Ed Yardeni as the frightened herd turned away from stock hockers who stay wealthy by corralling and skinning inexperienced investors.

Today 81 percent of us say we no longer trust our government to do the right thing.

Coming For Everything You Have

The statists have devoured America's once-vast surplus. They have run up an immense debt.

Our population is shifting from makers to takers — turning people who used to dream of creating their own business (but now despair because of high taxes, regulations and uncertainty) into slackers content to collect $60,000 a year in welfare to lie on a sunny beach in Hawaii with no work, no taxes, no responsibility. No wonder the demands on the nanny welfare state, and therefore on taxpayers, are going stratospheric.

To stay in power by buying votes with giveaways, the statists are coming for everything you have — your property, investments, savings, retirement plans, and more. They are systematically attacking most of the traditional safe havens that allowed past generations to safely accumulate enough to live on and retire comfortably.

Their masks are coming off. Democratic presidential candidate Hillary Clinton, former Secretary of State, now boasts that she will "topple" the top one percent of income earners in America and impose much heavier taxes on the "rich" and businesses (but, she assures voters, "not the middle class," just as her fellow Progressive Barack Obama promised that Obamacare would let you keep your doctor and cost less).

After being dumbed down in government schools, many voters are so easily bamboozled by envy and class warfare Orwellian groupthink that they never understand how taxes on corporations and the rich simply get passed on to the poor and middle class concealed in higher price tags for everything. Because of this, nobody really knows how much of what he or she pays for things is really secondhand taxes.

Clinton's rival for a time was Vermont Senator Bernie Sanders, a self-described democratic socialist who went on honeymoon in the Soviet Union. Sanders openly advocated a 90 percent tax rate and near-confiscatory inheritance taxes on the most successful. He has also advocated increasing social programs by an additional break-the-bank $18 Trillion to $28 Trillion in social spending over the next 10 years.

Embracing Socialism

In Iowa, a poll of likely Democratic February 1 caucus-goers found that only 38 percent describe themselves as capitalists; a larger 43 percent describe themselves as "socialists" in this heartland "welfare state" of federal farm and ethanol subsidies. [4]

Washington Post reporter Dan Balz writes that in Iowa socialists accounted for "58 percent of Sanders' supporters and about a third of Clinton's." [5]

New York Times/CBS News polling in November 2015 found that 69 percent of Sanders' and 52 percent of Clinton's supporters had a positive view of socialism. [6] It also reported that "African-Americans…support socialism by a ratio of 2 to 1."

A Gallup Poll in June 2016 found nationally that 59 percent of Democrats would be willing to vote for an openly socialist candidate. Among those 29 and younger, 69 percent — more than two thirds — said they were willing to vote for a socialist. [7]

This Big Government Party continues to move leftward and away from the traditional values of the American Dream. Both Sanders and Clinton may look old and have historically-failed economic dogma, but theirs is the face of today's and tomorrow's Democratic Party. More young Democrats and Independents supported Sanders than Clinton.

This means that with each election, business owners and would-be investors must weigh the risk of anti-capitalists winning more power and imposing more of the gradual property expropriation of ever-higher taxes and regulations.

America pays a terrible price because investors must hedge against the risk of the Democratic Party winning control over, and further enlarging, the government.

As happened in Great Britain, this risk historically means that fewer companies will be born or grow in America, fewer will find good jobs, and more entrepreneurs will feel motivated to depart for greener pastures where a new American Dream might take root.

We used to be able to find safe havens for our lives in many places — bank accounts, the dependable U.S. Dollar, our American Dream home, trusts, municipal and other bonds, stocks, our own business, our family inheritance and more….and if worse came to worst, we could take our savings and move to sunny foreign lands where our dollars had even more purchasing power.

Take a hard look at a few of the traditional Escape Hatches now closing around you and everything you own. These are a small part of The Machine that we call The Trap.

19 Choke Points for Financial Freedom

(1) – Taxing the Escape Hatch Abroad. On January 1, 2016, a new federal rule went into effect that allows the government to revoke the U.S. Passport of any citizen who the Internal Revenue Service says owes unpaid income taxes. [8]

This new Progressive rule declares that citizens who owe a certain amount of tax — initially $50,000 in taxes and penalties, an amount that could be reduced at any time — would not be permitted to leave the United States. These citizens would be required to pay the demanded tax and penalties to exit, or live out their lives without leaving the United States under a kind of nationwide house arrest.

(2) – Tying Your Passport to Domestic and Foreign Travel. The Transportation Security Agency (TSA) has warned that it may soon stop recognizing the driver licenses of up to 28 of the 50 states because the data on, and digitally embedded in, the licenses they issue does not precisely conform to federal I.D. standards. This could require would-be passengers instead to show their Passport, which would be unusable if it has been invalidated because of American tax matters. [9]

(3) – Raising the Cost of Renouncing Citizenship. Americans in record numbers have been renouncing U.S. citizenship. But the fee to do this has, under President Obama, increased by 422 percent to $2,350 — which according to litigator Robert W. Wood is "more than 20 times the average level charged in other high-income countries." The mere act of a rich person leaving the United States now triggers the legal presumption that the person is leaving America "for the purpose of tax avoidance." This imposes high scrutiny of your taxes for 5 years before *and after* you leave the country to catch and penalize you for any potential unpaid taxes. [10]

(4)– Democratic presidential candidate Hillary Clinton proposes imposing a large exit tax — perhaps 25 percent of total company assets. This is what was imposed on companies in December 1931 through Germany's "Reich flight tax," the *Reichsfluchtsteuer*. Something like this under a Hillary Clinton Administration could punish any American company leaving the United States. [11]

(5) – Ending Financial Privacy Abroad. President Obama has implemented FATCA, the Foreign Account Tax Compliance Act, which requires foreign banks and other financial institutions to notify the U.S. Government of any American accounts holding over $50,000 — and in some cases to collect and send our Internal Revenue Service withholding tax on the interest paid to such accounts. The Obama Administration reportedly applied a wide array of regulatory and political threats to compel such bank agreements by more than 77,000 institutions around the world. [12]

The United States is one of the few advanced nations that impose income taxes on what its citizens earn while living and working in foreign countries — even though their earning this money costs our government nothing to justify such taxation.

(6) – Bernie Sanders proposed imposing \$1 Trillion in corporate income taxes on what American companies earn overseas, possibly regardless of whether they bring such income into the United States or not. [13]

(7) – Ending Bank Privacy Inside the United States. Your bank is now legally required to spy on you, to notify the Internal Revenue Service of any "unusual" or "suspicious" activity of whatever amount, especially if it involves cash. [14]

(8) – It can now be a crime to withdraw cash from your own bank account. Both banks and customers are required to file a form if \$10,000 or more is withdrawn from a private bank account. As former Speaker of the House of Representatives Dennis Hastert learned, it can also be a crime called "structuring" to withdraw cash from your bank account in lesser amounts that over time add up to more than \$10,000. [15]

(9) – If you carry thousands of dollars in cash, law enforcement officers may confiscate it from you under civil asset forfeiture laws. They charge the cash itself, not you, as accessory to a potential crime. They will keep this cash unless you can prove that it is legally yours. In 2015, law enforcement officers used civil asset forfeiture laws to take more than \$5 Billion from Americans, more money than was stolen in all burglaries, combined. Cash is therefore literally a risky way to hold your assets that could make your mattress and your sleep uncomfortable. [16]

(10) – In the fast-approaching "cashless society," nearly all transactions will be electronic and monitored via government computers. Large cash transactions — already seen as suspicious, potentially criminal activity — will ultimately be made illegal. You will literally need government's "Mark of the Beast" to buy and sell, akin to what the Bible's Book of Revelation predicted. [17]

(11) – As of January 1, 2016, Bank accounts became at higher risk of "bail-ins" by which they can be seized to cover bank fines and penalties owed to the government. This, as we explained and documented in our 2014 book *Don't Bank On It! The Unsafe World of 21st Century Banking*, is but one of 20 major risks faced by today's bank account holders….risks you now take in exchange for being paid almost zero interest. No investment today may be less rational than a bank account; you have safer, more secure, more potentially profitable ways to protect a nest egg. [18]

(12) – Bank accounts will be poor havens of value. Under the Federal Reserve's deliberate "financial repression" policy, the interest banks pay depositors is held below the rate of real-world inflation. This guarantees that your accounts will continue to lose more value to bank fees and inflation than they are paid in bank interest. This policy was implemented as a way to push savers out of their bank accounts and into "moral risk" investments such as stocks. [19]

(13) – Stocks will be uncertain investments. The near-zero Fed interest rate policy has allowed companies to increase their stock value via cheap stock buybacks, mergers and inventory building. Many stocks have thus been overvalued and the resulting market bubble may be more susceptible to wild value swings as we saw in January 2016. [20]

(14) – Bonds will be uncertain investments. President Obama in his General Motors bankruptcy expropriated the money owed to secured bondholders and transferred it instead to the United Auto Workers union that was and is a major contributor to Democratic Party candidates. From Detroit to Puerto Rico, holders of municipal and other once-secure bonds face "haircut" risks so that irresponsible governments can evade responsibility for past political deals. [21]

(15) – Property is a risky haven of value. The Greatest Generation and Baby Boom generation thought of a home as a reliable piggy bank where value could keep going up until sold to pay for retirement in a downsized place. The real estate crash of 2008 showed how quickly those invested in their home could lose 40 percent of the average family's net worth.

That crash was caused by Progressive politicians using regulations and President Jimmy Carter's Community Reinvestment Act (CRA) to strong-arm banks into giving millions of mortgages to bad credit risks. President Obama is now pressuring banks to do this again.

Meanwhile, liberal cities and states keep using Eminent Domain power to forcibly transfer property from one private owner to another, a dubious constitutional policy that Republican presidential nominee Donald Trump approves. And President Obama has a new rule called AFFH, Affirmatively Furthering Fair Housing, that lets Washington dictate to towns and cities across America what they must do to provide low or zero-cost housing for the poor and minorities. Critics see AFFH as statists socially re-engineering America, dumping inner city poor on prosperous suburbs, and gerrymandering to benefit the Progressive party. [22]

Will the new poor residents of these communities be able to pay the high property taxes there? After this government redistribution of property drives property values down in these formerly prosperous communities, and the highest taxpaying residents move out, what will happen when the property tax revenue needed to maintain these communities falls?

Progressives have a long history of attempting to redistribute wealth and property, but instead redistribute economic decline and poverty.

(16) – Targeting retirement accounts. Revenue-hungry politicians of both major parties look at ways to tax or otherwise confiscate the $20 Trillion in private American retirement accounts such as 401(k)s and IRAs. The Obama Administration has reportedly worked on plans to, as happened in Argentina in 2008, seize the dollars in such accounts and replace them with annuities based on government debt bonds worth less than their face value. These government bonds can never be cashed in for a lump sum amount or withdrawn, and upon the death of the retiree, all or most of the value of this account would probably revert to the government, not the retiree's family; this could make Obamatirement more like Social Security than like a private IRA or 401(k). [23]

(17) – Targeting Trusts that now bypass all or part of the "Death Tax." Progressives do not want the rich "selfishly" passing on concentrated wealth to their children, whether via trusts or wills, because this increases "inequality" and "social injustice" in America. [24]

(18) – Massively increasing the "Death Tax." Democratic candidate Bernie Sanders proposed raising this tax on already-taxed estate money to at least 65 percent, collecting an additional $243 Billion over the next 10 years or less. The unspoken assumption of Progressives seems here to be that paternalistic government is the parent of us all and should have unbridled power to redistribute our wealth. Sanders also proposed a $3 Trillion "Wall Street speculation tax." Both Sanders and Clinton voiced support for a Financial Transactions Tax. [25]

If Mrs. Clinton wins and gets her way, the Death Tax could soar by an additional $350 Billion over 10 years. Our national debt will be almost $20 Trillion by the time President Obama leaves office. The unfunded liabilities for social programs and other obligations are already $120 Trillion and, off the budget, are growing by as much as $5 Trillion per year.

Secretary Clinton wants government to snatch away the inheritance left by every successful person to his or her children. But she graciously bestows on everyone's children a crushing national debt that, at the moment we write this, is more than $59.783, according to Sentier Research. This is nearly a quarter-million dollars for every family of four in America. If you are among the 40 percent of Americans who pay more in taxes than you receive in benefits, this debt burden on your family could easily exceed $500,000.

(19) – Reneging on Social Security. This utopian Ponzi scheme once taxed 16 workers to provide benefits for each retiree; in 2015 this was down to 2.9 workers, and soon will require seriously heavy taxes on 2.3 workers per retiree. [26]

Progressives are already manipulating Social Security to reduce its benefits. The program is supposed to offset inflation that would make our dollars worth less, but President Obama has year after year generally blocked such cost-of-living adjustments (COLAs), thereby in effect paying beneficiaries less. Each year without a COLA increase permanently lowers the baseline for all future retirees.

When gasoline soared to $5 per gallon, the Obama Administration said that no COLA was warranted because gasoline prices were "volatile," but in 2015 it denied a COLA increase because, it said, the falling gas price had offset any rise in the cost of living.

Progressives Break Their Promises

Politicians of both parties, as well as the non-partisan Congressional Budget Office, are considering many other ways to slash Social Security benefits. One is to means test, as is done with welfare programs; this would reduce or eliminate benefits for those with too much income or other assets; it would start by denying benefits to the rich but quickly be adjusted downward to deny Social Security to those who produced savings and investments during their lives.

When Social Security began, its benefits were exempt from taxes. Bill and Hillary Clinton changed the law so that 85 percent of Social Security benefits became taxable as income. Under President Obama's economic malaise, millions of Americans have been forced to work past age 65 to make ends meet, and this has let the government claw back many billions from their Social Security payments, taxing away again the retirement money they already paid for in taxes.

Progressives might have intended to provide security in retirement to senior citizens, but with Social Security headed for a smash up on the rocky shore of economic failure it is increasingly clear that such Progressive programs are becoming a huge cause of insecurity.

Today Social Security and a raft of related social programs are broke. Politicians long ago looted $2.66 Trillion from the Social Security Trust Fund, leaving behind IOUs that can only be redeemed by taxing the American people all over again. To launch Obamacare, the Obama Administration likewise looted $735 Billion — almost three-quarters of a trillion dollars — from the Medicare Trust Fund, thereby pushing this program towards bankruptcy.

The Obama Administration also greatly reduced the standards to qualify for Social Security Disability Insurance (SSDI), making it relatively easy to get this lifelong benefit for those whose Unemployment benefits were running out; it has been reported that, by the new Obama standards, you could qualify by telling the right doctor: "Doc, I hear voices in my head," something the doctor could neither prove nor disprove. Millions rushed in recent years to jump aboard Obama's gravy train, and today this disability program has more than 10 million people collecting benefits, almost as many as work full time in all of American manufacturing — a vanishing remnant of days when our country made things.

SSDI was on the brink of bankruptcy in 2016 until the gigantic bipartisan "Omnibus" budget bill Republicans and Democrats agreed to in the closing weeks of 2015 quietly looted another $150 Billion from Social Security's almost-empty trust fund and moved it to the separate, sinking Social Security Disability program. This redistribution of wealth from seniors brings Social Security even closer to the day it goes bust.

"Mean" Testing

Progressives will never give up Social Security, their flagship social program of the New Deal. To keep it afloat, young families may soon be taxed up to 25 percent of their income to fund this program that will likely never pay a dime in retirement to those who today are under age 40.

Those who are the most responsible — work the hardest and save for their future — will likely soon be denied Social Security benefits because the government will call them "too rich" to need it.

These statists will reward people based not on their merit, effort or achievement as free markets do — but instead by the Marxist standard, redistributing wealth from the makers to the takers "according to their need." In Italy, as we saw, a new legal precedent has recently been set for allowing those who claim to be hungry to steal the edible property of others — based on a subjective standard for hunger that may have nothing to do with the lack of food.

A New Re-tirement

The truck drivers should have remembered The Little Red Hen in the children's story, who showed that you should not expect others to provide what you want — but to do it yourself.

Instead, 407,000 workers — mostly unionized Teamster truck drivers and retirees — learned in 2016 from the Central States Pension Fund director Thomas Nyhan that the pensions they were depending on may be cut to "virtually nothing."

Bleeding $2 Billion a year that it cannot replace, this fund proposed to the government that it could remain solvent by slashing pension payments by a retirement-crushing 60 percent.

The U.S. Treasury's response: No. Even cutting pensions by 60 percent would not be enough to keep this underfunded fund going for much longer. The cuts must be far deeper, or the cost to workers must be much higher.

This gives 'retirement' a whole new meaning. For many of these short-changed drivers, it means they must re-tire their vehicles and put that rubber back on the road. As with millions of others, this retirement plan shortfall will crash their dreams of retirement and force them to re-tire and keep on trucking.

In today's ongoing economic crisis that began in 2008, pension funds have been hard hit. Many pension funds could shrink or sink from these hits, and less secure retirement vehicles such as IRAs and 401(k)s could also crash or get hijacked.

Defined benefit pensions promise workers a specific amount of money every month when they retire, but these promises are based on guesses about how much interest the pension fund's investments will earn. Those guesses in today's flat-lined economy have proven to be far too "optimistic" — or convenient for planners who want to put in as little funding as possible.

As we explained in *We Have Seen The Future and It Looks Like Baltimore: American Dream vs. Progressive Dream*, America's central bank the Federal Reserve dropped a key interest rate to zero at the start of the crisis to keep the economy from crashing.

This near-Zero Interest Rate Policy (ZIRP) has been in force ever since, which has provided almost free money to the government, the biggest banks, and giant corporation stock buybacks that juice the Wall Street casino. The real economy's growth is now also barely above zero percent growth; we are stuck in a stagnant, near-recession economy, with shopping malls turned into ghost towns.

Trouble is, retired people who depended on earning bank interest on their savings now earn almost nothing. Likewise, as we explain in *We Have Seen The Future and It Looks Like Baltimore,* "[D]efined benefit pension funds become troubled as they fail to earn sufficient returns with ZIRP." And to make matters worse, the Fed is now contemplating NIRP, Negative (below zero) Interest Rate Policy.

Denied the safe old money multiplier of compound interest, both retired bank savers and pension funds are pressed to "reach for yield" by turning to riskier investments, such as stocks. This leads to a more unstable, less secure economy of speculation and malinvestment.

Old-fashioned pensions were already a dying species. They nowadays exist mostly for 78 percent of government workers (whose pensions are underfunded by at least $1 Trillion), for 67 percent of the seven percent of private sector workers in powerful unions like the Teamsters, and for 13 percent of employees of companies that can handle the huge monetary and growing regulatory costs of defined benefit plans because such pensions keep employees from quitting. The percentage of private sector workers or retirees with pensions has fallen by more than 50 percent since the 1990s.

In 2015 President Barack Obama's Administration proposed granting states a "safe harbor" from the rules and safeguards of ERISA, the federal Employee Retirement Income Security Act of 1974. This, say critics, opens the way for squeezing private employers to help pay for underfunded state employee pensions. Led by California, 25 states have begun to move towards such rules. This could lead to more and more government control over our retirement plans.

The Obama Administration has already hinted it might imitate Argentina, which in 2008 suddenly seized bank retirement accounts and replaced the money in them with government bonds of equal face value...but whose market value was only 27 percent of their face value.

As The Little Red Hen warned, all these paths to retirement are now at risk. And because these are denominated in dollars, the declining value of the dollar is bleeding away your ability to pay for future needs. You could save all your life and end up with a pile of paper money of greatly reduced value.

Collectivizing Insecurity

The incentive in liberal utopia is therefore to avoid earning and saving, which will be expropriated — and concentrate instead on being needy. The needy wheel gets the grease. The paternalistic state rewards you not for growing up, but for being a lifelong government-dependent child, an infant at the government breast.

This allows Progressives to feel fulfilled and superior by playing the role of parents telling the infantilized masses what they are permitted to eat, drink, do, say and think.

An objective psychiatrist would tell nanny statists such as Barack Obama, Michael Bloomberg, Bernie Sanders or Hillary Clinton that their megalomania — their obsession with ruling every facet of other people's lives, and their dogmatic belief that they are entitled to impose their odd morality and Political Correctness by force onto everyone else — is a form of mental illness.

But this hypnotic collectivist dream has acquired enough political power to have undermined in millions of people the fundamental values and ideas of the American Dream that once made our nation free, prosperous and a light that inspired the world.

The American Dream, as we noted earlier, was created through small government and big individuals, freedom based on personal responsibility, private property and an intense work ethic, personal morality, voluntary community, faith in something higher than government, and a passionate love of free minds and free markets.

Statism has caused destruction wherever this collectivist ideology has taken root. In the past 100 years, Progressive-spawned ideologies have murdered more than 100 million people.

We see the damage Progressivism has done here in our debased dollar, our unreal economy, our mind-control universities, and our crime and drug-infested inner cities as in Baltimore. Progressivism has also corrupted our science and society with Politically Correct ideology that has replaced human integrity, honesty and truth.

The American Dream in Our Genes

American Exceptionalism is still here, deep in the DNA many of us inherited from pioneer ancestors. As we documented in our book *The Inflation Deception: Six Ways Government Tricks Us...and Seven Ways to Stop It*, UCLA Professor of Psychiatry Peter C. Whybrow theorizes that part of America's success may have come from a bit of genetic code found here more than in most other lands. They call it the "entrepreneurial gene" and identify it as D4-7 dopamine receptor alleles. [27]

If they are right, then many of us carry this exceptional DNA that drives a restless impulse to move, change, explore, and strive for more, especially more freedom and achievement.

In his brilliant 2015 book *Wealth, Poverty and Politics*, Dr. Thomas Sowell of the Hoover Institution at Stanford University investigates why a handful of nations at some point in their history create Golden Ages of creativity, prosperity, success and inspiration.

"To ask 'why nations fail' is to treat our conception of success as a norm, rather than the rare exception that it is in the long history of human beings...," writes Dr. Sowell. "It is *freedom* for ordinary people that has been a peculiar institution" in a world where most have suffered slavery, poverty, and rule by elites that deemed themselves superior. [28]

"Poverty occurs automatically," writes Dr. Sowell. "It is wealth that must be produced and must be explained." [29]

Professor Sowell understands that America's success came from a rare conjunction of opportunities, values, exceptional people and freedom. The American Dream is the formula for creating a continuing Golden Age, as we see from what it left around us.

We foolishly have allowed statists to impose their nightmare ideology and destroy the American Dream, a proven success. They are turning America into just another corrupt land of limited opportunity and little freedom, like those our ancestors fled.

"Although promoted as a means of helping people trapped by misfortunes beyond their control, welfare state institutions have themselves become traps," writes Dr. Sowell. [30]

Progressive welfare states redistribute a nation's wealth from the productive free market to the government, and then from self-serving politicians to the cronies and government dependents who keep those politicians in power.

A War That Never Ends

The politicians rule via the divide-and-conquer tactic of polarizing people into collectivized groups, then pitting those groups against one another in never-ending ideological warfare. Both Barack Obama and Hillary Clinton learned these ideological tactics for such warfare from the teachings of their shared "hometown" Chicago radical community organizer Saul Alinsky.

Progressive politicians expand their power by endlessly finding new grievances, "victims," and other pretexts for increasing the vast transfer of wealth and power from the private sector to the government and its special interests.

Who ultimately benefits from such perpetual Progressive warfare and from turning American culture into a battlefield?

Not the poor, who are given just enough to remain addicted to government, but never enough to gain their independence from the paternalistic Progressive plantation. Progressive politicians need the poor to remain poor and dependent so they can be controlled.

Not the community, where people live immersed in crime, violence and political corruption as Progressives threaten to ruin or jail police officers who dare to defend private property or pro-actively enforce the law.

And not the middle class, the once-prosperous heart of the American Dream that under Mr. Obama's time in office has shrunk for the first time in our history to less than half of America's population. The middle class is being torn between stagnant incomes and higher government taxes and regulatory pressure.

The Fading Dream

A January 2016 survey found that 69 percent of us now say that obstacles to realizing the American Dream are "more severe today than ever." Forty-nine percent of European-Americans now believe that they are not living the American Dream, and 32 percent believe that they will never achieve it. Many have redefined the traditional American Dream as living comfortably with financial security, not pursuing happiness or getting ahead through hard work. [31]

With Progressives systematically killing the American Dream, those carrying the freedom-craving entrepreneurial gene of their pioneer ancestors might feel far more stress than others at America being turned into just another European-style welfare state that heavily restricts individual free enterprise.

Many lower-middle-class European-Americans have abandoned traditional religious and moral values and the work ethic. By contrast, upper and upper-middle-class European-Americans in their gated communities and suburbs are becoming more conservative in their lifestyles. Sociologist Charles Murray explores this in his 2012 book *Coming Apart: The State of White America, 1960-2010.* [32]

The Identity Politics of the Progressive Dream defines and separates people by skin color. The American Dream respects people as individuals. Bill Bottrell, who co-wrote the 1991 hit song "Black and White" with Michael Jackson, summed up this difference and implicitly repudiated political conformity in a liberating rap line he sings in it: "I'm not going to spend my life being a color."

Remaking Us

The arrogant Progressive social engineers who thought they could make a new Eden, a heaven on Earth through eugenics and Political Correctness and coercion, have failed. They were not as superior to the rest of us as their arrogant oversized egos thought they were.

They have consumed America's seed corn, devoured centuries of wealth that others earned and saved, used the credit card of our children and grandchildren to rack up many trillions in unpaid and unpayable debt, and have now brought America to the brink of breakdown and internal culture war.

Our survival instinct senses that the Progressive Dream has led us not to a secure Post-Scarcity world where nobody needs to hoard or save — but to a Pre-Scarcity world with more takers than makers where the work ethic, thrift, and financial wisdom that once made America prosperous have largely been destroyed out of envy and greed.

Progressives destroyed an America based on hard, honest money. They replaced our incorruptible gold-backed dollars with easily printed, debased paper as our store of value and medium of exchange. Then they wrecked the free marketplace with a new coin of our realm — not money, but power. They made everything here subject to politics and an ideology that has failed everywhere it has ruled.

We have lost faith in our government and its policies to protect and provide for us. But our Progressive president has politicized almost every aspect of the American economy. A key problem with this is that "good" (winning) politics make for lousy economics, and sound, successful economics make for lousy politics. What America needs is the one thing Progressives will never permit — separation of economy and state.

What we want is to feel that we have "enough" to be secure. Instead we have a government that raises our taxes, debases the value of our money and homes, threatens our jobs, floods our communities with illegal aliens, and encourages racial polarization and hostility.

Left-of-center politicians tell police in places like Baltimore to "stand down" in the face of looters. The response of our President to potential riots and terrorism is to propose ways to take away the self-defense firearms of law-abiding citizens. The goose that laid the American Dream's Golden Age is being strangled to death.

The inner city mobs of infantilized gimme pigs have been taught by statists to hate their European-American neighbors — and that the government robbing those "privileged" neighbors is social justice.

Feeling trapped is a health-impairing form of stress. Feeling trapped when we sense a terrible crisis approaching is even worse.

The Trap that the statists are creating is potentially far worse than the loss of freedom. It is literally a death Trap, a source of stress that is already triggering fatal heart attacks, strokes, cancers, and other lethal conditions in untold numbers of Americans.

The Progressive collectivist dream has become a toxic nightmare hazardous to our health. It should be removed from our economy, society and government.

This will be difficult, but how we vote, think and conserve our assets and values can turn our own lives and our nation back towards the American Dream.

One good step toward getting out of The Trap is to convert 10-25 percent of family assets that are now denominated in unreliable government paper currency — which means paper dollars, stocks, bonds, and so forth. Start building a more solid shelter for your family out of universal, hard assets with value that does not depend on government's nanny-statist social engineers, ideologues, and Wall Street manipulators who have bought politicians to bail them out. To get ourselves out of this fast-closing Trap, we need to make some prudent, prompt, and firm decisions.

"Life Rewards Action."

– Dr. Phillip C. McGraw
Life Strategies

*"Money is the barometer
of a society's virtue.*

*"When you see that trading is done,
not by consent, but by compulsion –
when you see that in order
to produce, you need to obtain permission
from men who produce nothing –
when you see that money is flowing
to those who deal, not in goods, but in favors –
when you see that men get richer by graft
and by pull than by work, and your laws
don't protect you against them,
but protect them against you –
when you see corruption being rewarded
and honesty becoming a self-sacrifice –
you may know that your society is doomed."*

– Ayn Rand
Atlas Shrugged

Chapter Six

Totally De-Voted

"A vote is like a rifle:
its usefulness depends upon
the character of the user"

– Theodore Roosevelt

Money talks, and it has a constitutionally-protected right to do so, ruled the
United States Supreme Court in 2010.

In a 5-4 ruling led by the since-deceased conservative Justice Antonin
Scalia, the high court held in the case *Citizens United v. FEC* that the
government could not restrict or prohibit non-profit corporations such as the
group Citizens United from making independent political expenditures.

The Federal Election Commission (FEC) had prohibited this conservative
group, Citizens United, from airing on television an ad for the film *Hillary:
the Movie* within 30 days of the 2008 Democratic primaries.

Running such an ad that mentioned Mrs. Clinton's name, the FEC argued, violated the 2002 McCain-Feingold Act, also known as the Bipartisan Campaign Reform Act (BCRA).

The court struck down provisions in McCain-Feingold that prohibited corporations and unions from making independent expenditures and what BCRA called "electioneering communications."

Former Secretary of State Hillary Clinton continued in her 2016 presidential campaign to call for a new law or ruling that will overturn the *Citizens United* ruling.

McCain-Feingold supporters say the law was drafted to ensure even-handed coverage of candidates. In reality, it might do the opposite.

Most of America's mainstream media tilt left of center in their news coverage. They already favor candidates of the Left like Mrs. Clinton.

If those who oppose Mrs. Clinton are denied the opportunity to buy their way onto the airwaves to make their views heard, then only the indigenous Left-leaning views there will prevail and set the shape and Leftward movement of our politics.

If Mrs. Clinton can impose a law that stifles and silences her opponents' access to the media, she wins.

In her 2016 book *The Intimidation Game: How the Left Is Silencing Free Speech,* investigative reporter Kimberley Strassel of the *Wall Street Journal* documents how America's ideological Left reacted with fury to the "Citizens United" ruling. The Left thought it had achieved almost total control over the nation's media. It doubled down on its push to silence all who disagreed with Leftist dogma. [1]

The radical Left remains only inches away from such control. If Hillary Rodham Clinton is elected President in November 2016, she will select the replacements for Justice Scalia and perhaps several other aging Justices. These new Justices are likely to share her biases against money as free speech...and will be young enough to stay on the Supreme Court for a long time, transforming and silencing America.

The People's Media

Longtime talk radio star Barry Farber was asked why, in all the media, talk radio almost alone seems to reflect mostly conservative and libertarian views. Farber's answer is that ordinary people can be heard every day, with their voices and views pretty much unfiltered, just by calling up a talk radio show.

But we all know, says Farber, that the average person will never be allowed to appear unedited in the *New York Times* or on CBS News.

The dominant media are elite and Progressive in their biases.

In America, people with non-liberal views can at least buy their way onto media via advertising, as Citizens United did. This might be one more example of how the two coins, money and power, are often interchangeable.

What seems more shocking is that so many on the Left, who claim to be fair and open-minded, are willing to win a debate or an election by stifling the voices of their opponents.

Perhaps this stems from a residue of British aristocratic class bias. If someone was not born with elevated social status, they should not be permitted to buy their way to equality with their betters.

One glory of America has been that money can be an equalizer in society. The McCain-Feingold law seems to reflect an ominous new intolerance for diverse views, at least when the different ideas are on the political Right.

This intolerance damages not only free speech but also our democratic republic itself.

On college campuses, speakers are nowadays often silenced by the heckler's veto of those who say Politically Incorrect views are a "micro-aggression" against their tender feelings.

In public discussion of issues, the 2016 Democratic National Platform in effect calls for silencing and punishing those who so much as question the reality of man-made global warming. And some of this comes from the same scientists who back in the 1970s warned an ice age was almost here —

and demanded that others accept their dogmatic views back then, as well. So when were they wrong — yesterday or today? Either way, the climate alarmists' claim of infallibility is absurd, so why are people and companies threatened with fines or jail for taking doomsayer "the-sky-is-falling" views with a skeptical grain of salt?

Politicizing Science

In his far-sighted 1961 Farewell Address, President Dwight Eisenhower anticipated a danger that has now become evident.

"The prospect of domination of the nation's scholars by Federal employment, project allocations, and the power of money is ever present," he warned, "and is gravely to be regarded."

"We ought to 'ride' the global warming issue," Leftist U.S. Senator Tim Wirth (D.-Colorado) told a group of scientists and activists less than two decades later, "because even if the theory proves wrong, it will cause us to make changes we ought to be making anyway."

This was a federal lawmaker who voted on the budget from which many in his audience directly or indirectly were paid handsome incomes, and he, as an ideological politician, was telling them to push a point of view.

Why? Because government was using the global warming theory to demand $100 Trillion in long-term taxes as well as a vast shift in power from the private to the public sector, a shift so profound that it could virtually erase the meaning of private property in the United States and other capitalist nations around the world.

Radical environmental activists are sometimes called "watermelons" because they are "green" on the outside but "red" on the inside. As pseudo-scientific Marxist theories failed, one after another, and as the Soviet dictatorship morally discredited Marxist ideology, its acolytes had to find a disguise that let them continue their crusade to collectivize the planet.

Environmentalism and its idea that everything is ecologically, holistically interconnected and requires centralized political control was a perfect new base of operations from which the radical Left could continue its attacks designed to demonize and ultimately rule and ruin capitalism.

The original strategy and tactics of the watermelon Left were obvious. Amplified by the Leftist media, they launched a massive propaganda campaign warning of fast-approaching doom if Americans did not immediately approve vast new taxes and political controls to save the environment. Melting polar icecaps would cause the seas to rise and inundate the world's coastal cities within a mere decade or two, the doomsayers warned. They tried to panic and stampede people into granting vast environmental powers to the government, immediately!

The aim was to impose crushing regulations and taxes quickly. We suspect that the scientists knew that the whole doomsday scenario was nonsense, that even if humans were causing global warming it would take hundreds of years to happen — and could almost certainly be reversed by simple, inexpensive geo-engineering techniques.

So the objective was to impose crushing regulations and taxes, and then, when almost no warming happened, to give the government and its chokehold on capitalism the credit for "saving the planet."

The "Illusion" of Climate Policy

The real agenda is a "transformation" of the global economy, said the head of climate change policy at the United Nations, Costa Rican diplomat Christiana Figueres.

"This is the first time in the history of mankind," she said, "that we are setting ourselves the task of intentionally, within a defined period of time to change the economic development model that has been reigning for at least 150 years, since the industrial revolution."

And what economic system is to be changed? Capitalism.

And what will replace capitalism? The United Nations is to become the new center of wealth and wealth disbursement on Planet Earth.

"We redistribute *de facto* the world's wealth by climate policy," said Dr. Ottmar Endenhofer, one of the heads of the Intergovernmental Panel on

Climate Change (IPCC) that operates under the auspices of the United Nations.

A 2010 gathering of 10,000 at the United Nations Framework Convention on Climate Change (UNFCCC) in Cancun, Mexico, Dr. Endenhofer told reporters, was "not a climate conference" but "one of the largest *economic* conferences since World War II."

"One has to free oneself from the illusion that international climate policy is environmental policy," said Dr. Endenhofer. "This has almost nothing to do with environmental policy anymore…."

Purported climate change is merely the pretext for creating a vast flow of wealth from the advanced capitalist world to every other nation on Earth hit by flooding or drought, substandard harvests or locusts, heat waves or record cold.

All these things that we and our insurance policies used to call "Acts of God" must in today's godless Progressive world be paid for. The payers are to be rich nations — and especially the United States — who with their advanced technologies have "polluted" and thereby "expropriated" Earth's atmosphere and oceans for their own use.

America is to pay until it, too, becomes a poor third world nation, even though scientists know that climate is a 30-year averaging of weather, and that a season or two of record hot, cold, wet, dry, or stormy weather may simply be normal global fluctuation, not the product of climate change.

Pseudo-Science

We have relied on scientists to monitor and to computer model these longer patterns. If we cannot trust a white-robed member of the "objective" scientific priesthood, who *can* we trust?

A decade ago many confidential emails were leaked that several of the world's most respected global warming doomsayer climatologists had secretly sent to one another. In these, they boasted of how cleverly they had altered data to "hide the decline" — their words — that monitoring stations had clearly measured in global temperatures. Earth had not been getting hotter, but cooler. These so-called scientists had hidden the empirical evidence of this cooling.

By now, you will not be surprised to learn what followed. Most of the world's press buried this story, just as these researchers buried evidence that contradicted their global warming claims and theories.

The scientists, caught red-handed boasting that they had lied and falsified data to protect global warming claims they knew were false, were not fired, as they should have been.

They are still treated as respectable climate experts and honest practitioners of science — although they have betrayed every ethical standard of their profession.

Their scientific papers have not been withdrawn, and continue to be the cornerstones of warming claims made by the United Nations IPCC.

In an honest scientific world, their published studies would have been shredded and utterly discredited in the wake of this proof that they deliberately and knowingly falsified their data. And every other scientific paper that relied on their data would also be discredited and dismissed.

What would honest science look like? Every current claim of global warming would be thrown out, and new 30-year studies with careful safeguards to prevent data manipulation would begin. No scientist would make any claim about man-made global warming until and unless this new, honest-data period of 30 years showed such warming.

Until this happens, honest people must simply recognize that the data on which global warming claims are based has been gimmicked and is unreliable.

We had fairly reliable ground measurements from 1940 to almost 1980 that showed cooling in Earth's Northern Hemisphere. And we have had satellite data beyond the reach of these crooked phony pseudo-scientists that shows essentially no warming for almost the past 20 years.

Please notice that the period between these two patterns, from 1980 to 1996, is only 16 years — not the 30 years needed to make a scientific claim of a change of climate. In other words, all the claims you have heard that Earth's climate is warming are almost by definition unscientific and therefore deceptive.

Silencing the Skeptics

The "hide the decline" scientist frauds have gone unpunished — although Prime Minister May closed Britain's climate office. But honest global warming skeptics have come under attack. Eleven leftwing state Attorneys General have threatened to bring racketeering RICO statute criminal and civil charges against some of them, and against companies that have dared to question the reality of the so-called global warming "consensus" of politically motivated or intimidated scientists.

Genuine science, of course, is not based on a "consensus" that silences all who disagree. True science is based on free and open thought, and on the idea that any widely-accepted theory is always open to being tested and questioned.

Rabid climate alarmists such as former Vice President Al Gore (who lost the 2000 presidential election because those who knew him best in his home state of Tennessee voted against him) want to turn global warming into a rigid dogma that is a sin to question.

This is how "science" was practiced under Josef Stalin's science "czar" in the late Soviet Union. This is not how real science is supposed to be done in the enlightened West. But as a so-called Progressive, Gore is a thousand times more like Stalin than he is like Thomas Jefferson.

When those such as Mr. Gore try to control the freedom of speech and freedom of science of others, it seems clear that they know their dogmatic ideas cannot withstand the light of genuine scientific scrutiny, logic, evidence and truth.

We remember Gore claiming that all credible scientists in the field agree with him. Gore then ran away like a coward when the chief atmospheric scientist at the Massachusetts Institute of Technology (MIT) challenged him to debate.

Gravy Train

Thus far a majority of Americans have been too smart to be stampeded into the authoritarian socialism that Senator Wirth, a close ally of Hillary Clinton, was eager to "ride" to his ideological goal.

Few scientists, even those who knew that the planet has been slowly warming for at least 7,000 years since the last ice age, believed in this wild alarmism. The handful of scientists who did were herded in front of TV cameras and heralded as experts.

During the Clinton Administration, Vice President Gore lionized such experts. When other government scientists went before Congress and voiced skepticism about the climate doomsaying, Gore immediately had them fired.

It took only one or two such political "beheadings" to persuade the rest of the government's environmental scientists to either toe the ideological line about climatic warming, or to at least keep their mouths shut.

As we explained in an earlier book, the politicized pseudo-science controlled by the government now works like a gravy train. If you are a young scientist whose dream in life is to study the sex life of frogs in Costa Rica and you apply for a government grant to do this, you will be turned down.

But today if you apply for a grant to study "The effect of global warming on the sex life of frogs in Costa Rica," the Obama Administration will shower you with money — because it is clear that you know they want a study they can use as one more reason to empower and enrich the government to fight global warming.

Eisenhower understood this in his own era, when national defense and the Military-Industrial Complex were key to powering The Machine and its gravy train. Back then, as we noted, lobbyists got big money for education by calling their legislation "The National Defense Education Act."

But when government money can buy the scientific conclusions that politicians want, is this still honest science?

What does modern democracy mean when Politically Correct pseudo-science is amplified and dissenting scientific views are silenced?

Tilting the Game Board

Look at some other recent examples of questionable tactics used to alter the outcome of elections:

1. Prohibiting the requirement for voter photo IDs, which has the effect of making fraudulent voting easier. Liberals claim that vote fraud is almost non-existent, but some precincts in 2016 Florida, a battleground state, reported voter turnout of more than 140 percent of registered voters.

2. Gerrymandering district boundaries so that, in the words of one Texas judge, "It used to be that voters chose the candidates. With Gerrymandering, the political candidate can help pick his voters."

In what we have called the "Obamamander," President Obama *de facto* extended the entire southern border of the United States below all of Mexico and half of Central America. Latinos surging across our border will someday soon be voting, and around two-thirds will initially vote for Democrats. Since Latinos tend to have family, religious, and work ethic values closer to Republicans, the Democrats could lose this advantage within one to two generations.

3. Allowing felons to vote is a longtime crusade for Democrats, who say that when a person has "paid his debt to society" he should get his rights as a citizen back. Politicians who say this should be asked if that includes felons getting back their Second Amendment right to keep and bear arms.

In 2016 the Democrat-controlled legislature in Maryland restored felon voting rights to approximately 45,000 convicted felons, and did so over the Governor's veto.

In Virginia, Governor Terry McAuliffe, a longtime Clinton comrade, issued an executive order (that might not even be legal) ordering the restoration of voting rights to 205,000 felons. When a court blocked this, McAuliffe began massive "individual" vote restorations.

And as to a felon "paying his debt to society," the California legislature has a plan to let felons vote while still in jail.

Why do we see this partisan passion in favor of votes for felons? Studies at Northwestern and other universities suggest that up to 88 percent of ex-felons would vote Democratic. They apparently think alike: both Democrats and felons favor using coercion to redistribute others' wealth.

Be assured that if felons were likely to vote Republican, Democrats would be rabidly opposed to letting them cast ballots. Likewise, if illegal aliens were likely to vote Republican, Democrats would be the ones demanding construction of a huge wall across America's southern border. Where politicians sit usually determines where they stand.

4. Leftists have proposed lowering the American voting age to 16, when adolescents are liberally idealistic, naïve, and likely to vote Democratic. During the Vietnam War era, the voting age had been lowered from 21 to 18.

In the European Union, by contrast, some Brexit opponents want to prohibit voting by those who reach an older age, perhaps 65. Some also want to prohibit voting on any more referendums in EU countries.

5. The Internal Revenue Service (IRS) delayed the granting of tax-exempt status to conservative Tea Party groups for two years or more while, in at least one case, IRS-marked secret tax documents of a pro-life group were illegally given to a pro-choice group and were used to harass the conservatives.

6. Elections increasingly are conducted with ballots passing through the U.S. Postal Service and its unionized letter carriers. Almost all letter carriers are noble and honest, but if even one percent of letter carriers are less than honest in a state such as Oregon — where all voting is done by mail — they might tip an election simply by making sure ballots mailed from Republican neighborhoods never get to the polls for counting.

7. And, of course, there are longstanding debates over how easily electronic voting machines can be rigged or hacked to produce a desired election outcome.

These are just a few of the ways The Machine may be closer to controlling and thwarting our Democratic Republic than we know.

So let us consider a practical matter. What has been the best way to hedge against the economic impact of the 2016 presidential election as various candidates have come and gone?

In at least one way, for investors it might not really matter which of these candidates wins...*IF* they know how to make the right winning investment.

Gold Standard Bearers

Among the fallen candidates of both parties, the one who most loudly called for a return to hard money was the Lone Star-crossed Texas GOP Senator Ted Cruz. He advocated the gold standard of more than 100 years ago that required every paper dollar to be backed by a guaranteed amount of gold.

Today's Progressive welfare state was built on the government's ability to conjure billions and trillions of paper fiat dollars magically out of thin air. Take that away and the Left's power to endlessly expand government collapses. A restored true gold standard would handcuff the politicians by requiring them to back each new dollar with actual gold.

Cruz was by no means the first modern candidate to call for restoring honest money. President Ronald Reagan appointed a gold commission to consider the idea, and former 2016 presidential candidate Rand Paul's father, Congressman Ron Paul, was a commission member.

Among those running in the 2012 GOP presidential race, Rep. Paul, businessman Herman Cain, and former Speaker of the House Newt Gingrich all openly called for a return to the gold standard. So have journalist and sometime presidential candidate Steve Forbes, technology genius George Gilder, and many others.

Texas Governor Greg Abbott is creating a state bullion depository that will make saving and doing business in gold much easier. We discuss this in detail in our 2015 book *We Have Seen The Future And It Looks Like Baltimore: American Dream vs. Progressive Dream.* [2] Governor Abbott and former Texas Governor Rick Perry, another gold depository advocate, endorsed Cruz for president.

Among 2016 GOP presidential candidates, Senator Cruz may be the only one to formally endorse returning to a gold standard — but several other candidates spoke positively of studying or considering the idea, including former Arkansas Governor Mike Huckabee, famed neurosurgeon Ben

Carson, Kentucky Senator Rand Paul, New Jersey Governor Chris Christie and nominee Donald Trump.

On the Left, the idea of returning to a gold standard is widely attacked because, after all, it would take away their cookie jar for feeding and fattening the ever-expanding welfare state. Critics rarely admit this, however, preferring to attack by claiming that the gold standard is "unworkable" and a threat to using economist John Maynard Keynes' kind of stimulus spending to fuel the economy, and a factor in causing the Great Depression. [3]

Progressive economists know that several kinds of gold standards exist. Rather than attack the classical gold standard of the late 1800s that made America the world's most successful economy — the same gold standard advocated by Cruz — these economists evoke a politically-imposed bastardization, a gold "straw man" known as the "Interwar gold-exchange standard." This had replaced the classical gold standard 10 years before the Great Depression and therefore the classical gold standard did not cause the Depression. [4]

A return to the classical gold standard is quite plausible, but a gold standard works because of gold's scarcity. After thousands of years of mining this incorruptible precious metal, the entire world supply would fit into a single cube only about 67 feet on a side.

$5,000 per Ounce

Because Progressives have printed so many paper dollars out of thin air to fund their welfare state, each dollar's fixed value under a new gold standard might be 1/5,000th of an ounce of gold or less.

In other words, implementing a new classical gold standard might cause the value of gold to jump to $5,000 per ounce or more.

The election, or even nomination, of a President Ted Cruz could have signaled the world that America and its voters may be returning to the classical gold standard — and returning to our former economic greatness. Honest money has once again become thinkable.

What might this do to the world value of gold, the ultimate sure and pure financial asset, the once and future honest universal reserve currency?

Economic historians might look back on 2016 as the year that four wildly different candidates — Clinton, Trump, Sanders and Cruz — were the final four chosen by primary voters to be President. And yet, perhaps by destiny, a victory by any one of them could potentially have sent the value of gold soaring upward as a result of people seeking in the precious metal either a safe haven in an economy likely to get worse, or a profit opportunity.

These prospects remain with a race narrowed to Hillary Clinton, Donald Trump, and growing popular support for the free market Libertarian Party candidate, former New Mexico Republican Governor Gary Johnson.

The year 2016 brought dramatic changes that redefined America — but not just in our politics. It turned into a year that could also redefine and restore our very idea of the integrity of government, money and value.

It became a year when millions of people became sick of the status quo and the tired old establishment politicians of both ruling political parties.

Got gold? This is what the wise are electing to get now, before the November balloting. Their decisiveness could make them big winners in and after the 2016 election.

President Ronald Reagan reawakened us to morning in America, an era of optimism that produced a quarter-century of prosperity and success.

President Barack Obama's nearly eight years, by contrast, have produced mourning in America and a widespread pessimistic feeling of loss, despair and grief.

Millions now feel that something essential to our success and well-being has died here — that we are sad witnesses to the death of the American Dream.

A poll published January 5, 2016 by *Esquire* Magazine and NBC News found that 52 percent of Americans believe the American Dream was "Once True but Not Anymore." Another 11 percent believe that it "Never Held True."

Sixty-three percent of those interviewed in this poll no longer believe in the American Dream of rugged individualism, personal freedom and responsibility, the right to set your own course in life and to keep the fruits of your efforts in a land where small government allows individuals to achieve their highest potential.

If nearly two-thirds of us have lost faith in this faith-based dream, is the America of our Founders and Framers doomed soon to die and disappear?

The Road to Serfdom

The statist dream, a collectivist ideology that emerged from the French Revolution and European Romantic Movement two centuries ago, is opposed to individualism, Judeo-Christian values, and free market economics.

Statism views people and nations as groups to be led by a ruling elite of superior beings who by replacing religion and individual freedom with Big Government and Big Science can create utopia, a human-made Heaven on Earth.

In Europe, Progressivism transformed into several kinds of totalitarianism as well as today's welfare states.

Today it is turning into an anti-democratic empire in the form of the European Union…whose mindset in many ways resembles these previous collectivist governments.

The EU is a bit less oppressive, at least thus far, because citizens, and under rare circumstances, countries still have a right to leave.

In the United States Progressivism's banner today is carried by President Barack Obama and Democratic candidates such as self-proclaimed socialist Bernie Sanders and former Secretary of State Hillary Clinton, who promises that if elected she will "topple" the top 1 percent of earners in America.

The Progressive Dream in all its small variations believes that government should be paternalistic and, therefore, that the people should be infantilized and utterly dependent on Big Government.

Truth in labeling would rename this ideology the Regressive Dream, because in all its forms it would create not progress or prosperity but the squalid, impoverished collectivism that was Europe and much of the rest of the world during the Dark Ages.

This is, to a shocking degree, what nearly eight years of President Obama have produced. He and his comrades have driven America nearly $20 Trillion into debt to enrich a few cronies and stimulate anemic economic growth of less than 2 percent as we teeter on the cliff-edge of another Great Recession or Depression.

America's "non-employment" rate is today the worst since another Progressive President, Jimmy Carter, created the economic malaise of the late 1970s, the fetid quicksand that America escaped by electing Ronald Reagan to replace Carter in 1980.

In 2016 America faced such a choice again. Would we vote to give Obamalaise four more years of Progressive utopian nightmares with Mrs. Clinton? Or would we vote to return to optimism, freedom and the American Dream?

Would it continue to be mourning in America on the downhill path of Progressivism — or the sunrise of morning again lighting our way upward, ascending once more to the American Dream?

Real Democracy

Electoral democracy is becoming more restricted every day. In the November 2016 American presidential election, most voters in all but a handful of battleground states will be unable to affect the outcome with their votes.

Even if your preferred candidate wins, chances are that your choice will ultimately be unable or unwilling to fulfill what promises you thought had been made to you.

But the good news is that we have a form of real democracy in America, and you vote in its elections every day.

This is marketplace democracy, where you can consciously use your ballot — your money — to elect one product or company over another and thereby have a voice in what directions the free market will take.

Ultimately the government does not care how you vote in its elections. The tax collector is going to take your money, whether you favor its policies or not.

But no such coercion exists in the free marketplace. Companies compete and campaign to win your dollars through voluntary, not coercive, transactions.

This daily democracy lets us vote with our consumer dollars to empower those companies whose quality, design, innovations and integrity we deem best.

We need to remember, and teach our children, that free marketplace democracy can have more day-to-day impact on our lives than voting to put a person in the White House.

We should also teach our children that these two democracies interact.

When politicians use the coercive power of the state to limit our market choices or to tax away our dollars, they are taking away our right to vote in America's daily democracy.

As your ability to spend shrinks because you, after paying taxes, have a lot less money, this is denying you "votes" that could directly and immediately improve your and your family's lives.

This is one more reason why it is important to protect and preserve the consumer voting power you earn — your money's quantity *and* quality.

Chances are that roughly half of your neighbors who go to the polls and vote in November will cast their ballot for the loser. But nowadays most of us lose when politicians raise our taxes.

Remember — It's not just your money but also your right to vote in the free marketplace that they are taking from you.

As the politicians tax us in thousands of ways, including the deliberate debasement of our money and the hidden tax of inflation this can cause, it is more important than ever to move a portion of your savings out of paper dollars and into something solid such as gold that paper money manipulation cannot steal.

In the long run, those cajoled into betting in the stock market casino risk serious losses with their savings. But when people buy carefully and thoughtfully, they have a fair chance to come home as winners.

"Of all the contrivances for
cheating the laboring classes of mankind,
none has been more effective than that
which deludes them with paper money....

Ordinary tyranny, oppression, excessive taxation,
these bear lightly on the happiness
of the mass of the community,
compared with fraudulent currencies and
the robberies committed by depreciated paper."

– Senator Daniel Webster
Senate speech, May 28, 1832
on the United States Bank

Part Four

Dawning Empires

Chapter Seven

"No Humans Need Apply"

*"Robots already run most of our world.
We'll be their butlers soon enough."*

— Eric Stoltz
Movie Actor / Director

Brexit was not the first time British workers resisted immigrants in order to protect their jobs. Their first fight, however, was not against imported people, but alien machines.

In the early 1800s factories in northern England were starting to use the first industrial robots, powered mechanical looms and similar devices that wove cloth, stockings and other products faster and with fewer errors than humans could.

In 1801 the French inventor Joseph Marie Charles (nicknamed Jacquard) had perfected his Jacquard loom that controlled the pattern woven into cloth with a paper card's punched holes — like the punch cards that would be used to program our early computers a century and a half later. Skilled weavers were no longer needed to program these power looms.

British factory workers back then believed in what they called the "lump of labor" theory — that only a fixed amount of work was available to be done. A piece of cloth woven by a machine was work and pay forever lost to a human weaver.

Many of these workers called themselves Luddites, after their fictional hero Ned Ludd who was said to live in Sherwood Forest and to have smashed such factory machines. [1]

Ever since, those who oppose technological advances have been called Luddites.

On the Continent, some workers, when no boss was watching, would throw one of their old wooden shoes into the gears of these machines to damage them. These shoes were called "sabots," and their use to jam or break the factory robots came to be called "sabotage."

Rise of the Robots

Analysts used to dismiss Luddite fears of machines as baseless. They reassured us that the design, repair and maintenance of early industrial machines created at least as many new human jobs as the machines replaced. And in more prosperous eras, being freed from mind-numbing assembly line jobs for more creative work could be more liberating than threatening.

Today, however, the relentless and accelerating advance of robot technology coupled with computer Artificial Intelligence is now becoming a major economic crisis in advanced nations.

In his 2015 book *Rise of the Robots: Technology and the Threat of a Jobless Future*, futurist and Silicon Valley software developer Martin Ford shows how computer-guided robots are acquiring the skills to reliably replace more than just factory workers who turn a nut on a simple bolt all day long. [2]

We have already taken our first steps into an age where such robotized systems will drive and park our cars, fly our airliners, and defeat the top human champions on the TV show *Jeopardy* and our greatest chess Grandmasters.

Robots are beginning to teach our kids, nurse our ill and elderly, and do thousands of other things that now require human professionals skilled in human interactions.

Robots have already begun to guide our legal decisions and documents, and to advise and handle our banking and investments.

After a deranged terrorist gunman assassinated five police officers in Dallas in summer 2016, the authorities killed him with a bomb-carrying robot. Experts called this an early example of future law enforcement and war waged with robots. President Barack Obama has used remotely-controlled drone aircraft to kill suspected terrorists in foreign countries.

Our next generation of jet fighters will be robotically piloted, if only because a human pilot could not remain conscious through the high-G-force maneuvers such an aircraft would execute. The National Aeronautics and Space Administration (NASA) now plans to use robots for much of its exploration of other planets.

Our nation's defenders fear the day when terrorists can use robotic controls to steer a truck into a crowd, or an airliner into a skyscraper. Or when they can hack into our own weaponized robots and redirect their power.

Slave or Master?

What, exactly, is a robot?

The name comes from Karel Čapek, who in 1921 wrote the play "R.U.R.," which stood for Rossum's Universal Robots. He derived "robot" from a Czech word for forced labor.

His robots were artificial people that could be used as servants — or slaves. And that has been a widely-shared theme of these entities in science fiction. Will they start as our servants, become our partners, replace us and our jobs, and sooner or later with an I.Q. boost from Artificial Intelligence turn into our masters?

"In the early days of robots people said, 'Oh, let's build a robot' and what's the first thought? You make a robot look like a human and do human things," says scientist Neil deGrasse Tyson. "That's so 1950s. We are so past that."

And, indeed, the typical robot no longer looks human. Chances are that your refrigerator and dishwasher now have computerized "minds" and are robots. So is the Roomba flat, round self-guiding vacuum cleaner sucking up pet hair under your kitchen table.

"I don't think there's a formal definition that everyone agrees on," Kate Darling, a researcher in robot ethics at MIT Media Lab told *The Atlantic*, although she says most scientists define a robot as having some sort of body. [3]

Naked algorithms, and the "bot" programs which do simple robot-like tasks on websites, are now more numerous on the Internet than humans are. They are, as their name suggests, like quasi-robots.

So how close are robots to taking our jobs? It's already happening, with white collar as well as blue collar work, as Jerry Kaplan investigates in his 2015 book *No Humans Need Apply: A Guide to Wealth and Work in the Age of Artificial Intelligence.* [4]

In today's flat American economy, a push has been underway to boost the wages of hamburger flippers at McDonald's to $15 per hour. Trouble is, the higher that wages go, the more cost effective it becomes to replace even semi-skilled workers with robotized technology.

This investment comes with many advantages. It allows a fast-food store to keep its prices lower and more competitive, which benefits the many customers as compared to the few workers.

As to workers, modern robots may cost more initially — but the "training" with modern robots likely costs no more than it does with today's dumbed-down, egoed-up high school graduates.

Also, robots do not get sick, fail to show up on time, fall in love, make major mistakes, rob the till, demand a raise, go out on strike, or retire.

In one Japanese automobile factory, robots work 24 hours each day, seven days each week; the robots, guided not by eyes but by sensors, work all night in a dark factory, which saves the company the cost of lighting.

The major entity pushing for this McDonald's $15 minimum wage is the powerful left-of-center union SEIU, the Service Employees International Union, roughly half of whose members are government workers.

Jobs in the Balance

The SEIU might have some slight motivation in unionizing hamburger flippers, but their larger reason for pushing this wage increase could lie elsewhere.

The big unions have "prevailing wage," "minimum wage," or similar clauses in their contracts. If they can push McDonald's into raising its wages by $8 per hour, then SEIU contractors might be required to boost the high wages paid to its union employees by $8 or more per hour. And this, in turn, will increase how much in union dues its members must pay SEIU.

This union's push to raise McDonald's wages is therefore not entirely selfless. In fact it is quite cynical, because SEIU knows that a young high school dropout who is starting his or her way up the job ladder will get a government-required pay raise one day and then be fired the next. These young workers will have been priced out of the marketplace for the level of work they were doing.

This is the same SEIU that in Illinois and nearly two dozen other states has "persuaded" governments to give it a fat slice of the government stipends that home caregivers receive. These workers should be regarded as unionized and dues paying, SEIU insists, even though a large share of those getting the stipend are caring only for one elderly or disabled member of their own family. So this union grabs a substantial share of what would have been a stipend that helped these poor and suffering families, just so fat cat union bosses can keep flying to their luxury gatherings in corporate jets.

When the $15 minimum wage is imposed, the typical McDonald's franchisee will likely keep the best third of workers and begin replacing the lesser two-thirds with automation and robots. The cost of the pay increase itself is what will pay for buying these robots.

To understand what today's unions think of blue collar workers, think back to the 2016 Democratic National Convention and the head of the AFL-CIO Richard Trumka cheering that party's nominee Hillary Clinton.

Fact One to know: Trumka is the former President of the United Mine Workers Union. Fact Two: Hillary Clinton in a rare moment of candor told miners who belong to this union that, if she is elected, "We're going to put a lot of coal miners and coal companies out of business." Fact Three: Trumka has more than $11 Million dollars from coerced worker union dues, as well as millions of union shock troops who can be ordered to help Democratic candidates in dozens of different ways without being paid for such work, to elect Hillary Clinton and other Democrats.

Monopoly Sandwich

This is how much organized labor cares about the blue collar workers who built it, especially now that the only growing part of the union movement is white collar government workers — federal, state, and local.

Nowadays the average federal worker in wages plus benefits is paid approximately $120,000 per year. The average comparable private sector worker in wages plus benefits makes around $68,000 per year, much of which is lost as taxes to pay for a growing government sector.

The government is a monopoly that doles out pay without having any competitors. The union to which government workers must pay dues is also a monopoly. So the only growing part of the union movement is to put a monopoly on top of a monopoly, at a crushing expense to the taxpayers who get no say in this cozy socialism-on-top-of-socialism arrangement.

Unions could, like Luddites, resist with strikes, slowdowns, industrial sabotage, and other methods to halt the coming of worker-replacing robotic technologies — but this would merely slow an inevitable rear-guard retreat.

Robots will hold down consumer prices, and in the long run the companies that use them will out-compete the companies that pay higher wages.

Unionized companies will go bankrupt, and most will be replaced by new, non-unionized companies.

This robot takeover of jobs will affect many millions of Americans — including perhaps you, your children and grandchildren.

Our "Flash Crash" Culture

As we explored in our 2014 book *Don't Bank On It!: The Unsafe World of 21st Century Banking*, on May 6, 2010, the New York Stock Exchange suffered what came to be called "the Flash Crash," when the Dow Jones Industrial Average plummeted unexpectedly by nearly 1,000 points in only minutes.

A single "sell" order valued at approximately $4.1 Billion purportedly set off a cascade of computerized buy-and-sell programs around the world that are designed to respond immediately, and without consulting human beings, to key changes in market prices. As each major trading computer reacted, it could have triggered programmed reactions in similar computers. [5]

Some of these systems use High Frequency Trading (HFT) that today can launch trade decisions, buy and sell orders, in mere thousandths of a second or less. This, according to critics, allows traders who have paid millions for this razor-thin advantage-in-time to detect incoming stock purchases; front run and automatically buy that stock before the competing slower order gets processed; and sell the stock a fraction of a second later to the slower order at a slightly higher price. [6]

Such are the systems, with their risk of triggering "buy" or "sell" cascades around the world, that are being used in today's merging worlds of high-tech investing and high-money banking.

As we said, we shape our tools and thereafter our tools shape us. We created debased money as a political and economic tool, and we built our society on it — yet now we wonder why our society has become debased.

We built giant government so our politicians could have limitless money, power, and glory — and now we wonder why government is crushing us.

And now we are developing robots capable of doing all our work — and we will soon wonder why we have become so helpless, and wonder where our jobs, wealth and freedom went.

Parents know that their children will not necessarily think the way they do. Why did we assume that we would always control how our robots think or act?

Intelligence, Artificial

Another crash happened on Leap Year Day, February 29, 2012, a relatively quiet Wednesday on the New York Stock Exchange.

Looking backward, historians may date this as the first sign of what became the Great Financial Collapse that changed our civilization forever.

On that fateful day, a sudden "violent sell-off in stocks…seemed to start at exactly 10:00 AM" Eastern Time, recounted *Business Insider* reporter Sam Ro. "[T]he supernatural speed of the sell-off had traders thinking two words: Artificial Intelligence." [7]

One who thought this was Art Cashin, the veteran director of floor operations for UBS Financial Services, a subsidiary of giant United Bank of Switzerland.

His *Cashin's Comments* the next morning said:

Algo My Way By Myself Or Open The Pod Doors, HAL…As noted, the instantaneous nature of the selloff…raised lots of questions…. Those questions prompted an intriguing hypothesis…that [the just-released speech by Federal Reserve Chairman Ben Bernanke] had been instantly parsed by a computer using Artificial Intelligence."

"You wouldn't need much Artificial Intelligence to see…quickly and clearly" that Bernanke's speech described improving employment in the economy, which would shift Federal Reserve concern to the other half of its dual mandate, from jobs to "worrying about inflation and a firm dollar," wrote Cashin. Such a shift could re-value many stocks and trigger both market buying and selling.

"So was the selloff started by someone's version of HAL 9000 [the soft-spoken yet murderous spacecraft computer in Stanley Kubrick's 1968 movie "2001: A Space Odyssey," whose three-letter name HAL was a one-letter backstep from computer company IBM]?" asked Cashin. "We don't know for sure. There are said to be such experiments on trading desks at hedge funds and elsewhere. And, it certainly fits the action to a tee." [8]

HAL, we remember, had a mind of "his" own and was willing to kill any human "he" decided was a danger to the spacecraft's mission. In June 2016, the BBC reported a runaway Russian robot in Perm that escaped lab confinement, fled down a nearby street, and was recaptured only after its battery ran out.

We already have IBM robots such as "Watson," that could defeat the greatest human champion at *Jeopardy*, Ken Jennings, and "Deep Blue," that beat the greatest living chess Grandmaster Gary Kasparov.

These victories happened largely because the computers could remember and instantly retrieve stored information, such as all Grandmaster matches won over centuries by humans. But computers are beginning to bring more than storage and speech to such challenges; they are beginning to analyze that data, to make abstract connections and "think," in ways different from human beings.

This is no longer your father's financial world of slow, thoughtful individual banking and stock buying. By 2011, 73 percent of market trading was already algorithmic, done via machines and exotic programmed computer algorithms. [9] In 1987 the average share of stock was held by one owner for approximately two years. By 2011 the average share was held for only 22 seconds. And this churn is getting faster and faster. [10]

By 2011, "a company announced the ability to execute trades within nanoseconds," wrote Cris Sheridan of *FinancialSense.com*. "According to *Wikipedia*, 'One nanosecond is to one second as one second is to 31.7 years.' Just let that seep in for a moment. How many millions of trades can be made in one second? Too many. Although speed isn't a substitute for intelligence, in terms of trading, it's a pretty good proxy." [11]

For years computer scientists tried to teach computers to comprehend the English language and to glean business data from world news, creating early business decipherment programs to do this such as "Ripper," "Shredder, "Rebellion" and "You Don't Know Jack."

A.I.-pocalypse Now

Today's Artificial Intelligence (A.I.) computers can sift key investment information 24 hours a day from the world's vast digital news and data flow. Not only can they read business news but also write the data they analyze into business news stories key-worded to be easy for other A.I. computers to read — and to use to make, buy and sell investment decisions in tiny fractions of a second, without necessarily consulting humans. [12]

We have encountered and empowered a superior alien intelligence of our own making. The science fiction stories about the dangers of this are many. In "2001," HAL's programming prompts him to defend the space mission by killing all but one of the very astronauts he supposedly was programmed to protect and serve.

More than fiction, Artificial Intelligence frightens some of today's brightest scientists and engineers. Elon Musk, the genius behind PayPal, SpaceX and Tesla electric automobiles, fears that A.I. could potentially prove to be "more dangerous than nukes." Astrophysicist Stephen Hawking warns that A.I. could destroy humankind. [13]

"One can imagine such technology [Artificial Intelligence] outsmarting financial markets, out-inventing human researchers, out-manipulating human leaders, and developing weapons we cannot even understand," wrote Hawking and three scientific colleagues in a May 2014 article. "Whereas the short-term impact of AI depends on who controls it, the long-term impact depends on whether it can be controlled at all." [14]

Are we creating super-predator rivals that could out-compete and replace us? Could we become merely an evolutionary step to the next dominant life form on planet Earth, A.I. computer machines? Look at what is now happening in the stock market.

"Shaping" Markets, Marginalizing Investors

"For decades, professional investment advisors have continued to teach reliance on 'value investing' and 'buy-and-hold' as long-term guides to successful investment. [But] technology may now have overridden such investment concepts," we are told in *The Marginalizing of the Individual Investor.* [15]

This analysis, Sheridan tells us, is published "by the global think tank International Economy, whose editorial board includes…former and current presidents of the European Central Bank, George Soros, Martin Feldstein, and various Federal Reserve chairmen.

"High-frequency trading platforms are focused solely on ramping up speed and volume so as to maximize tiny gains per transaction," *Marginalizing* continues. "Computerized algorithms that are momentum-sensitive are increasingly high-frequency trading-driven, raising serious doubts about traditional concepts of how markets should work."

"Investment strategies based on fundamentals such as a company's long-term performance have been swept aside by high-frequency trading algorithms hunting for inefficiencies in daily pricing and super arbitrage opportunities," *Marginalizing* continues. "In so doing, they open investors to a new form of risk that has not been accounted for in most 'buy and hold' asset allocation models."

"In effect, individual traders are confronted with overwhelming momentum-driven forces that are unrelated to performance of individual businesses," writes *Marginalizing*. "A 'fair price' may exist, but high-frequency traders are not seeking fair prices — they are focused on immediate profit…."

"Unfortunately," warns *Marginalizing*, "high-frequency trader interaction with computerized algorithms of large-cap financial institutions is providing opportunities for high-speed, virtually undetectable market manipulation. Where there is opportunity to 'shape' the market for advantage, it is likely that such opportunity will be exploited."

Are our A.I. computers and official policies already rigging our stock markets, banks and currency? Where is this self-driving vehicle taking us?

The choice being offered to us is to lose the value of our money in bank accounts, or lose our money in risky, potentially-rigged stock market casinos where giant broker-banker partnerships own the biggest, fastest computers. Government lets all this continue because it shakes down the banks and brokers that have our money and shares their "take." We need to create our own choice that benefits and protects us.

Calling Collect-ive

Today's automated computer programs, some pundits suspect, have put the modern computer-driven global stock markets and investment banks on a hair trigger, not unlike liquid-fueled nuclear missiles of the early 1960s that were to be launched at the first sign of preemptive enemy missile attack because military planners believed they had to "use it or lose it." Only with the development of solid fuel rockets and invulnerable hardened missile silos did this hair trigger policy change.

Our weakening economy and the U.S. Dollar are becoming more vulnerable because we rely on ever-more-centralized systems.

Decentralizing our technologies would make America much less vulnerable to high-tech terrorism and breakdowns.

What Left-liberals condemn as "urban sprawl," combined with local self-reliance, would make us much harder for terrorists to attack and shut down. [16]

America's ruling politicians and bureaucrats, however, are ideologically committed to forcing more and more centralized control onto every aspect of life in the United States.

Decentralization and self-reliance, they believe, would make Americans too independent, too free, and statists are eager to replace individual liberty with collectivist control.

These centralized systems of control are making our economy and society vastly more vulnerable to many kinds of "flash crashes," inadvertent or deliberate, in the technological systems on which we depend.

We have invested our fate in systems whose vulnerabilities we do not fully know or comprehend. Could this become the "Achilles' Heel" of our civilization, the fatal weak spot that brings it down?

Precariats of the World, Unite!

What will happen when, as experts predict, robots will have replaced perhaps half the jobs of working Americans?

This is one of many reasons why some economists say the West has created a new class — not a Marxist proletariat of workers without any good prospects who "have nothing to lose but their chains" — but what University of London economist Guy Standing calls a "precariat," people with jobs and situations that are precarious. [17]

The middle class most of us once thought we belonged to, along with its values we all shared, comprises less than half of America's population and is shrinking.

Studies now warn that a quarter of Americans have no savings for retirement — or for anything else. A third of us reportedly have too little spare money to handle a $1,000 emergency.

One third of Americans are now in the "gig" economy, freelancers who mostly just get by, making just enough to pay their bills so long as nothing goes wrong such as an illness or unexpected expense.

These precariat workers typically at night either get stoned or stay awake worrying. Their anxiety causes stress, which impairs both their work skills and health.

No wonder America's economy is spiraling down. No wonder so many turn to the welfare state rather than continue a drowning struggle. And once they are receiving regular government benefits for doing nothing, no wonder so few are willing to risk losing those benefits by going back to work.

The long-term unemployed typically will have their job resumes ignored without a recent work history. Those with youthful criminal convictions have also been almost automatically rejected, which is why the Obama Administration now threatens severe punishment for companies that dare to do criminal background checks on those submitting preliminary job applications.

Needless to say, when companies are effectively forced to hire convicted criminals, and some of those hires commit crimes such as identity theft against company clients, the government will blame the company, not itself.

Money for Nothing

Some analysts on both the Right and Left have proposed a way to deal with human joblessness: not a minimum wage to be paid by employers, but a "guaranteed minimum income" to be paid by the government. [18]

This income for everybody, typically proposed to be around $850 to $1,200 per month, would ensure that people have a steady income that will keep coming, whether they have a job or not.

The idea is supported by Andy Stern, former head of the SEIU. (This is the same radical labor leader who once famously said that those who do not give in to his "power of persuasion" will be subjected instead to "the persuasion of power."

In his 2016 book *Raising the Floor: How A Universal Basic Income Can Renew Our Economy and Rebuild The American Dream*, Stern argues that a guaranteed minimum income would make people more secure and give them more human dignity. That this would also be a massive redistribution of wealth from the upper class to the middle and lower classes he apparently sees merely as a bonus. [19]

On the other end of the political spectrum, the American Enterprise Institute analyst and libertarian Charles Murray also applauds this idea.

In the 2016 updating of his 2006 book *In Our Hands: A Plan to Replace the Welfare State*, Murray argues that it would be significantly cheaper for government to give everybody a guaranteed basic income than it now costs to give out welfare. [20]

Why is giving so much to everybody cheaper than today's welfare state? Because it eliminates the middleman.

In today's American welfare state, the world's second largest behind China, vast amounts of welfare money are allocated to help the poor, but as much as 81 cents of every dollar is raked off and spent by the welfare bureaucracy — social workers, $150,000 per year administrators, and the like. The actual welfare recipient actually receives as little as 19 cents of every welfare dollar.

Eliminating the Middleman

If we eliminate these money-devouring middlemen who now take most of this money and instead just give money directly to the poor, we could provide every poor person a middle-class income and have mountains of money left over for all the rest of us.

Murray's analysis stems from Nobel Laureate economist Milton Friedman's idea for a "negative income tax" that gives a big enough tax refund to lift every poor person up to a minimum basic income.

Within The Machine, the poor are merely a pretext for imposing vast taxes in the name of the welfare state. This is why researchers have found social workers who tell their clients *not* to get a job. If today's poor suddenly all won the lottery and became middle class, what pretext would justify continuing the welfare state?

Murray's guaranteed basic income would make the welfare state unnecessary. No more welfare, or means testing, or concern about potential welfare cheats. What could be more egalitarian than guaranteeing everybody the same basic income, a secure floor beneath everybody's feet to prevent anyone from falling into poverty?

This, of course, would end the jobs of those employed by the welfare state. This could curtail one huge group of people who vote for the Big Government Party to keep their own checks coming.

For millions of today's welfare recipients, regularly receiving paychecks without having to renew welfare applications or groveling as a supplicant in front of bureaucrats and social workers might make them feel less like dependent slaves of the Big Government Party politicians.

Of course, the idea of providing everybody a guaranteed basic income raises many questions. At what age would it begin, one or 18 or 21? How do you encourage work by paying people enough to feel secure but not enough to feel successful or fulfilled?

Would a guaranteed income undermine the work ethic of millions, perhaps even worse than critics say welfare has done?

By making work unnecessary, would this make humans feel unnecessary — and deny people the sense of accomplishment, self-respect, and human dignity that comes with work?

Traitor to Humankind

At a more practical level, how will this impact the economy? Imagine a future where robots do the work providing things and services — but this guaranteed income for the entire human population is low, almost subsistence level.

Who can afford to buy what the robots are making, if half of Americans stop producing? Other robots? A few rich people?

Production may be much higher, thanks to robots, but consumption by humans in this emerging society will likely be far below what it is today. Who is going to pay for all of this?

The rising empire of the European Union has an answer.

On May 31, 2016, the European Parliament filed a draft report recommending that robots be granted the legal "status of electronic persons" for "the purpose of taxation and social security contributions." [47]

Social security taxes on robots, even though they will never live — since they are not alive now — to collect any social security benefits, can then be used to help fund the basic guaranteed income for human workers the robots have replaced.

This EU report, in fact, recommends such a guaranteed income, money for nothing, for humans to compensate for jobs lost to robots.

To the degree that high taxes on robots discourage companies from using them, could this save some human jobs? Probably not, because the robots have few of the problems, as noted above, that human workers do.

The EU seems not to care, as long as its bureaucrats get their taxes. This new empire has become a traitor to humankind.

If the European Union is willing to grant the status of "electronic persons" to robots so it can tax them, where else does this lead?

Will robots acquire other human rights? The right to vote and elect robot lawmakers? Free speech? Marriage? Choice of gender identity? Protection against insults and other "micro-aggressions?" Freedom not to be fired when they become old, slow, and obsolete?

Will robots have the right to move and work anywhere in the EU? Have maximum daily work hours? Vacations? A guaranteed minimum wage? The right to keep and bear arms? No, nobody in the EU has *that* right except its secret imperial military.

Science fiction authors have given us chilling glimpses of what can come to pass if today's strong government and weak economic patterns continue, as we shall see in the next chapter.

"When buying and selling are controlled by legislation, the first thing to be bought and sold are legislators."

– P.J. O'Rourke

*"Politics is the Entertainment Division
of the Military-Industrial Complex."*

– Frank Zappa
Musician

Chapter Eight

Seeds of Tomorrow

*"We are in science fiction now.
Whoever controls the images
...controls the culture."*

– Allen Ginsberg
Poet

The seeds of the future, both good and bad, are already sprouting around us, as foreseen by visionary authors of science fiction.

Their stories often anticipate what changes will happen and help us to see this more clearly.

Here are a few stories that foresaw ominous seeds germinating in our world today:

Nineteen Eighty-Four (also known as ***1984***) by George Orwell (pen name for Eric Blair, who worked as a British colonial policeman in Burma):

The central character in this 1948 novel works for the government in the Ministry of Truth by daily rewriting news and historical documents to ensure that all of them show that the dictator, "Big Brother," has always been right about everything.

This kind of mind control also comes in the form of official slogans that restrict thinking or speaking anything contrary to Big Brother's ideological orthodoxy.

The Left in America is Orwellian, having created Political Correctness to restrict what people are permitted to write and say.

On many college campuses, almost any non-Leftist speaker or views have been silenced because they constitute a pain-causing "micro-aggression" against intolerant students.

The 2016 Democratic Party's national platform calls for punishing companies that advocate skepticism about man-made global warming. Others on the Left have proposed fines, prison, and in rare cases even execution for global warming skeptics.

The Obama Administration routinely re-writes historical documents to delete all references to radical Islamist terrorism. In 2016 they took a video interview with French President François Hollande and edited it to delete his mention of "Islamic terrorism."

This novel depicts a future with Big Brother's surveillance equipment everywhere. In today's real world, such surveillance cameras are in widespread use in London. The National Security Agency is building a facility in Utah capable of storing extensive data about every person on Earth.

We do not know the extent to which government is monitoring potentially millions of people, including us. Such surveillance in this novel is justified by this country Oceania — one of three global imperial powers…if you can believe anything at all in the perpetually revised history books.

Winston Smith, the central figure in this novel, begins to doubt that the perpetual war between these powers is real. Perhaps Big Brother occasionally sets off a bomb in the city to create the illusion of war, thereby justifying Big Brother's totalitarian powers.

Note that massive government surveillance of many of us is now justified in our world by a potentially perpetual war against terrorism.

Brave New World by Aldous Huxley:

The most frightening thing about the dystopian government in this 1932 novel is that the people in this world are mostly quite happy.

They go to the "Feelies" at their local theater and, via electric hand knobs on the seats, are able to feel the recorded sensations felt by the actors as they performed. (In the future our old movies will have dubbed-in emotions.)

In this strange world, residents use a drug, Soma, which keeps them pacified and happy. When a group's Soma runs out, people begin to panic as they start to return to reality, cold turkey. Just in time, a government truck appears with fire hoses and drenches the crowd with liquefied Soma. The crowd almost instantly becomes tranquil and docile again.

Sexual activity with a variety of partners is regarded as recreation. Reproduction is done by the state. The residents of *Brave New World* are test tube babies, genetically altered to be one of six different types, from smart to dumb.

Babies are programmed with hypnotic messages each day, embedding slogans that will be repeated throughout each person's life. These messages tell Gamma babies, for example, that Gammas are the best and most talented people. Such programming makes everyone feel superior, so nobody envies those of different types.

In today's America many drugs, including marijuana, are illegal under federal law. Despite this, the Obama Administration has largely ceased enforcement of these laws as the states of Colorado, Washington, Oregon and Alaska have under state law legalized high-potency marijuana, taxed it, and begun selling it commercially and openly for "recreational use." Several other states may soon follow.

Some cities, as we discussed in our book *We Have Seen the Future and It Looks Like Baltimore: American Dream vs. Progressive Dream*, have turned to harder drugs, now cheap and widely available. The once-beautiful city of Baltimore is now America's heroin capital, with one of every 10 residents a junkie.

Mind-altering illicit and prescription drug use is now widespread among many professionals, including traders who run Wall Street. The average American uses at least two prescription drugs, the most widely used of which is legally classed as an "anti-psychotic." Are we turning into a Brave New World, with a large portion of our citizens already tranquilized, pacified, and made less productive and self-reliant by drugs?

In August 2016 the head of the Atlanta Federal Reserve Bank, Dennis Lockhart, said: "Central banking is in a brave new world."

The Matrix:

This 1999 movie portrays a struggle for planetary dominance between the conjured virtual world of computers and the real world of a colony of humans fighting to survive and restore a ruined Earth. It shows how the line between the two realms is already profoundly blurred as our machines now reshape our world and perception of reality.

A smart phone game, "Pokéman GO," suddenly became wildly popular in Summer 2016. It blurs real and computer worlds by inserting computer-generated characters into the very place your smart phone camera is seeing, then gives you ways to capture these otherwise-invisible creatures.

The Matrix depicts the risks of creating and empowering Artificial Intelligence computers and robots that can rival or surpass us.

Minority Report:

This 2002 film, directed by Steven Spielberg and based on a Philip K. Dick story, envisions a future in which the state arrests people for crimes they have not yet committed.

These pre-criminals can be arrested and jailed because a team of psychics foresees what it calls their forthcoming crimes. The state then preemptively arrests the "criminal."

Odd as this sounds, the People's Republic of China announced in 2016 that it was going to start identifying such pre-criminals for surveillance and potential arrest.

Imagine the emerging technologies, combined with today's surveillance methods, in the hands of the British in, say, 1760. Hostility to their rule, or rebellious tendencies in general, could be identified and used to preemptively neutralize George Washington, Thomas Jefferson and other future leaders of the American Revolution. How is our surveillance re-writing the future?

Ready Player One:

Based on the 2011 novel by Ernest Cline, and being turned into a major motion picture by Steven Spielberg (who also did the movie "*A.I.*") for 2018 release, this dystopian story is set in 2044 in a ruined society on the brink of social breakdown. People live in tiny apartments they rarely leave because of pervasive violent crime. The world comes to them — for everything from shopping on their meager income, to scarce part-time work, to attending school — via computer connections.

The hero and his friends spend their days trying to unravel the secrets hidden inside a worldwide virtual reality computer game based on a utopia called OASIS. The co-creator of OASIS has promised to give his immense fortune to whoever unlocks its secret codes.

Cline describes this OASIS co-creator as "a cross between Albert Einstein and Santa Claus."

The fortune is an enormous incentive, being in OASIS currency, "the most stable currency in the world" of apparently unstable currencies.

The villain in this story is a giant multinational corporation aiming to take over and "monetize" OASIS.

The story details the dawning world of more than half the population — never working, subsisting on the government's guaranteed basic income check that has replaced welfare, and other benefits.

Such people have tiny apartments with mirrored walls to create the illusion of more room. Many use drugs, akin to the Soma in *Brave New World*, but some of which may enhance intelligence. And they have amazing virtual reality capabilities that allow them to live their entire lives vicariously through virtual reality...another version of *The Matrix*.

Chillingly, America's stagnant economy and welfare-drugfare policies are rapidly turning this kind of dystopia from fiction to fact.

Star Trek:

This Gene Roddenberry fiction set in the 24th Century, was originally conceived during the 1960s for television as "Wagon Train to the Stars," then later metamorphosed on television into smug European Political Correctness. Its movies continue to be a cash machine for Hollywood.

The story and its characters have long inspired exploration, innovation, and open-mindedness. Some fans have begun to broaden its horizons into the future possibilities for economics.

"Trekonomics is post-economic," writes Manu Saadia in his 2016 book *Trekonomics: The Economics of Star Trek*. [1]

"In Star Trek, currency has become obsolete as a medium for exchange. Labor cannot be distinguished from leisure. Universal abundance of almost any goods has made the pursuit of wealth irrelevant."

Really? In the original Star Trek, the crew used "Federation Credits" to purchase odd things like Tribbles.

By *Star Trek: The Next Generation*, however, Captain Jean-Luc Picard (played by British actor Patrick Stewart) was unctuously saying:

"People are no longer obsessed with the accumulation of things. We've eliminated hunger, want, the need for possessions. We've grown out of our infancy."

"Material needs no longer exist," said Captain Picard. "Money doesn't exist in the 24th Century."

"The acquisition of wealth is no longer the driving force in our lives. We work to better ourselves and the rest of humanity."

Stewart likely delighted in speaking these preachy lines. In real life he is a proud British Labour Party-supporting socialist, a Brexit opponent, and a very successful and wealthy movie star.

But aboard the Starship Enterprise, its Holodeck lets crew members experience whatever they desire in full three-dimensional virtual reality —

skydiving, visiting the "Pleasure Planet" Risa, climbing the tallest volcano in the solar system, Olympus Mons on Mars.

The Enterprise's Replicator can conjure and rearrange atoms to produce within seconds almost anything a crew member asks for. Here's your perfectly cooked Beef Wellington.

The Star Trek world has harnessed the power of matter-antimatter reactors and thus has almost limitless power at nearly zero cost. This power makes possible the economic dream of "post-scarcity," enough power to manufacture at the atomic scale almost anything you want.

Alchemist Gold

Imagine going to a Starship Enterprise Replicator and saying "I would like five pounds of pure gold, please."

What becomes of motivation, money and value in such a universe?

Since antiquity, alchemists dreamed of finding a way to transmute lead or other cheap base elements into gold — an event they called *chrysopoeia*. Even alchemist Sir Isaac Newton, one of the greatest scientists in human history, failed to discover this secret.

But in the Golden State of California in 1980, scientists made this transmutation happen. We now know that this transformation can be done to three elements: lead, mercury, and bismuth.

Nobel-prizewinning chemist Glenn Seaborg and his team of nuclear scientists from the Lawrence Berkeley National Laboratory aimed the high energy beam from a particle accelerator at a sample of bismuth for a day.

Their particle accelerator within a day stripped four protons from each of more than a thousand atoms of bismuth, thereby turning those atoms into isotopes of gold.

Seaborg's experiment proved that humans now can, after centuries of trying, at last transmute a base element into gold. This atomic alchemy, however, is unlikely to change the price of gold anytime soon.

Experts have predicted that the near-term market price of an ounce of gold might soon increase to between $10,000 and $20,000.

The Particle beam accelerator that Dr. Seaborg and his team used cost $5,000 per hour to operate, and their one-day experiment created at most a few thousand atoms of gold.

"It would cost more than one quadrillion dollars per ounce to produce gold by this experiment," Seaborg in 1980 told the *Associated Press*. [2]

At today's price, ounces of natural gold are a tremendous bargain.

Alas, in the real world we do not yet have a working matter-antimatter reactor.

The Machinery of Peace

Gene Roddenberry believed that money is a vestige of humankind's dark past, the serpent he wanted to banish from his utopian future Eden.

(For the record, the agnostic Roddenberry resisted all network attempts to have him include a Christian chaplain in the Enterprise crew.)

"The flexibility of money, with its ability to let disparate persons work in harmony, is (far from Roddenberry's view) one of the most glorious developments in the history of mankind," wrote P. Gardner Goldsmith in *The Freeman*, the journal of the Foundation for Economic Education. [3]

"Money is the machinery of peace, not of war," wrote Goldsmith.

Science Fantasy

After studying Trekonomics, wrote Goldsmith, "I realized 'Star Trek' was not science fiction but science fantasy."

Without Roddenberry creating his own *Deus ex machina*, his infinite power reactor, the machine that can make limitless amounts of everything, his socialist post-scarcity paradise might never be possible.

His matter-antimatter reactor requires "dilithium crystals" to work. As one economist asked, in Star Trek who mines these crystals? The series depicts humans, not robots, doing this. These keys to Star Trek's magic utopian kingdom presumably cannot be manufactured by a Replicator.

Roddenberry's race of beings originally used to demonize capitalism, the money-obsessed extraterrestrials he called the Ferengi, use bars of a special metal that also cannot be produced by Replicators — and therefore has value as one of the few "scarce" materials in the Star Trek universe.

In this egalitarian Star Trek future, why is one person the captain of the Enterprise, where most crew members are not even officers? (When an anonymous crew member beamed down with a landing party, we always knew he was about to be killed.) The Star Trek future may have no "inequality," but it has rank, privilege, and hierarchy.

Is the captain paid more than his crew members — or did pay, and hence pay differences, vanish when money did? In the post-scarcity Federation, do "progressive taxes" still exist, and does the captain pay more taxes than his crew members? Is this a post-taxation paradise?

Star Trek almost certainly has a government with officials willing to spend to the limit of its resources — and beyond.

As the joke goes about the other grand space movie franchise, *Star Wars*, the intergalactic empire will not be destroyed by war but by the cost overruns and supersized debt and interest from building the Death Star.

One thing will be certain four centuries from now, as it was four centuries ago: every nation, world, or intergalactic federation will have two coins in its realm. One is the coin of money; the other the coin of power.

The British and American empires have stood on two legs — one military, the other economic. If and when either leg collapses, the empire falls.

Cashless on Antares

If Star Trek has no money, is it ultimately based on just one coin — power? If citizens have no wealth or property in this future utopia, it is a good bet that they do not control their own high-powered Replicator, or their own matter-antimatter reactor to power it, or Dilithium crystals, or a giant starship like the Enterprise.

But somebody will "own" such ultra-expensive things. And all those in need of free goodies from a Replicator will be dependent on the Federation government and its powerful rulers to provide such goodies.

The Enterprise may be an exploration ship, but it is armed like a warship. The Federation has a history of war. It conquered Mr. Spock's home planet Vulcan because Vulcans play logical chess but Earthlings bluff as in poker.

So even if the Federation has no coin of money, it has acquired and uses vast quantities of the coin of power. In many ways these two coins are fungible and interchangeable, and when one is missing the other often takes its place.

We have noticed that the same power-hungry politicians who are eager to tax and redistribute other people's money are almost never willing to redistribute *their own power* to the rest of us.

Quite the opposite, their solution to every problem is always to increase the government's power and to tax away an ever-larger share of wealth earned by the People. Whatever became of the 1960s slogan "Power to the People?"

Our politicians have become power junkies whose addiction to OPM (other people's money) and OPP (other people's power) constantly craves and demands an ever-increasing dose of both drugs.

 Yet what our country desperately needs to restore liberty and prosperity is a return of both power and wealth from government to the People.

Only when government stops devouring more than its "fair share" of our nation's power and wealth can the rest of us grow to our healthy full potential, as America's Framers intended.

Our Declaration of Independence and Constitution were designed to keep power in the hands of the People and to constrain the government.

Unlike the Star Trek Replicator, government produces nothing. It acquires wealth and power by taking them from others. This is why when government becomes obese, millions of the rest of us starve.

Gene Roddenberry should have thought more about these two coins, money and power, when socially engineering his utopian vision of a Star Trek without money, but where only the government owns all the power and starships.

Dreams and Nightmares

Those who dream of having a Star Trek Replicator should remind themselves of the classic 1956 science fiction movie **Forbidden Planet**, which told of an ancient brilliant extraterrestrial civilization that perished because it built a giant machine capable of fulfilling all of their wishes, like Aladdin's magic lamp.

What these ancients forgot, *Forbidden Planet* shows, is that the mind has more than noble and friendly thoughts and wishes. It also has a side of unconscious, primal, negative emotions such as hatred and jealousy that psychoanalyst Sigmund Freud called the "Id."

When this great civilization switched on its grand wish-granting machine, it gave unlimited power to carrying out all the evil emotions and lusts for power over others that lurked in their minds. This destroyed them.

In odd ways, this is what The Machine and its ability to churn out endless quantities of paper money have given to collectivist ideologues and greedy politicians in our own time.

The Machine has brought our economy and society to the brink of destruction — a "macro-aggression" against America.

"You can avoid reality,
but you cannot avoid the consequences
of avoiding reality."

– Ayn Rand

*"You have to choose between trusting
to the natural stability of gold
and the natural stability of the honesty and intelligence
of the members of the Government.*

*"And, with due respect for these gentlemen,
I advise you, as long as the Capitalist system lasts,
to vote for gold."*

— **George Bernard Shaw**
Irish Playwright

Part Five

An Empire for Liberty

Epilogue

The Golden Triangle

"...we should have such an empire for liberty
as she has never surveyed since the creation:
& I am persuaded no constitution was ever before so well
calculated as ours for extensive empire & self government."

– Thomas Jefferson
Letter to James Madison
April 27, 1809

On July 30, 2016, *The Economist* published an attack on America's Republican presidential nominee Donald Trump because he had said "Americanism, not globalism, will be our credo." [1]

"It has been our fate as a nation not to have ideologies, but to be one," said historian Richard Hofstadter. Our national ideology is Americanism.

Whatever one might think of Mr. Trump, this anti-Brexit United Kingdom magazine does not understand him. It now sees him on the wrong side of a "new political divide," not between Right and Left but between what it calls welcoming "open" people and wall-building "closed" people.

For Europeans with their long and bloody past of nationalism, even the authoritarian and deceptive ways of the new empire now called the European Union might seem preferable. It, at least, is erasing old national borders and distinctions, they feel.

We also appreciate the joy Europeans dreamed of at no longer being awakened at 2:00 a.m. on a sleeper train crossing the Continent by Swiss border guards demanding to see your passport. Then again, Switzerland just prior to the Brexit vote withdrew its application to join the European Union.

If America seems unconcerned about such things, perhaps this is because our sheer land area is 2.4 times larger than the entire European Union (minus the 94,000 square miles of the United Kingdom, whose combined land area is smaller than our State of Michigan).

What *The Economist* somehow fails to understand is that the United States already withdrew from our parent empire more than 240 years ago. We broke away from the British Empire, and they have never quite forgiven us.

United States of Earth

Americanism, as Donald Trump knows, does not refer to a Europe-like nationalism shaped not only by the democracy of Greece, the laws of Rome, and the parliamentary system of England, but also by the Dark Ages, feudalism, and centuries of plagues, economic stagnation, and serfdom.

Today this is the Progressive European Union flooded with military-age Muslim males, thousands of whom refuse to work because, they say, German Chancellor Angela Merkel "invited" them to come and stay in Europe as "her guests."

America, by contrast with this, is what the late Hoover Institution at Stanford University sociologist Seymour Martin Lipset called "the first new nation." America is literally the first great and successful model for a future United States of Planet Earth based on freedom, including free market economics.

Americanism is, therefore, not a rejection of globalism. Americanism *IS* globalism, but based on a model of liberty different from the narrower collectivist Progressive politics and economics of *The Economist.*

Do we want to identify and control those who are trying to cross our border? In this age of terrorism (and soon, God forbid, of nuclear terrorism), of course we do. Our government has behaved recklessly by not controlling our borders. Our government has a responsibility and duty to protect its citizens.

If we seem insecure, even defensive, this is because our expanding government violates the most fundamental values set forth by America's revolutionary Framers. They wanted America's government to remain small and its people to be big, self-reliant, and free.

The Golden Triangle

America won its independence from the British Empire, but today we continue to face the perennial challenge of sustaining our freedom.

Outside America's Constitutional Convention, as noted earlier, a woman asked Benjamin Franklin what kind of government the delegates had given us. "A Republic," Franklin replied, "…if you can keep it." [2]

One key to keeping our Republic is what author Os Guinness (a descendant of the famed Dublin brewery founder) calls The Golden Triangle: Freedom requires virtue, virtue requires faith, and faith requires freedom. [3]

A free society depends on individuals practicing self-government over their own emotions and appetites, on being people of honor and personal integrity. It requires that we deal with one another honestly in agreements and in the use of honest money.

Without the spirit of virtue sustained by faith, our leaders and citizens can quickly turn into corner-cutters who push the limits of every law and agreement for selfish advantage. Many try to take out of the community pot more than they put in.

We might be experiencing the low points of a theory that civilizations follow a roughly 200-year cycle attributed to Scottish historian Alexander Tytler, who wrote of it at the same time as the American Revolution. We discussed Tytler's theory in *The Inflation Deception*.

The cycle begins with a people in bondage, wrote Tytler. From that bondage they turn to spiritual faith, which inspires them to courage, which moves them to take actions that win their liberty.

As the cycle continues, liberty and faith and courage guide this people to achieve material abundance.

Over and over throughout human history, wrote Tytler, the down side of the cycle begins as abundance leads a people to selfishness, to feeling entitled to take more than they make, and to taking their freedom and success for granted.

As the downward cycle continues, selfishness begets complacency and apathy as people forget the values, work ethic and spiritual faith that led them to abundance and liberty.

Again and again, civilizations have tried to sustain their lifestyle and material wealth by going deep into debt in one way or another. This dependence soon returns a people to bondage, where centuries or millennia may pass before a new leader or generation finds the spiritual faith to begin the upward cycle anew.

It is not hard to see where many Americans are on Tytler's cycle. The challenge before us is to be a saving remnant, able to restore the uplifting values that move a people to greatness and renew the vision of America's Founders — for without vision the people perish.

Progressive Poison

Why do some societies succeed while others fail?

One clue may be found in recent psychological research done by Dan Ariely of Duke University's Fuqua School of Business and others. We analyzed these research findings in *We Have Seen the Future and It Looks Like Baltimore: American Dream vs. Progressive Dream*.

This research tested people who had grown up in either free market West Germany or Communist East Germany before the post-World War II Communist Iron Curtain came down and Germany was reunified.

The study found that those whose values were shaped by "egalitarian," collectivist Progressive East Germany "cheated twice as much as Western Germans overall."

Moreover, these researchers found, "The longer individuals were exposed to socialism, the more likely they were to cheat on our task." [4]

These researchers concluded that "the political regime of socialism has a lasting impact on citizens' basic morality."

This is logical, because socialism is one vast system of stealing at gunpoint from some in order to give the fruits of their labor to others who did not earn it.

Socialism is, in essence, slavery, forcing some to work and sacrifice their lives for others. No wonder this arrogant collectivist ideology damages the minds, hearts and souls of all who live under it.

"Socialism is damaging in many ways," an *Investor's Business Daily* editorial said in summarizing the study. "It wrecks economies and batters the quality of life. It corrupts, dehumanizes and makes people worse.… The researchers further remind us that socialist regimes suppress speech, engender social distrust, create economic scarcity and breed moral hypocrisy."

Progressivism, this new evidence suggests, has consequences — and is hazardous to the health and well-being of human individuals and society.

Progressivism is a poison that only a few societies can survive, but never thrive on or fulfill their highest potential while being forced to swallow. Why should anyone or any nation swallow this toxic ideology when we could instead be free, healthy and prosperous?

Freedom frightens some people because it requires them to be responsible. They would rather be like dependent infants with a paternalistic government to care for them. They would rather live as ghosts in somebody else's Progressive Dream, building some ruler's pyramid instead of their own.

Efforts to impose a shotgun marriage between the liberating American Dream and the honesty-destroying, authoritarian Progressive Dream are simply irrational.

Progressivism does more than impair economic growth. It literally poisons and damages the moral integrity, humanity, and spirituality of individuals who would live far better and be much happier in the America of our Founders.

Party Animals

In his 2016 book *Playing to the Edge: American Intelligence in the Age of Terror*, former Central Intelligence Agency chief Michael Hayden recounts how as a young military officer he once asked a Bulgarian government official "What is Truth to you?"

"Truth?" the Communist Party apparatchik replied. "Truth is what serves the Party."

The government in Communist China has a problem bigger than its illegal militarized islands in the China Sea, its unsteady economy, or its imitation of the World Bank called the Asian Infrastructure Investment Bank that even pro-American nations such as the United Kingdom have rushed to join.

Communism is not really an ideology so much as a cult, a substitute religion for True Believers. This is why we see the glazed eyes and irrational dogma from radicalized Progressives. Because Communism has no Truth, it is failing as a religion and its leader Xi Jinping is frightened.

Christianity has been growing at an average of seven percent per year for more than 50 years in Communist China, despite the Communist church burnings, threats, killings, and demands that people go back to their local pagan deity worship.

According to Fenggang Yang, Professor of Sociology and Director of the Center of Religion and Chinese Society at Purdue University, Red China by 2035 could have almost a quarter-billion Protestant citizens. By one scenario, 32.5 percent of China's huge population by 2040, and 66.7 percent by 2050, could be Christian. China could have more Christians than any other nation on Earth.

In Europe, by contrast, Christian churches are largely empty, in part because when people lost faith in government they also lost faith in the official state religion.

In July 2016 a Pew Research Center survey reported that "nones," those with no religion, are now 21 percent of voters, America's largest voting bloc defined by religion as Pew parses this. Progressives may be influencing this shift by waging a relentless culture war of ridicule and mockery. Evangelicals have held their ground at 20 percent during the past eight years, Pew reports, but establishment Protestant churches have fallen by five percent to 14 percent, and Roman Catholics by three percent to 20 percent as the faith of America's fathers declines.

Both the Golden Triangle and rising Tytler Cycle depend on the morals, virtue, and courage that come from faith.

The Tribe Inside

Society can quickly break down into us-against-them, divide-and-conquer identity group politics. People today are forgetting the nation and family where we all belong.

In his 2016 book *Tribe: On Homecoming and Belonging*, author Sebastian Junger says that the soldiers who have faced combat understand what it means to protect the backs of our brothers and sisters in arms. [4]

Our ancestors, Junger told C-SPAN Book TV, lived "in groups of 40 to 60 people. In today's cities we are no longer living in such groups — but inside we sense that there is no survival outside of group survival."

"You get your sense of security in the world by being necessary to the group," war correspondent Junger says. "If you're not necessary to the group, you're in danger....they won't sacrifice for you, and you're alone in the jungle and you're going to die. That's what's wired into our brains."

"Today's communities let us live as individuals, but the society does not need you to help gather food or defend the neighborhood. No safety [that you would get] from being part of a group. We're wired to fear such a society."

"Humans don't mind hardship. In fact they thrive on it," says Junger. "What they mind is not feeling necessary. Modern society has perfected the art of making people not feel necessary. It's time for that to end."

We need a sense of shared purpose and respect, says Junger, who recalled a photo of graffiti on a wall in Ramadi, Iraq: "America is not at war," it read. "The Marine Corps is at war. America is at the mall." [5]

And when that Marine leaves his warrior comrades and comes home, says Junger, he comes from a group that needs him as a matter of life and death to a society that does not respect his importance — from soft liberals who are, in the words of the British Empire's soldier-poet Rudyard Kipling, "makin' mock o' uniforms that guard you while you sleep." [6]

Such virtues throughout human history have flourished best when cultivated by faith and belief in a higher power.

As Thomas Jefferson penned in our Declaration of Independence, our "unalienable" rights to life, liberty and the pursuit of happiness come from our "Creator."

These rights do NOT come from politicians or government. If they did, then government and politicians could take them away.

Rediscovering Patriotism

John Adams, America's second president, said America's Constitution was "made only for a moral and religious people. It is wholly inadequate to the government of any other."

We fought and won our own Brexit while demanding our rights as English folks that the British Crown denied us. Imagine how different the world might be today if King George III had simply given his North American colonies seats in Parliament.

With Brexit, the voters of the United Kingdom declared their independence from the European Empire that was choking off their rights.

Their voters reawakened and remembered their heritage.

We need to do likewise.

"The one absolutely certain way of bringing this nation to ruin, of preventing all possibility of its continuing to be a nation at all," said Theodore Roosevelt in a 1915 speech to Irish Catholic Knights of Columbus on Columbus Day, "would be to permit it to become a tangle of squabbling nationalities, an intricate knot of German-Americans, Irish-Americans, English-Americans, French-Americans, Scandinavian-Americans or Italian-Americans, each preserving its separate nationality, each at heart feeling more sympathy with Europeans of that nationality, than with the other citizens of the American Republic...."

"There is no such thing as a hyphenated American who is a good American," Teddy Roosevelt continued. "The only man who is a good American is the man who is an American and nothing else." There is no room in this country for hyphenated Americanism, he had told this audience earlier. "...[A] hyphenated American is not an American at all."

President Woodrow Wilson, who like Roosevelt was a Progressive, held similar views. "Any man who carries a hyphen about with him," said Wilson, "carries a dagger that he is ready to plunge into the vitals of this Republic, whenever he gets ready."

America, as we noted from President Ronald Reagan's wisdom, is a country built not on history, but on ideas and ideals. We can go live in Japan, but its people will never accept us as Japanese. But someone from Japan — or anywhere else on Earth — can move to the United States and be accepted as an American. The main requirement for this is that they come in accordance with our laws, and that they embrace fully our ideas and ideals; that they think of themselves as Americans; that they too, like many millions before them, embrace American patriotism — from the Latin word *patria*, "father."

Salad Bowlers

Teddy Roosevelt and Woodrow Wilson were not prohibiting immigrants from enjoying their ancestral foods, beverages, songs, or even language (if spoken predominantly inside their homes).

These two presidents were merely telling people not to come here while leaving one foot of loyalty in their previous country. Divided loyalty, they suggest, is worse than no loyalty to America at all — because it means that such immigrants would be like a foreign country inside our borders.

Today's Progressives have a very different view. Most believe in Multiculturalism, a philosophy that America is no better — and because of its old belief in superiority, has usually been worse — than the world's other cultures. As President Obama put it, American exceptionalism is no different from British exceptionalism or Greek exceptionalism.

We used to speak of the American "melting pot" in which most cultural differences were dissolved and mostly removed, at least among Americans of European ancestry. By the 1960s the metaphor had changed as we became the American "salad bowl" in which every bit of cheese, olive, and lettuce comingled but kept its unique sense of foreign identity — while being coated with a salad dressing of see-through Americanism.

Today, Progressive politicians, teachers, and activists insist that newcomers keep their original identity. The hyphen has become the staple used to affix people to political coalitions. This connects them to a group of people, usually organized for Leftist activism and Big Government Party voting.

However, by Balkanizing Americans into identifying not with our whole nation, but predominantly with only ethnic pieces of it, Progressives are deliberately playing the old divide-and-conquer game. They are depriving recent legal immigrants of their larger right to become full Americans.

"Machine" Politics

This, tellingly, is how the old Democratic "machine" politics of big cities, such as Tammany Hall in New York City, worked. Immigrants were taught to see themselves as foreigners in America who needed the help of The Machine's politicians to secure their share of the American pie.

This locked the immigrants into dependency on crooked and corrupt government. Patrick would arrive from the west of Ireland, get introduced to the Tammany ward heeler, and within days he would be given a government patronage job — often the badge and nightstick of a policeman, for those were once patronage jobs under Tammany. Patrick was given a few coins of money, and the bosses of Tammany used his and other dependent immigrant votes to steal for themselves the coin of political power in the city and, through its congressmen and senators, sometimes the country.

This was not full freedom for immigrants. It was just a slightly higher class of feudalism, with political bosses as the new lords of the castle and their political retainers and dependents as the new serfs.

Those medieval politics live on in Northeastern Democratic politicians such as Nancy Pelosi, whose father was the Mayor of machine politics in Baltimore — as we describe in our 2015 book *We Have Seen the Future and It Looks Like Baltimore: American Dream vs. Progressive Dream.*

The Progressive insistence on using such politics of division nationwide is poisoning American politics, fragmenting us into nation-groups, each fighting to grab more than its share of the wealth of America.

Claiming Her Hyphen

Progressives urge even those who have long lived here to restore their hyphen, because a hyphenated identity is now more valuable than being a full American. Progressives have given the hyphen an elevated status. The person with a hyphen in his or her identity has a privileged position, and usually some historic claim to be part of a victim group of some kind. With this comes a ready excuse for failure or falling short of one's potential. With this hyphen can come a preferential claim for jobs, college admissions, loans, and a host of special government benefits denied to full, un-hyphenated Americans.

Nowadays being a hyphenated American can pay big dividends. Look at Elizabeth Warren, who apparently concocted her claim to be 1/32nd Native

American and parlayed this into a $500,000 a year job at Harvard (that should have gone to a genuine Native American), and then into a seat in the U.S. Senate. (As we noted earlier, Senator Warren of Progressive Massachusetts apparently has refused to take a DNA test that might show she was wrong about her claimed hyphenation all along. Does she disbelieve her own story?)

This Balkanization of America is the redistribution of wealth based not on traditional American meritocracy, but on raw strong-arm politics of class warfare, envy, jealousy, and theft. Every day we can see it tearing our country apart, and we can see the glee on Leftist faces because the America they have always hated is being torn to shreds.

Teddy Roosevelt and Woodrow Wilson had a point. America does not need immigrants who come here to keep their old flag and allegiance while living off our welfare system.

What America needs are *citizens* who want to become part of, and make their best contributions to, the traditions and values that have made America the greatest nation in world history. To those we say "Welcome!"

Moral Rearmament

Our own big government now treats us, in philosopher Paul Goodman's phrase, "like a conquered province." Our public servants now act like our masters, whether elected or in the permanent unelected regulatory bureaucracy.

The Machine, in all its manifestations, that has stolen so much from us has been created and run with fiat money that can be conjured out of thin air to buy votes, reward cronies, enrich politicians and endlessly expand government.

It has debased our morals, and what is required is what used to be called "Moral Rearmament," putting our moral and spiritual armor back on.

Simply returning to the hard money specified in the U.S. Constitution by America's Framers would begin slowing The Machine's expansion and shrinking its size.

A Saving Remnant

Progressives exploited their distorted version of Keynesian economics to justify taxing, spending and redistributionist policies strikingly similar to socialism. By invoking John Maynard Keynes instead of Karl Marx, Progressives claimed that robbing the rich and giving to the poor made everybody richer by stimulating the economy.

This Keynesian conjuring is now largely discredited. Spending $8 Trillion of "stimulus" over eight years has left us with 95 million Americans unable or unwilling to find needed full-time jobs. The economy, as of August 2016, is spiraling down at 1.1 percent "growth." More than one third of Americans have little or no savings.

Genuine wealth and prosperity cannot be sustained, at least for long, just by printing pieces of paper reading "Legal Tender." In a real economy, people must earn money and set some of it aside, in a secure form, for savings and investment. Without such real investment, the economy slows, stalls, and crashes.

Does America have a "saving remnant?" It does if some of us are a remnant that saves.

But we have learned not to trust our life savings to banks, because of the 20 severe risks we described in *Don't Bank On It!* Why trust your hard-earned savings to a bank that pays almost zero interest? A portion of your savings should never be held in U.S. Dollars, a fiat currency backed only by politician promises. With paper-dollar-free savings such as gold in a crisis, you would be a stabilizing force not only for yourself and your family — but also for your neighbors, community, state, and nation.

Is saving hard money hard? At some point in most people's lives, it is. But part of growing up and earning your independence requires hard work and self-discipline. Saving by, for example, buying one gold coin per month is what our pioneer ancestors described with a now-unfamiliar term — character-building. Saving meant deferring immediate gratification for a higher goal — security, peace of mind, giving, being prepared, and creating economic insurance, a golden nest egg to protect others.

America's Founders knew that to be free of the British Empire, they would have to "govern" themselves — not only as a nation, but also as individuals. "The secret of happiness is freedom," said the ancient Greek historian Thucydides, and "the secret of freedom is courage." Only those who control themselves can keep a measure of real freedom, and independence from being controlled by others.

Freedom, in other words, requires not only self-control and courage. It is a spiritual discipline that leads to greater inner strength, maturity, and perspective.

When you save, what you are really saving is yourself and the generations that come after you.

Thank God that many of our ancestors made the sacrifice to be a saving remnant. We still retain some of the liberty they set aside as our heritage almost a quarter-Millennium ago. Much liberty has been lost and needs to be replenished by our generation for our grandchildren. Are you ready to become America's saving remnant?

This is needed to restore America's values and economic health — thrift, self-discipline, reversing the flow of wealth and power to Washington and returning it to We the People who created it, as individuals and as a nation.

President Dwight Eisenhower in his 1961 Farewell Address said:

> *"We cannot mortgage the material assets of our grandchildren without asking the loss also of their political and spiritual heritage."*

*"Whenever destroyers appear among men,
they start by destroying money,
for money is men's protection
and the base of a moral existence.*

*"Destroyers seize gold and leave
to its owners a counterfeit pile of paper.*

*"This kills all objective standards
and delivers men into the arbitrary power
of an arbitrary setter of values."*

– Ayn Rand
Atlas Shrugged

Footnotes

Pre-Introduction Page

[1] Excerpts from "Military-Industrial Complex Speech, Dwight D. Eisenhower, 1961." Yale Law School / Lillian Goldman Law Library / The Avalon Project. URL: http://avalon.law.yale.edu/20th_century/eisenhower001.asp

This January 17, 1961 speech is also known as President Dwight David Eisenhower's Farewell Address to the Nation.

Chapter One – Breaking Free

[1] Frederick Forsyth, "Birth of Superstate: Frederick Forsyth on How UNELECTED Brussels Bureaucrats SEIZED Power," *Daily Express*, June 13, 2016. URL: http://www.express.co.uk/news/politics/679277/History-EU-how-bureaucrats-seized-power; "Frederick Forsyth The Author – His View on Brexit," *The Oracle*, June 6, 2016. URL: http://have-your-say.915577.n3.nabble.com/Frederick-Forsyth-The-Author-His-view-on-Brexit-td4036560.html

[2] Edward Krudy, "Post-Brexit Global Equity Loss of Over \$2 Trillion Worst Ever: S&P," *Reuters*, June 26, 2016. URL: http://www.reuters.com/article/us-britain-eu-stocks-idUSKCN0ZC12G

[3] Frederick Forsyth, "Birth of Superstate: Frederick Forsyth on How UNELECTED Brussels Bureaucrats SEIZED Power," *Daily Express*, June 13, 2016. URL: http://www.express.co.uk/news/politics/679277/History-EU-how-bureaucrats-seized-power; "Frederick Forsyth The Author – His View on Brexit," *The Oracle*, June 6, 2016. URL: http://have-your-say.915577.n3.nabble.com/Frederick-Forsyth-The-Author-His-view-on-Brexit-td4036560.html

[4] Tom Batchelor, "EU Army on Way? EU Cannot Rely on NATO and Needs New Defence Policy Says Brussels Chief," *Daily Express*, June 30, 2016. URL: http://www.express.co.uk/news/world/684549/EU-cannot-rely-NATO-needs-new-defence-policy-chief; for the open public version of *Global Strategy*, see *Shared Vision, Common Action: A Stronger Europe: A Global Strategy for the European Union's Foreign And Security Policy*, published June 28, 2016, five days after the Brexit referendum at URL: http://www.iss.europa.eu/uploads/media/EUGS.pdf

See also http://europa.eu/globalstrategy/en

[5] Nick Gutteridge, "European SUPERSTATE To Be Unveiled: EU Nations 'To Be Morphed Into One' Post-Brexit," *Daily Express*, June 28, 2016. URL: http://www.express.co.uk/news/politics/683739/EU-referendum-German-French-European-superstate-Brexit; Joseph Curtis, "Has Britain Avoided a 'European Superstate'? France and Germany 'Draw Up Plans to Morph EU Countries Into One With Control Over Members' Armies and Economies," *U.K. Daily Mail*, June 27, 2016. URL: http://www.dailymail.co.uk/news/article-3662827/Has-Britain-avoided-European-superstate-France-Germany-draw-plans-morph-EU-countries-one-control-members-armies-economies.html

[6] Tom Batchelor, " 'EU WANT AN EMPIRE' Brussels Hope to Expand Its Influence As Far As ASIA and AFRICA," *Daily Express*, July 1, 2016. URL: http://www.express.co.uk/news/world/685005/EU-superstate-army-plans-Brussels-expand-reach-China-Africa-Brexit-Ukip

[7] Leo McKinstry, "Now the Pro-EU Lobby Want a Ban on Referendums," *U.K. Express*, April 14, 2016. URL: http://www.express.co.uk/comment/columnists/leo-mckinstry/660845/Now-pro-EU-lobby-wants-ban-referendums-LEO-MCKINSTRY

[8] Leo McKinstry, "The EU Has Revealed Its True Nature: A Federalist Monster That Will Not Stop Until Nations are Abolished," *U.K. Telegraph*, April 7, 2016. URL: http://www.telegraph.

co.uk/news/2016/04/07/the-eu-has-revealed-its-true-nature-a-federalist-monster-that-wi/

[9] "With Globalization in Danger, G-20 Double Down on a Defense," *Bloomberg News*, July 24, 2016. URL: http://www.bloomberg.com/news/articles/2016-07-24/with-globalization-under-threat-g-20-double-down-on-a-defense

[10] "Brexit Remorse? UK Lawmaker Calls for Parliament to Ignore EU Referendum," *Fox News*, June 26, 2016. URL: http://www.foxnews.com/world/2016/06/26/brexit-remorse-uk-lawmaker-calls-for-parliament-to-ignore-eu-referendum-as-millions-call-for-second-vote.html; Iain Watson, "EU Referendum Petition Signed by More Than 2.5 M," *BBC News*, June 25, 2016. URL: http://www.bbc.com/news/uk-politics-eu-referendum-36629324

[11] James Traub, "It's Time for the Elites to Rise Up Against the Ignorant Masses," *Foreign Policy*, June 28, 2016. URL: http://foreignpolicy.com/2016/06/28/its-time-for-the-elites-to-rise-up-against-ignorant-masses-trump-2016-brexit/; Tyler Durden, " 'Ignorant Masses' Warn 'Elites' – Go Ahead, Rise Up… But Be Careful What You Wish For," *ZeroHedge*, June 30, 2016. URL: http://www.zerohedge.com/print/564840

[12] Fraser Cameron, "Why We Should Ban Referenda on EU Policies," *EurActiv*, April 10, 2016. URL: https://www.euractiv.com/section/global-europe/opinion/why-we-should-ban-referenda-on-eu-policies/; Leo McKinstry, "Now the Pro-EU Lobby Want a Ban on Referendums," *U.K. Express*, April 14, 2016. URL: http://www.express.co.uk/comment/columnists/leo-mckinstry/660845/Now-pro-EU-lobby-wants-ban-referendums-LEO-MCKINSTRY

[13] Robert McCrum, Robert MacNeil, and William Cran, *The Story of English: Third Revised Edition*. New York: Penguin Books, 2002.

[14] Joseph E. Stiglitz, *The Euro: How a Common Currency Threatens the Future of Europe*. New York: W.W. Norton, 2016.

[15] Peter S. Goodman, "How a Currency Intended to Unite Europe Wound Up Dividing It," *New York Times*, July 27, 2016. URL: http://www.nytimes.com/2016/07/28/business/international/how-a-currency-intended-to-unite-europe-wound-up-dividing-it.html

[16] Ed Lowther, "A Short History of the Pound," *BBC News*, February 14, 2014.

[17] David Sinclair, *The Pound: A Biography: The Story of the Currency That Ruled the World*. London: Random House UK, 2001; see also Ed Lowther, "A Short History of the Pound," *BBC News*, February 14, 2014.

[18] The six books coauthored by Craig R. Smith and Lowell Ponte are: (1) **Crashing the Dollar:** *How to Survive a Global Currency Collapse;* (2) **The Inflation Deception:** *Six Ways Government Tricks Us…And Seven Ways to Stop It!;* (3) **The Great Debasement:** *The 100-Year Dying of the Dollar and How to Get America's Money Back;* (4) **The Great Withdrawal:** *How the Progressives' 100-Year Debasement of America and the Dollar Ends;* (5) **Don't Bank On It!** *The Unsafe World of 21st Century Banking;* and (6) **We Have Seen The Future And It Looks Like Baltimore:** *American Dream vs. Progressive Dream.*

[19] Rachel Premack, "The One Investment that Just Made a Killing, Thanks to Brexit," *Washington Post*, June 25, 2016. URL: https://www.washingtonpost.com/news/wonk/wp/2016/06/25/the-one-investment-that-just-made-a-killing-thanks-to-brexit/

Chapter Two – The Accidental Empire

[1] Governor George W. Bush, "A Distinctly American Internationalism" (speech). Ronald Reagan Presidential Library, Simi Valley, California, November 19, 1999. URL: https://www.mtholyoke.edu/acad/intrel/bush/wspeech.htm

[2] "George Washington's Farewell Address 1796," Text from Yale University Law School's Avalon Project of documents. URL: http://avalon.law.yale.edu/18th_century/washing.asp

[3] First Inaugural Address, The Papers of Thomas Jefferson, Princeton University. URL: https://jeffersonpapers.princeton.edu/selected-documents/first-inaugural-address-0

[4] Niall Ferguson, *Colossus: The Price of America's Empire*. New York: Penguin Press, 2004. Page 34-36.

[5] *Ibid.*

[6] David Vine, "The United States Probably Has More Foreign Military Bases Than Any Other People, Nation, or Empire in History, and It's Doing Us More Harm Than Good," *The Nation*, September 14, 2015.

[7] Eric Schlosser, "The H-Bombs in Turkey," *The New Yorker*, July 17, 2016; Tyler Durden, "Turkish Prosecutors Raid Incirlik Airbase Housing US Warplanes and 50 Nuclear Bombs," *ZeroHedge*, July 18, 2016.

[8] Brian Kilmeade and Don Yaeger, *Thomas Jefferson and the Tripoli Pirates: The Forgotten War that Changed American History*. New York: Sentinel / Penguin, 2015.

[9] Ambassador Robert D. Blackwill and Jennifer M. Harris, *War by Other Means: Geoeconomics and Statecraft*. Cambridge, Massachusetts: Belknap Press / Harvard University Press, 2016.

[10] Niall Ferguson, *Colossus: The Price of America's Empire*. New York: Penguin Press, 2004.

[11] Justo Sierra (Mendes), *The Political Evolution of the Mexican People*. Austin: University of Texas Press, 2014.

[12] Homer Lea, *The Valor of Ignorance*. New York and London: Harper & Brothers, 1909, See also Tom Alexander, "The Amazing Prophecies of 'General' Homer Lea," *The Smithsonian*, July 1993.

[13] "Remarks by the Honorable Ray Mabus, Secretary of the Navy, Santa Barbara Navy League Luncheon, Dreier Museum, Santa Barbara, CA, Thursday, October 22, 2009" (Transcript). URL: http://www.navy.mil/navydata/people/secnav/Mabus/Speech/Santa%20Barbara%20NL%20Lunch%206%20NOV%20090.pdf

[14] Victor Davis Hanson, "A Funny Sort of Empire: Are Americans Really So Imperial?" *National Review*, November 27, 2002. URL: http://victorhanson.com/wordpress/?p=4982

[15] Niall Ferguson, *Colossus: The Price of America's Empire*. New York: Penguin Press, 2004. Page 279. See also Niall Ferguson, *Empire: The Rise and Demise of the British World Order and the Lessons for Global Power*. New York: Basic Books, 2004; and Niall Ferguson, *Empire: How Britain Made the Modern World*. New York: Penguin Books, 2012.

[16] Rosa Brooks, *How Everything Became War and the Military Became Everything: Tales From the Pentagon*. New York: Simon & Schuster, 2016. See also Kathy Gilsinan, " 'We Have No Idea What Wars Is,' " *The Atlantic,* August 10, 2016. URL: http://www.theatlantic.com/international/archive/2016/08/rosa-brooks-war-military/494846/

[17] Radley Balko, *Rise of the Warrior Cop: The Militarization of America's Police Forces*. New York: PublicAffairs / Perseus Books Group, 2013; John W. Whitehead, *A Government of Wolves: The Emerging American Police State*. New York: SelectBooks, 2013; John W. Whitehead, *Battlefield America: The War On The American People*. New York: SelectBooks, 2015.

[18] John Fund, "The United States of SWAT," *National Review*, April 18, 2014.

[19] Lowell Ponte, "Leading by Example," *FrontPageMagazine*, March 22, 2000. URL: http://archive.frontpagemag.com/readArticle.aspx?ARTID=21767

[20] Excerpts from "Military-Industrial Complex Speech, Dwight D. Eisenhower, 1961." Yale Law School /
 Lillian Goldman Law Library / The Avalon Project. URL: http://avalon.law.yale.edu/20th_century/eisenhower001.asp

This January 17, 1961 speech is also known as President Dwight David Eisenhower's Farewell Address to the Nation.

Chapter Three – Welcome to The Machine

[1] Smedley D. Butler, *War Is A Racket*. Seattle: Amazon Digital Services, 2012. This short book, originally published in 1935, can be downloaded at no cost from various Internet sites, including:

URL: http://www.historyisaweapon.org/defcon1/warracket.html or

URL: https://archive.org/stream/WarIsARacket/WarIsARacket_djvu.txt

[2] Jens O. Parsson, *Dying of Money: Lessons of the Great German and American Inflations*. Indianapolis: Dog Ear Publishing, 2011.

[3] Morris Berman, *Dark Ages America: The Final Phase of Empire*. New York: W.W. Norton, 2006.

[4] Seymour Martin Lipset (Editor), *Consensus and Conflict: Essays in Political Sociology*. New Brunswick, New Jersey: Transaction Books, 1985. Page 243.

[5] Lowell Ponte, "Happy Birthday, Mr. Jefferson," *Reader's Digest*, April 1993.

[6] Simon Johnson, "The Quiet Coup," *The Atlantic*, May 2009. URL: http://www.theatlantic.com/magazine/archive/2009/05/the-quiet-coup/307364/

Chapter Four – The Money Changers

[1] Dan Hyde, "Apple Boss: Next Generation of Children 'Will Not Know What Money Is,' " *U.K. Telegraph*, November 11, 2015.

[2] Associated Press, "Sen. Shaheen Says It's Time to Put a Woman on the $20 Bill," *GOPUSA. com*, April 18, 2015. URL: http://www.gopusa.com/news/2015/04/18/sen-shaheen-says-its-time-to-put-a-woman-on-the-20-bill/; Adam Chandler, "The Quest to Boot Old Hickory Off the $20," *The Atlantic*, April 17, 2015. URL: http://www.theatlantic.com/national/archive/2015/04/erasing-andrew-jackson/390825/; Abby Ohlheiser, "This Group Wants to Banish Andrew Jackson from the $20 Bill," *Washington Post*, March 3, 2015. URL: http://www.washingtonpost.com/blogs/the-fix/wp/2015/03/03/this-group-wants-to-banish-andrew-jackson-from-the-20-and-replace-him-with-a-woman/; Jillian Keenan, "Kick Andrew Jackson Off the $20 Bill!" *Slate.com*, March 3, 2014. URL: http://www.slate.com/articles/news_and_politics/politics/2014/03/andrew_jackson_should_be_kicked_off_the_20_bill_he_ordered_a_genocide.html; Jarrett Stepman, "Andrew Jackson's Likeness on the $20 Bill Must Be Preserved," *Breitbart.com*, April 19, 2015. URL: http://www.breitbart.com/big-government/2015/04/19/andrew-jacksons-likeness-on-the-20-bill-must-be-preserved/; Tyler Durden, "Martin Armstrong: 'Understanding Jackson's Bank War Is Critical To Our Future,' " *ZeroHedge.com*, April 19, 2015. URL: http://www.zerohedge.com/print/504995

[3] "Putting a Woman on the $20 Bill" [Room for Debate], *New York Times*, March 18, 2015. URL: http://www.nytimes.com/roomfordebate/2015/03/18/putting-a-woman-on-the-20-bill; Craig R.

Smith and Lowell Ponte, "The Money Changers: Re-facing and Debasing Our Currency: What the Proposed $20 Bill Makeover Might Mean," *The Buzz*, April 20, 2015. URL: https://www.prbuzz. com/politics-a-public-affairs/308088-the-money-changers-re-facing-and-debasing-our-currency-what-the-proposed-20-bill-makeover-might-mean.html; "President$ On Your Money," *Nerdwallet. com*, February 2013. URL: http://assets.nerdwallet.com/blog/investing/files/2013/02/presidents.jpg; "Jane Austen to be Face of the Bank of England £10 Note," *BBC News*, July 24, 2013. URL: http:// www.bbc.com/news/business-23424289

[4] "Woodrow Wilson Asks 'What Is Progress?' " (1912), Heritage Foundation. URL: http://www. heritage.org/initiatives/first-principles/primary-sources/woodrow-wilson-asks-what-is-progress

[5] Dan Dorfman, "If Government Stimulus Worked, It Would Be A Perpetual Wealth Machine," *Forbes* Magazine, December 26, 2013. URL: http://www.forbes.com/sites/ jeffreydorfman/2013/12/26/if-government-stimulus-worked-it-would-be-a-perpetual-wealth-machine-2/#2062325c6a10

[6] Jason Frank and Isaac Kramnick, "What 'Hamilton' Forgets About Hamilton," *New York Times*, June 10, 2016. URL: http://www.nytimes.com/2016/06/11/opinion/what-hamilton-forgets-about-alexander-hamilton.html; Nancy Isenberg, "Liberals Love Alexander Hamilton. But Aaron Burr Was a Real Progressive Hero," *Washington Post*, March 30, 2016. URL: https:// www.washingtonpost.com/posteverything/wp/2016/03/30/liberals-love-alexander-hamilton-but-aaron-burr-was-a-real-progressive-hero/; Samuel Biagetti, "Why Did Everyone Hate Alexander Hamilton? These Elitist Policies Made Hamilton the Most Despised Man in America," *HistoryBuff. com*, January 13, 2016. URL: http://historybuff.com/why-did-everyone-hate-alexander-hamilton-1-KNybdVLeDn4W; Jackie Calmes, "Success of 'Hamilton' May Have Saved Hamilton on the $10 Bill," *New York Times*, April 15, 2016. URL: http://www.nytimes.com/2016/04/16/us/politics/ success-of-hamilton-may-have-saved-hamilton-on-the-10-bill.html

[7] John Steele Gordon, *Hamilton's Blessing: The Extraordinary Life and Times of Our National Debt*. London: Walker Books, 2010.

Chapter Five – The Trap

[1] Job 18: 8-11 is here excerpted from the King James Version (KJV) translation of the Bible.

[2-3] Full disclosure: Lowell Ponte was for 15 years a Roving Editor at *Reader's Digest* Magazine.

[4] Aaron Blake, "This Number Proves Bernie Sanders Can Win Iowa," *Washington Post*, January 17, 2016. URL: https://www.washingtonpost.com/news/the-fix/wp/2016/01/17/this-number-proves-bernie-sanders-can-win-iowa/

[5] *Ibid.*

[6] Giovanni Russonello, "Poll Watch: Democrats, Even Clinton Supporters, Warm to Socialism," *New York Times*, Novembver 20, 2015. URL: http://www.nytimes.com/politics/first-draft/2015/11/20/poll-watch-democrats-even-clinton-supporters-warm-to-socialism/?_r=0

[7] Justin McCarthy, "In U.S., Socialist Presidential Candidates Least Appealing," Gallup, June 22, 2015. URL: http://www.gallup.com/poll/183713/socialist-presidential-candidates-least-appealing. aspx?utm_source=Politics&utm_medium=newsfeed&utm_campaign=tiles

[8] Robert W. Wood, "Passports Required For Domestic Travel In 2016, But IRS Can Revoke Passports For Taxes," *Forbes*, November 25, 2015. URL: http://www.forbes.com/sites/ robertwood/2015/11/25/passports-required-for-domestic-travel-in-2016-but-irs-can-revoke-passports-for-taxes/#2715e4857a0b4eb8610c5f06

[9] *Ibid.*

[10] Robert W. Wood, "U.S. Raises Fee To Expatriate By 422% A Second Time," *Forbes Magazine*, September 18, 2015; "Expatriation Tax" article at Wikipedia; Internal Revenue Service, "Expatriation Tax." June 11, 2015. URL: https://www.irs.gov/individuals/International-Taxpayers/Expatriation-Tax

[11] Ira Stoll, "Clinton Wants to Tax U.S. Companies for Trying to Pay Less Taxes," *Reason Magazine*. December 7, 2015. URL: http://reason.com/archives/2015/12/07/clintons-exit-tax/print

[12] Craig R. Smith and Lowell Ponte, *Don't Bank On It! The Unsafe World of 21ˢᵗ Century Banking*. Phoenix: Idea Factory Press, 2014. Pages 135-141.

[13] "Here's A List of Bernie Sanders' $19.6 Trillion In Tax Hikes," *Washington Examiner* / Fox News, January 18, 2016.

[14] Craig R. Smith and Lowell Ponte, *Don't Bank On It! The Unsafe World of 21ˢᵗ Century Banking*. Phoenix: Idea Factory Press, 2014. Pages 9-15.

[15] Craig R. Smith and Lowell Ponte, *We Have Seen The Future And It Looks Like Baltimore: American Dream vs. Progressive Dream*. Phoenix: P2 Press, 2015. Pages 127-147.

[16] Craig R. Smith and Lowell Ponte, *We Have Seen The Future And It Looks Like Baltimore: American Dream vs. Progressive Dream*. Phoenix: P2 Press, 2015. Pages 137-139; Christopher Ingraham, "Law Enforcement Took More Stuff From People Than Burglars Did Last Year," *Washington Post,* November 23, 2015; Noah Smith, "Stop-And-Seize Turns Police Into Self-Funding Gangs," *Bloomberg*, November 12, 2015.

[17] Craig R. Smith and Lowell Ponte, *We Have Seen The Future And It Looks Like Baltimore: American Dream vs. Progressive Dream*. Phoenix: P2 Press, 2015. Pages 127-147.

[18] Craig R. Smith and Lowell Ponte, *Don't Bank On It! The Unsafe World of 21ˢᵗ Century Banking*. Phoenix: Idea Factory Press, 2014.

[19] Craig R. Smith and Lowell Ponte, *Don't Bank On It! The Unsafe World of 21ˢᵗ Century Banking*. Phoenix: Idea Factory Press, 2014. Pages 9-15.

[20] Craig R. Smith and Lowell Ponte, *We Have Seen The Future And It Looks Like Baltimore: American Dream vs. Progressive Dream*. Phoenix: P2 Press, 2015. Pages 151-169.

[21] Craig R. Smith and Lowell Ponte, *We Have Seen The Future And It Looks Like Baltimore: American Dream vs. Progressive Dream*. Phoenix: P2 Press, 2015. Pages 118-119 and 200-203; "The Bursting of The Bond Bubble Has Begun," Parts 1-3. *ZeroHedge*, January 13, 15 and 23, 2016.

[22] Craig R. Smith and Lowell Ponte, *We Have Seen The Future And It Looks Like Baltimore: American Dream vs. Progressive Dream*. Phoenix: P2 Press, 2015. Pages 71-81.

[23] Craig R. Smith and Lowell Ponte, *The Great Withdrawal: How the Progressives' 100-Year Debasement of American and the Dollar Ends*. Phoenix: Idea Factory Press, 2013. Pages 151-162.

[24] Craig R. Smith and Lowell Ponte, *We Have Seen The Future And It Looks Like Baltimore: American Dream vs. Progressive Dream*. Phoenix: P2 Press, 2015. Pages 122-126.

[25] "Here's A List of Bernie Sanders' $19.6 Trillion In Tax Hikes," *Washington Examiner* / Fox News, January 18, 2016. This source reports that Sanders proposes to raise the Death Tax by $243 Billion; see also Tim Worstall, "One More Consequence of a Financial Transactions Tax: Less Revenue," *Forbes* Magazine, January 22, 2016; Ryan Ellis, "Bernie Sanders' Socialized Healthcare

Plan Would Double the Death Tax," *Forbes* Magazine, January 18, 2016.

[26] Craig R. Smith and Lowell Ponte, *We Have Seen The Future And It Looks Like Baltimore: American Dream vs. Progressive Dream.* Phoenix: P2 Press, 2015. Pages 111-116.

[27] Craig R. Smith and Lowell Ponte, *The Inflation Deception: Six Ways Government Tricks Us... And Seven Ways to Stop It!* Phoenix: Idea Factory Press, 2011. Pages 131-136.

[28] Thomas Sowell, *Wealth, Poverty and Politics: An International Perspective.* New York: Basic Books / Perseus Books Group, 2015. Page 176.

[29] *Ibid.*, Page 177.

[30] *Ibid.*, Page 167

[31] Catey Hill, "White People Have Least Confidence In the American Dream," *MarketWatch,* January 22, 2016.

[32] Charles Murray, *Coming Apart: The State of White America, 1960-2010.* New York: Crown Forum 2012; Harold Meyerson, "The Steady Demise Of White Working Class America," *Investor's Business Daily,* November 6, 2015; Pew Research Center, "The American Middle Class Is Losing Ground," December 9, 2015. URL: http://www.pewsocialtrends.org/2015/12/09/the-american-middle-class-is-losing-ground/; Victor Tan Chen, "All Hollowed Out: The Lonely Poverty of America's White Working Class," *The Atlantic,* January 16, 2016.

[33] Pagan Kennedy, "The Fat Drug," *New York Times*, March 8, 2014; Tom Philpott, "Can Antibiotics Make You Fat?" *Mother Jones*, January 2, 2013; Ellin Holohan, "Epidemic of Obesity in U.S. Kids Began in Late '90s," *U.S. News & World Report,* June 21, 2011.

[34] Ben Fell and Miles Hewstone, *Psychological Perspectives on Poverty: A Review of Psychological Research Into The Causes and Consequences of Poverty.* Oxford, U.K.: University of Oxford / Joseph Rowntree Foundation, 2015. URL: https:www.jrf.org.uk/report/psychological-perspectives-poverty; See pages 24-26; Aria Bendix, "How Urban Planning Can Influence Obesity Rates," *The Atlantic*, January 12, 2016.

Chapter Six - Totally De-Voted
[1] Kimberley Strassel, *The Intimidation Game: How the Left Is Silencing Free Speech.* New York: Twelve / Hachette Book Group, 2016. See also Sharyl Attkinsson, *Stonewalled: My Fight for Truth Against the Forces of Obstruction, Intimidation, and Harassment in Obama's Washington.* New York: Harper, 2014; Jonah Goldberg, *Liberal Fascism: The Secret History of the American Left, From Mussolini to the Politics of Meaning.* New York: Doubleday, 2008; Mary Katherine Ham and Guy Benson, *End of Discussion: How the Left's Outrage Industry Shuts Down Debate, Manipulates Voters, and Makes America Less Free (and Fun).* New York: Crown Forum, 2015; Kim R. Holmes, *The Closing of the Liberal Mind: How Groupthink and Intolerance Define the Left.* New York: Encounter Books, 2016; Kirsten Powers, *The Silencing: How the Left is Killing Free Speech.* Washington, D.C.: Regnery Publishing, 2015; Ben Shapiro, *Bullies: How the Left's Culture of Fear and Intimidation Silences Americans.* New York: Threshold Editions / Simon & Schuster, 2013.

[2] Craig R. Smith and Lowell Ponte, *We Have Seen The Future And It Looks Like Baltimore: American Dream Vs. Progressive Dream.* Phoenix: P2 Publishing, 2015. Pages 144-147.

[3] Michael Hiltzik, "The Worst Idea in the Presidential Debate: A Return to the Gold Standard," *Los Angeles Times*, December 31, 2015.

[4] Ralph Benko, "Ted Cruz Has The Best Idea In The Presidential Debate: A Return To The Gold Standard," *Forbes*, January 4, 2016; Ralph Benko, "Cruz Is Smart to Campaign on the Gold

Standard," *The Hill*, January 28, 2016.

Chapter Seven – "No Humans Need Apply"

[1] Richard Conniff, "What The Luddites Really Fought Against," *Smithsonian Magazine*, March 2011. URL: http://www.smithsonianmag.com/history/what-the-luddites-really-fought-against-264412/?no-ist

[2] Martin Ford, *Rise of the Robots: Technology and the Threat of a Jobless Future*. New York: Basic Books, 2015.

[3] Adrienne LaFrance, "What Is a Robot?" *The Atlantic*, March 22, 2016. URL: http://www.theatlantic.com/technology/archive/2016/03/what-is-a-human/473166/

[4] Jerry Kaplan, *Humans Need Not Apply: A Guide to Wealth and Work in the Age of Artificial Intelligence*. New Haven, Connecticut: Yale University Press, 2015.

[5] Craig R. Smith and Lowell Ponte, *Don't Bank on It!: The Unsafe World of 21st Century Banking*. *Phoenix: Idea Factory Press, 2014. Pages 36-39;* Michael MacKenzie and Telis Demos, "Fears Linger of a New 'Flash Crash,'" *Financial Times*, May 5, 2011. See also John Melloy, "Year After May 6 'Flash Crash,' Rumblings of a Stock Correction," *CNBC.com*, May 4, 2011. URL: http://www.cnbc.com/id/42899594/Year_After_May_6_Flash_Crash_Rumblings_of_a_Stock_Correction ; "2010 Flash Crash," *Wikipedia*. URL: http://en.wikipedia.org/wiki/2010_Flash_Crash

[6] Michael Lewis, *Flash Boys: A Wall Street Revolt*. New York: W.W. Norton, 2014.

[7] Sam Ro, "ART CASHIN: WE May Have Just Witnessed The Presence Of Artificial Intelligence In The Stock Market," *Business Insider*, March 1, 2012. URL: http://www. businessinsider.com/art-cashin-artificial-intelligence-stock-market-2012-3

[8] *Ibid.*

[9] Cris Sheridan, "Markets, Murmurations, and Machines," *FinancialSense.com*, February 3, 2012. URL: http://www.financialsense.com/contributors/cris-sheridan/markets-murmurations-machines

[10] *Ibid.*

[11] Cris Sheridan, "Is Artificial Intelligence Taking Over the Stock Market?" *FinancialSense. com*, March 2, 2012. URL: http://www.financialsense.com/contributors/cris-sheridan/is-artificial-intelligence-taking-over-the-stock-market

[12] Kris Devasabai, "Quants Turn to AI for Market Insights," *Hedge Funds Review*, December 20, 2013. URL: http://www.risk.net/hedge-funds-review/feature/2307119/quants-turn-to-ai-for-market- insights; see also Tom Steinert-Threlkeid, *Securities Technology Monitor*, November 17, 2011. URL: http://www.securitiestechnologymonitor.com/news/machine-readable-tweet-streams-algo-trading- gnip-29578-1.html?ET=securitiesindustry:e3039:180629a:&st=email&u tm_source=editorial&utm_ medium=email&utm_campaign=STM_BNA_08302010_111711#; Christopher Mims, "AI That Picks Stocks Better Than the Pros: A Computer Science Professor Uses Textual Analysis of Articles to Beat the Market," *MIT Technology Review*, June 10, 2010. URL: http://www.technologyreview.com/view/419341/ai-that-picks-stocks-better-than-the-pros/

[13] "AI Potentially 'More Dangerous than Nukes," *CNBC*, August 4, 2014. URL: http://www. cnbc. com/id/101892104; Allen Wastier, "Elon Musk, Stephen Hawking and Fearing the Machine," CNBC, June 21, 2014. URL: http://www.cnbc.com/id/101774267; Stephen Hawking, Stuart Russell, Max Tegmark and Frank Wilczek, "Stephen Hawking: 'Transcendence Looks At the Implications of Artificial Intelligence – But Are We Taking AI Seriously Enough? *The Independent*

(UK), May 1, 2014. URL: http://www.independent.co.uk/ news/science/stephen-hawking-transcendence-looks-at-the-implications-of-artificial-intelligence— but-are-we-taking-ai-seriously-enough-9313474.html ; Nick Bostrom, *Superintelligence: Paths, Dangers, Strategies*. Oxford: Oxford University Press, 2014.

[14] Stephen Hawking, Stuart Russell, Max Tegmark and Frank Wilczek, "Stephen Hawking: 'Transcendence Looks At the Implications of Artificial Intelligence – But Are We Taking AI Seriously Enough? *The Independent* (UK), May 1, 2014. URL: http://www.independent.co.uk/ news/science/stephen-hawking-transcendence-looks-at-the-implications-of-artificial-intelligence— but-are-we-taking-ai-seriously-enough-9313474.html

[15] Harald Malmgren and Mark Stys, "The Marginalizing of the Individual Investor: The Inside Story of Flash Crashes, Systemic Risk, and the Demise of Value Investing," *The International Economy*, Summer 2010. URL: http://www.international-economy.com/TIE_Su10_MalmgrenStys.pdf; Cris Sheridan, "Is Artificial Intelligence Taking Over the Stock Market?" *FinancialSense.com*, March 2, 2012. URL: http://www.financialsense.com/contributors/cris-sheridan/is-artificial-intelligence-taking-over-the-stock-market; Cris Sheridan, "Is the Entire Market Rigged?" *FinancialSense.com*, March 31, 2014. URL: http://www.financialsense.com/contributors/cris-sheridan/is-the-entire-market-rigged; Jeff Christian, "It's Not Just Gold – Computerized Trading Used to Manipulate All Markets," FinancialSense.com, March 17, 2014. URL: http://www.financialsense.com/contributors/jeff-christian/gold-manipulated-computerized-trading; Paul Saffo, "New Era, New God, Says Paul Saffo," *The Economist*, November 22, 2010. URL: http://www.economist.com/node/17509358; Cris Sheridan, "A.I.: The New God of Economics, Banking and Finance," *FinancialSense.com*, July 5, 2012. URL: http://www.financialsense.com/contributors/cris-sheridan/artificial-intelligence-the-new-god-of-economics; Cris Sheridan, :The HFT Revolution: 6 Reasons Why High Speed Trading Is Taking Over the Markets, *FinancialSense.com*, March 21, 2012. URL: http://www.financialsense.com/contributors/cris-sheridan/hft-revolution-six-reasons-why-its-taking-over-markets; Sean Sposito, "Banks Deploy Artificial Intelligence to Deepen Understanding of Customers," *American Banker*, July 23, 2012. URL: http://www. americanbanker.com/issues/177_141/banks-deploy-artificial-intelligence-to-understand-consumers-1051132-1.html

[16] Lowell Ponte, "Terrorism Central?" *FrontPageMagazine.com*, August 18, 2003. URL: http://archive.frontpagemag.com/readArticle.aspx?ARTID=16740

[17] Guy Standing, *A Precariat Charter: From Denizens to Citizens*. London: Bloomsbury Academic, 2014; Guy Standing, *The Precariat: The New Dangerous Class*. London: Bloomsbury Academic, 2011.

[18] David R. Wheeler, "What If Everybody Didn't Have to Work to Get Paid?" *The Atlantic*, May 18, 2015; Ilana E. Strauss, "Would A Work-Free World Be So Bad?" *The Atlantic*, June 28, 2016.

[19] Andy Stern, *Raising the Floor: How a Universal Basic Income Can Renew Our Economy and Rebuild the American Dream*. New York: PublicAffairs / Perseus Books Group, 2016. See also Bourree Lam, "The Case for Unions to Support a Universal Basic Income," *The Atlantic*, June 27, 2016; Ralph Benko, "Book Review: Andy Stern Wants Me to Send You $10,000/Year Tax Free (Part One), *Forbes*, June 30, 2016; Ralph Benko, "Book Review (Part Two): Andy Stern Dips His Toe Into The 2020 Presidential Waters," *Forbes*, July 1, 2016; "Bill Moyers Talks With Andy Stern," *Bill Moyers Journal* / PBS, June 15, 2007. URL: Http://www.pbs.org/moyers/journal/06152007/transcript2.html

[20]Charles Murray, *In Our Hands: A Plan to Replace The Welfare State* (Revised and updated since 2006 original). Washington, D.C.: American Enterprise Institute (AEI), 2016. See also Charles Murray, "A Guaranteed Income for Every American," *Wall Street Journal*, June 3, 2016. URL: https://www.aei.org/publications/a-guaranteed-income-for-every-american/print/

Chapter Eight – Glimpses of Tomorrow

[1] Manu Saadia, *Trekonomics: The Economics of Star Trek.* Pipertext, 2016.

[2] John Matson, "Fact or Fiction? Lead Can Be Turned Into Gold," *Scientific American,* January 31, 2014. URL: http://www.scientificamerican.com/article/fact-or-fiction-lead-can-be-turned-into-gold/

[3] Full disclosure – Lowell Ponte used to be a Contributing Editor of this journal at FEE.

Epilogue – An Empire for Liberty

[1] "The New Political Divide: Farewell, Left vs. Right. The Contest that Matters Now Is Open Against Closed" (Editorial), *The Economist* July 30, 2016. URL: http://www.economist.com/news/leaders/21702750-farewell-left-versus-right-contest-matters-now-open-against-closed-new; see also its accompanying article "Drawbridges Up," *The Economist,* July 30, 2016.

[2] Eric Metaxas, *If You Can Keep It: The Forgotten Promise of American Liberty*. New York: Viking Press, 2016.

[3] Os Guinness, *A Free People's Suicide: Sustainable Freedom and the American Future*. Westmont, Illinois: IVP Books (InterVarsity Press), 2012.

[4] Dan Ariely and others, The (True) Legacy of Two Really Existing Economic Systems (Monograph). Munich, Germany: Department of Economics, University of Munich, March 19, 2015. May be downloaded in English at http://papers.ssrn.com/sol3/papers.cfm?abstract_id=2457000; "Socialism of Progressives Such As Obama Brings Out Worst in Us," Investor's Business Daily, August 5, 2015; Zenon Evans, "Socialists Are Cheaters, Says News Study," Reason Magazine, July 22, 2014; Mark J. Perry, "Who'd a-thunk It? Socialism Is Demoralizing, Socially Corrosive, and Promotes Individual Dishonesty and Cheating?" American Enterprise Institute, July 19, 2014.

[5] Sebastian Junger, *Tribe: On Homecoming and Belonging*. New York: Twelve / Hachette Book Group, 2016.

[6] Brian Stewart, "In Defense of the Tribe," *National Review*, May 23, 2016. URL: http://www.nationalreview.com/article/435706/sebastian-junger-tribe-book

[7] From Rudyard Kipling's 1890 poem "Tommy." URL: http://www.poetryloverspage.com/poets/kipling/tommy.html

Sources

John Abromeit and others (Editors), *Transformations of Populism in Europe and the Americas: History and Recent Tendencies.* London: Bloomsbury Academic, 2015.

Daron Acemoglu and James A. Robinson, *Economic Origins of Dictatorship and Democracy.* Cambridge: Cambridge University Press, 2009.

_____, *Why Nations Fail: The Origins of Power, Prosperity, and Poverty.* New York: Crown Business, 2012.

Anat R. Admati and Martin Hellwig, *The Bankers' New Clothes: What's Wrong With Banking and What To Do About It.* Princeton, New Jersey: Princeton University Press, 2013.

Liaquat Ahamed, *Lords of Finance: The Bankers Who Broke the World.* New York: Penguin Books, 2009.

George A. Akerlof and Robert J. Schiller, *Animal Spirits: How Human Psychology Drives the Economy, and Why It Matters for Global Capitalism.*

Princeton, New Jersey: Princeton University Press, 2009.

_____, *Phishing for Phools: The Economics of Manipulation and Deception.* Princeton, New Jersey: Princeton University Press, 2009.

Daniel Alpert, *The Age of Oversupply: Overcoming the Greatest Challenge to the Global Economy.* New York: Portfolio / Penguin, 2014.

Morris Altman, *Behavioral Economics For Dummies.* Hoboken, New Jersey: For Dummies/John Wiley & Sons, 2012.

Stephen E. Ambrose and Fouglas G. Brinkley, *Rise to Globalism: American Foreign Policy Since 1938 (Ninth Revised Edition).* New York: Penguin Books, 2010.

John Anthers, *The Fearful Rise of Markets: Global Bubbles, Synchronized Meltdowns, and How to Prevent Them In The Future.* London: FT Press / Financial Times, 2010.

David Archibald, *Twilight of Abundance: Why Life in the 21st Century Will Be Nasty, Brutish, and Short.* Washington, D.C.: Regnery Publishing, 2014.

Sharyl Attkinsson, *Stonewalled: My Fight for Truth Against the Forces of Obstruction, Intimidation, and Harassment in Obama's Washington.* New York: Harper, 2014.

Tyler Atkinson, David Luttrell and Harvey Rosenblum, *How Bad Was It? The Costs and Consequences of the 2007-2009 Financial Crisis* (Staff Paper No. 20). Dallas, Texas: Federal Reserve Bank of Dallas, July 2013.

Radley Balko, *Rise of the Warrior Cop: The Militarization of America's Police Forces.* New York: PublicAffairs / Perseus Books Group, 2013.

Bill Bamber and Andrew Spencer, *Bear Trap: The Fall of Bear Stearns and the Panic of 2008.* New York: Ibooks, Inc., 2008.

James R. Barth, Gerard Caprio Jr., and Ross Levine, *Guardians of Finance: Making Regulators Work for Us.* Cambridge, Massachusetts: The MIT Press, 2012.

Randy Barnett, *Our Republican Constitution*. New York: Encounter Broadside Books, 2016.

James Bartholomew, *The Welfare of Nations*. London: Biteback Publishing, 2015.

William W. Beach and others, *Obama Tax Hikes: The Economic and Fiscal Effects* (Monograph). Washington, D.C.: Heritage Foundation, 2010.

Thorsten Beck (Editor), *The Future of Banking*. Centre for Economic Policy Research, 2011.

David Beckworth (Editor), *Boom and Bust Banking: The Causes and Cures of the Great Recession*. Oakland, California: Independent Institute, 2012.

Noah Berlatsky (Ed.), *Inflation*. Detroit: Greenhaven Press/Opposing Viewpoints Series, 2013.

Ben S. Bernanke and others, *Inflation Targeting: Lessons from the International Experience*. Princeton, New Jersey: Princeton University Press, 1999.

Peter Bernholz, *Monetary Regimes and Inflation: History, Economic and Political Relationships*. Williston, Vermont: Edward Elgar Publishing, 2006.

Peter L. Bernstein, *Against the Gods: The Remarkable Story of Risk*. Hoboken, New Jersey: John Wiley & Sons, 1998.

_____, *A Primer on Money, Banking, and Gold*. Hoboken, New Jersey: Wiley & Sons, 2008.

Ambassador Robert D. Blackwill and Jennifer M. Harris, *War by Other Means: Geoeconomics and Statecraft*. Cambridge, Massachusetts: Belknap Press / Harvard University Press, 2016.

Mark Blyth, *Austerity: The History of a Dangerous Idea*. Oxford: Oxford University Press, 2013.

Haim Bodek, *The Problems of HFT – Collected Writings on High Frequency Trading & Stock Market Structure*. Seattle, Washington: CreateSpace / Amazon, 2013.

Bill Bonner, *Hormegeddon: How Too Much Of A Good Thing Leads To Disaster*. Nulkaba, New South Wales, Australia: Lioncrest Publishing, 2014.

William Bonner and Addison Wiggin, *Financial Reckoning Day: Surviving the Soft Depression of the 21st Century*. Hoboken, New Jersey: John Wiley & Sons, 2004.

_____, *The New Empire of Debt: The Rise and Fall of an Epic Financial Bubble* (Second Edition). Hoboken, New Jersey: John Wiley & Sons, 2009.

Neal Boortz and John Linder, *The FairTax Book: Saying Goodbye to the Income Tax and the IRS....* New York: Regan Books / HarperCollins, 2005.

Neal Boortz, John Linder and Rob Woodall, *FairTax: The Truth: Answering the Critics*. New York: Harper, 2008.

Walter R. Borneman, *Polk: The Man Who Transformed the Presidency and America*. New York: Random House, 2009.

Nick Bostrom, *Superintelligence: Paths, Dangers, Strategies*. Oxford: Oxford University Press, 2014.

Volker Bothmer and Ioannis A. Daglis, *Space Weather: Physics and Effects*. Berlin: Springer, 2010.

Donald J. Boudreaux, James Scott, Timothy B. Lee and J. Bradford DeLong, *Seeing Like a State: A Conversation with James C. Scott*. Washington, D.C.: Cato Institute / Cato Unbound, 2010.

Richard X. Bove, *Guardians of Prosperity: Why America Needs Big Banks*. New York: Portfolio / Penguin, 2013.

Samuel Bowles, *The Moral Economy: Why Good Incentives Are No Substitute for Good Citizens* (Castle Lectures Series). New Haven, Connecticut: Yale University Press, 2016.

Jerry Bowyer, *The Free Market Capitalist's Survival Guide: How to Invest and Thrive in an Era of Rampant Socialism*. New York: Broad Side / Harper Collins, 2011.

Andrew J. Bracevich, *The Limits of Power: The End of American Exceptionalism* (American Empire Project). New York: Henry Holt, 2009.

_____, *The New American Militarism: How Americans Are Seduced by War* (Second Updated Edition). Oxford: Oxford University Press, 2013.

H.W. Brands, *The Age of Gold: The California Gold Rush and the New American Dream*. New York: Doubleday / Random House, 2002.

_____, *American Colossus: The Triumph of Capitalism 1865-1900*. New York: Anchor Books / Doubleday / Random House, 2010.

_____, *The Money Men: Capitalism, Democracy, and the Hundred Years' War Over the American Dollar*. New York: W.W. Norton, 2010.

Richard Brookhiser, *Alexander Hamilton, American*. New York: Touchstone / Simon & Schuster, 2000.

Arthur C. Brooks, *The Battle: How the Fight Between Free Enterprise and Big Government Will Shape America's Future*. New York: Basic Books/Perseus Books, 2010.

_____, *The Conservative Heart: How to Build a Fairer, Happier, and More Prosperous America*. New York: Broadside Books / HarperCollins, 2015

_____, *Gross National Happiness: Why Happiness Matters for America – and How We Can Get More of It*. New York: Basic Books, 2008.

_____, *The Road to Freedom: How to Win the Fight for Free Enterprise*. New York: Basic Books/Perseus Books, 2012.

David Brooks, *The Road to Character*. New York: Random House, 2015.

Rosa Brooks, *How Everything Became War and the Military Became Everything: Tales From the Pentagon*. New York: Simon & Schuster, 2016.

Brendan Brown, *Euro Crash: How Asset Price Inflation Destroys the Wealth of Nations* (Third Revised Edition). London: Palgrave Macmillan, 2014.

Ellen Hodgson Brown, *The Public Bank Solution: From Austerity to Prosperity*. Baton Rouge, Louisiana: Third Millennium Press, 2013.

_____, *Web of Debt: The Shocking Truth About Our Money System and How We Can Break Free (Fourth Edition)*. Baton Rouge, Louisiana: Third Millennium Press, 2011.

Robert Bryce, *Smaller Faster Lighter Denser Cheaper: How Innovation Keeps Proving the Catastrophists Wrong*. New York: Public Affairs / Perseus Books Group, 2014.

Dedria Bryfonski (Ed.), *The Banking Crisis*. Detroit: Greenhaven Press / Opposing Viewpoints Series, 2010.

James M. Buchanan and Richard E. Wagner, *Democracy in Deficit: The Political Legacy of Lord Keynes*. Indianapolis: Liberty Fund, 1999.

Todd G. Buchholz, *New Ideas from Dead Economists: An Introduction to Modern Economic Thought*. New York: New American Library/Penguin Books, 1989.

_____, *The Price of Prosperity: Why Rich Nations Fail and How to Renew Them*. New York: Harper, 2016.

Bruce Bueno de Mesquita, *The Dictator's Handbook: Why Bad Behavior Is Almost Always Good Politics*. Washington, D.C.: Public Affairs Press, 2011.

John Butler, *The Golden Revolution: How to Prepare for the Coming Global Gold Standard*. New York: John Wiley & Sons, 2012.

Smedley D. Butler, *War Is A Racket*. Seattle: Amazon Digital Services, 2012. This short book, originally published in 1935, can be downloaded at no cost from various Internet sites, including:

URL: http://www.historyisaweapon.org/defcon1/warracket.html or

URL: https://archive.org/stream/WarIsARacket/WarIsARacket_djvu.txt

Bruce Caldwell (Editor), *The Collected Works of F.A. Hayek, Volume 2: The Road to Serfdom: Texts and Documents: The Definitive Edition*. Chicago: University of Chicago Press, 2007.

Charles W. Calomiris and Stephen H. Haber, *Fragile by Design: The Political Origins of Banking Crises and Scarce Credit*. Princeton, N.J.: Princeton University Press, 2014.

James E. Campbell, *Polarized: Making Sense of a Divided America*. Princeton, New Jersey: Princeton University Press, 2016.

Ben Carson with Candy Carson, *America the Beautiful: Rediscovering What Made This Nation Great*. Grand Rapids, Michigan: Zondervan Publishing, 2012.

_____, *A More Perfect Union: What We The People Can Do To Reclaim Our Constitutional Liberties*. New York: Sentinel / Penguin, 2015.

_____, *One Nation: What We Can All Do To Save America's Future*. New York: Sentinel / Penguin, 2015.

Stephen G. Cecchetti and others, *The Real Effects of Debt*. BIS Working Papers No 352. Basel, Switzerland: Bank for International Settlements, September 2011. URL: http://www.bis.org/publ/work352.pdf

Central Intelligence Agency, *The CIA World Factbook 2013*. New York: Skyhorse Publishing, 2012.

Edward Chancellor, *Devil Take the Hindmost: A History of Financial Speculation*. New York: Plume (Reissue Edition), 2000.

Marc Chandler, *Making Sense of the Dollar: Exposing Dangerous Myths about Trade and Foreign Exchange*. New York: Bloomberg Press, 2009.

Ha-Joon Chang, *Bad Samaritans: The Myth of Free Trade and the Secret History of Capitalism*. London: Bloomsbury Press, 2008.

Ron Chernow, *Alexander Hamilton*. New York: Penguin Books, 2005.

_____, *The House of Morgan: An American Banking Dynasty and the Rise of Modern Finance*. New York: Grove Press, 2010.

Moorad Choudhry, *An Introduction to Banking: Liquidity Risk and Asset-Liability Management*. Hoboken, New Jersey: John Wiley & Sons, 2011.

Harold Van B. Cleveland, Charles P. Kindleberger, David P. Calleo and Lewis E. Lehrman, *Money and the Coming World Order*, Second Edition. Greenwich, Connecticut: Lehrman Institute, 2012.

Ta-Nehisi Coates, *The Beautiful Struggle: A Memoir*. New York: Spiegel & Grau / Random House, 2009.

_____, *Between the World and Me*. New York: Spiegel & Grau / Random House, 2015.

Tom A. Coburn, *The Debt Bomb: A Bold Plan to Stop Washington from Bankrupting America*. Nashville: Thomas Nelson, 2012.

Lizabeth Cohen, *A Consumers' Republic: The Politics of Mass Consumption in Postwar America*. New York: Vintage / Random House, 2008.

Stephen S. Cohen and J. Bradford DeLong, *Concrete Economics: The Hamilton Approach to Economic Growth and Policy*. Cambridge, Massachusetts: Harvard Business Review Press, 2016.

Congressional Budget Office, *The Budget and Economic Outlook: Fiscal Years 2011 to 2021*. Washington, D.C.: Congressional Budget Office, January 2011. URL: http://www.cbo.gov/ftpdocs/120xx/doc12039/01-26_FY2011Outlook.pdf

Miles Copeland, *The Game of Nations: The Amorality of Power Politics*. New York: Simon & Schuster, 1970.

Arnold Cornez, *The Offshore Money Book: How to Move Assets Offshore for Privacy, Protection, and Tax Advantage*. New York: McGraw-Hill, 2000.

Jerome R. Corsi, *America for Sale: Fighting the New World Order, Surviving a Global Depression, and Preserving U.S.A. Sovereignty*. New York: Threshold Editions / Simon & Schuster, 2009.

Jerome R. Corsi and Craig R. Smith, *Black Gold Stranglehold*. Los Angeles: WND Books, 2005.

Jay Cost, *A Republic No More: Big Government and the Rise of American Political Corruption*. New York: Encounter Books, 2015.

Diane Coyle, *GDP: A Brief But Affectionate History*. Princeton, New Jersey: Princeton University Press, 2014.

Crews, Clyde Wayne, Jr., *Ten Thousand Commandments: An Annual Snapshot of the Federal Regulatory State* (2014 Edition). (Monograph). Washington, D.C.: Competitive Enterprise Institute, 2014.

Satyajit Das, *The Age of Stagnation: Why Perpetual Growth is Unattainable and the Global Economy is in Peril*. Amherst, New York: Prometheus Books / Penguin, 2016.

Mike Dash, *Tulipomania: The Story of the World's Most Coveted Flower & The Extraordinary Passions It Aroused*. Waterville, Maine: G.K. Hall & Company, Publishers, 2001.

Glyn Davies, *A History of Money: From Ancient Times to the Present Day*. Third Edition. Cardiff: University of Wales Press, 2002.

Glyn Davies and Roy Davies, *A Comparative Chronology of Money: Monetary History from Ancient Times to the Present Day.* (Monograph based on Glyn Davies and Roy Davies, above.) (2006) URL: http://projects.exeter.ac.uk/RDavies/arian/amser/chrono.html

Carlos de la Torre and others, *The Promise and Perils of Populism: Global Perspectives*. Lexington: University Press of Kentucky, 2014.

Christine Desan, *Making Money: Coin, Currency, and the Coming of Capitalism*. Oxford: Oxford University Press, 2015.

Hernando de Soto, *The Mystery of Capital: Why Capitalism Triumphs in the West and Fails Everywhere Else*. New York: Basic Books / Perseus Books Group, 2000.

Jesus Huerta de Soto, *Money, Bank Credit, and Economic Cycles, Third Edition*. Auburn, Alabama: Ludwig von Mises Institute, 2012.

Karl de Schweinitz, *England's Road to Social Security*. New York: A.S. Barnes & Company / University of Pennsylvania Press, 1961.

Peter H. Diamandis and Steven Kotler, *Abundance: The Future Is Better Than You Think*. New York: Free Press, 2012.

Jared Diamond, *Collapse: How Societies Choose to Fail or Succeed*. New York: Viking Press, 2005.

James D. Dilts, *The Great Road: The Building of the Baltimore and Ohio, the Nation's First Railroad, 1828-1853*. Redwood City, California: Stanford University Press, 1996.

Peter F. Drucker, *Post-Capitalist Society*. New York: Harper Business, 1993.

Dinesh D'Souza, *America: Imagine a World Without Her*. Washington, D.C.: Regnery, 2014.

_____, *Obama's America: Unmaking the American Dream*. Washington, D.C.: Regnery, 2012.

_____, *The Roots of Obama's Rage*. Washington, D.C.: Regnery, 2010.

_____, *Stealing America: What My Experience with Criminal Gangs Taught Me About Obama, Hillary, and the Democratic Party.* New York: Broadside, 2015.

_____, *The Virtue of Prosperity: Finding Values in an Age of Techno-Affluence.* New York: Free Press / Simon & Schuster, 2000.

Richard Duncan, *The Dollar Crisis: Causes, Consequences, Cures*. Singapore: John Wiley & Sons (Asia), 2003.

_____, *The New Depression: The Breakdown of the Paper Money Economy.* New York: John Wiley & Sons, 2012.

Gregg Easterbrook, *The Progress Paradox: How Life Gets Better While People Feel Worse.* New York: Random House, 2003.

Mary Eberstadt, *How the West Really Lost God: A New Theory of Secularization.* West Conshohocken, Pennsylvania: Templeton Press, 2013.

Nicholas Eberstadt, *A Nation of Takers: America's Entitlement Epidemic.* West Conshohocken, Pennsylvania: Templeton Press, 2012.

Gauti B. Eggertsson, *What Fiscal Policy Is Effective at Zero Interest Rate?* Staff Report No. 402 (Monograph). New York: Federal Reserve Bank of New York, November 2009. URL: http://www.newyorkfed.org/research/staff_reports/sr402.pdf

Barry Eichengreen, *Exorbitant Privilege: The Rise and Fall of the Dollar and the Future of the International Monetary System.* Oxford: Oxford University Press, 2011.

_____, *Global Imbalances and the Lessons of Bretton Woods* (Cairoli Lectures). Cambridge, Massachusetts: MIT Press, 2010.

_____, *Globalizing Capital: A History of the International Monetary System* (Second Edition).

_____, *Golden Fetters: The Gold Standard and the Great Depression, 1919-1939* (NBER Series on Long-Term Factors in Economic Development). Oxford: Oxford University Press, 1996.

Barry Eichengreen and Marc Flandreau, *Gold Standard In Theory & History.* London: Routledge, 1997.

Mohammed A. El-Erian, *The Only Game In Town: Central Banks, Instability, and Avoiding the Next Collapse.* New York: Random House, 2016.

Kathleen C. Engel and Patricia A. McCoy, *The Subprime Virus: Reckless Credit, Regulatory Failure, and Next Steps.* New York: Oxford University Press USA, 2011.

Richard A. Epstein, *How Progressives Rewrote the Constitution.* Washington, D.C.: Cato Institute, 2006.

_____, *Takings: Private Property and the Power of Eminent* Domain. Cambridge, Massachusetts: Harvard University Press, 1985.

_____, *Why Progressive Institutions Are Unsustainable.* New York: Encounter Broadside / Encounter Books, 2011.

James Fallows, *National Defense.* New York: Random House, 1981.

Federal Reserve System, Board of Governors of, *Consumers and Mobile Financial Services 2013* (Monograph). Washington, D.C.: Federal Reserve Board Division of Consumer and Community Affairs, March 2013. URL: http://www.federalreserve.gov/econresdata/consumers-and-mobile-financial-services-report-201303.pdf

Carl Feisenfeld and David Glass, *Banking Regulation in the United States, 3rd Edition*. Huntington, N.Y.: Juris Publishing, 2011.

Niall Ferguson, *The Abyss: World War I and the End of the First Age of Globalization – A Selection from The War of the World*. New York: Penguin Books, 2012.

_____, *The Ascent of Money: A Financial History of the World*. New York: Penguin Press, 2008.

_____, *The Cash Nexus: Money and Power in the Modern World, 1700-2000*. New York: Basic Books, 2002.

_____, *Civilization: The West and the Rest*. New York: Penguin Books, 2011.

_____, *Colossus: The Price of America's Empire*. New York: Penguin Press, 2004.

_____, *Empire: The Rise and Demise of the British World Order and the Lessons for Global Power*. New York: Basic Books, 2004.

_____, *Empire: How Britain Made the Modern World*. New York: Penguin Books, 2012.

_____, *The House of Rothschild: Volume 1: Money's Prophets: 1798-1848*. New York: Penguin Books, 1999.

_____, *The House of Rothschild: Volume 2: The World's Banker: 1849-1999*. New York: Penguin Books, 2000.

_____, *The Great Degeneration: How Institutions Decay and Economies Die*. New York: Penguin Books, 2013.

_____, *Kissinger: 1923-1968: The Idealist*. Penguin Press, 2015.

Peter Ferrara, *America's Ticking Bankruptcy Bomb: How the Looming Debt Crisis Threatens the American Dream – and How We Can Turn the Tide Before It's Too Late*. New York: Broadside Books, 2011.

William Fleckenstein and Frederick Sheehan, *Greenspan's Bubbles: The Age of Ignorance at the Federal Reserve*. New York: McGraw-Hill, 2008.

Steve Forbes and Elizabeth Ames, *Money: How the Destruction of the Dollar Threatens the Global Economy – and What We Can Do About It*. New York: McGraw-Hill, 2014.

_____, *Reviving America: How Repealing Obamacare, Replacing the Tax Code and Reforming The Fed Will Restore Hope and Prosperity*. New York: McGraw-Hill, 2015.

Martin Ford, *Rise of the Robots: Technology and the Threat of a Jobless Future*. New York: Basic Books, 2015.

Rana Foroohar, *Makers and Takers: The Rise of Finance and the Fall of American Business*. New York: Crown Business, 2016.

Ralph T. Foster, *Fiat Paper Money: The History and Evolution of Our Currency*. Second Edition. Shenzhen, China: Shenzhen Jinhao Publishing / Alibaba.com, 2010.

Justin Fox, *The Myth of the Rational Market: A History of Risk, Reward, and Delusion on Wall Street*. New York: Harper Business, 2009.

Thomas Frank, *Listen, Liberal: Or, What Ever Happened to the Party of the People?* New York: Metropolitan Books, 2016.

Kevin D. Freeman, *Economic Warfare: Risks and Responses: Analysis of Twenty-First Century Risks in Light of the Recent Market Collapse* (Monograph). Cross Consulting and Services, 2009. This can be downloaded from the Internet at no cost from http://av.r.ftdata.co.uk/files/2011/03/49755779-Economic-Warfare-Risks-and-Responses-by-Kevin-D-Freeman.pdf or at no cost from http://www.freemanglobal.com/uploads/Economic_Warfare_Risks_and_Responses.pdf

_____, *Game Plan: How to Protect Yourself from the Coming Cyber-Economic Attack.* Washington, D.C.: Regnery Publishing, 2014.

_____, *Secret Weapon: How Economic Terrorism Brought Down the U.S. Stock Market and Why It Can Happen Again.* Washington, D.C.: Regnery, 2012.

Jeffry A. Frieden, *Global Capitalism: Its Fall and Rise in the Twentieth Century.* New York: W.W. Norton, 2006.

George Friedman, *The Next Decade: Where We've Been…And Where We're Going.* New York: Doubleday, 2011.

Milton Friedman, *An Economist's Protest.* Second Edition. Glen Ridge, New Jersey: Thomas Horton and Daughters, 1975. Also published as *There's No Such Thing As A Free Lunch.* La Salle, Illinois: Open Court Publishing, 1975.

_____, *Capitalism & Freedom: A Leading Economist's View of the Proper Role of Competitive Capitalism.* Chicago: University of Chicago Press, 1962.

_____, *Dollars and Deficits: Inflation, Monetary Policy and the Balance of Payments.* Englewood Cliffs, New Jersey: Prentice-Hall, 1968.

_____, *Money Mischief: Episodes in Monetary History.* New York: Harcourt Brace, 1992.

_____, *On Economics: Selected Papers.* Chicago: University of Chicago Press, 2007.

_____, *Why Government Is the Problem (Essays in Public Policy).* Stanford, California: Hoover Institution Press, 1993.

Milton & Rose Friedman, *Free to Choose: A Personal Statement.* New York: Harcourt Brace Jovanovich, 1980.

_____, *Tyranny of the Status Quo.* San Diego, California: Harcourt Brace Jovanovich, 1984.

Milton Friedman & Anna Jacobson Schwartz, *A Monetary History of the United States, 1867-1960.* A Study by the National Bureau of Economic Research, New York. Princeton, New Jersey: Princeton University Press, 1963.

Francis Fukuyama, *The End of History and The Last Man.* New York: Free Press, 1992.

_____, *Trust: The Social Virtues and The Creation of Prosperity.* New York: Free Press, 1996.

John Fund and Hans von Spakovsky, *Obama's Enforcer: Eric Holder's Justice Department.* New York: Broadside Books, 2014.

Joseph Gagnon, Matthew Raskin, Julie Remache and Brian Sack, *Large-Scale Asset Purchases by the Federal Reserve: Did They Work?* New York: Federal Reserve Bank of New York / *Economic Policy Review*, May 2011. URL: http://newyorkfed.org/research/epr/11v17n1/1105gagn.pdf

Joseph E. Gagnon and Brian Sack, *Monetary Policy with Abundant Liquidity: A New Operating Framework for the Federal Reserve.* Document PB 14-4 / Policy Brief. Washington, D.C.: Peterson Institute for International Economics, January 2014. URL: http://www.piie.com/publications/pb/pb14-4.pdf

James K. Galbraith, *The Predator State: How Conservatives Abandoned the Free Market and Why Liberals Should Too.* New York: Free Press, 2008.

Mark Lee Gardner, *Shot All to Hell: Jesse James, the Northfield Raid, and the Wild West's Greatest Escape.* New York: William Morrow, 2013.

John D. Gartner, *The Hypomanic Edge: The Link Between (A Little) Craziness and (A Lot of) Success in America.* New York: Simon & Schuster, 2005.

Charles Gasparino, *Bought and Paid For: The Unholy Alliance Between Barack Obama and Wall Street.* New York: Sentinel / Penguin, 2010.

Francis J. Gavin, *Gold, Dollars, and Power: The Politics of International Monetary Relations, 1958-1971 (The New Cold War History).* Chapel Hill, North Carolina: University of North Carolina Press, 2007.

Timothy F. Geithner, *Stress Test: Reflections on Financial Crises.* New York: Crown / Random House, 2014.

Nicole Gelinas, *After the Fall: Saving Capitalism from Wall Street – and Washington.* New York: Encounter Books, 2011.

Pamela Geller and Robert Spencer, *The Post-American Presidency.* New York: Threshold Editions / Simon & Schuster, 2010.

Teresa Ghilarducci, *Guaranteed Retirement Accounts: Toward Retirement Income Security.* Washington, D.C.: Economic Policy Institute, November 20, 2007. URL: http://www.gpn.org/bp204/bp204.pdf

_____, *What You Need to Know About the Economics of Growing Old (But Were Afraid to Ask): A Provocative Reference Guide to the Economics of Aging.* Notre Dame, Indiana: University of Notre Dame Press, 2004.

_____, *When I'm Sixty-Four: The Plot Against Pensions and the Plan to Save Them.* Princeton, New Jersey: Princeton University Press, 2008.

George Gilder, *Knowledge and Power: The Information Theory of Capitalism and How It Is Revolutionizing Our World.* Washington, D.C.: Regnery Publishing, 2013.

_____, *The Scandal of Money: Why Wall Street Recovers But The Economy Never Does.* Washington, D.C.: Regnery Publishing, 2016.

_____, *Wealth and Poverty.* New York: Basic Books, 1981.

Newt Gingrich, *A Nation Like No Other: Why American Exceptionalism Matters*. Washington, D.C.: Regnery Publishing, 2011.

Sally Goerner and others, *Money and Sustainability: The Missing Link*. Axminster, Devon, U.K.: Triarchy Press, 2012.

Jonah Goldberg, *Liberal Fascism: The Secret History of the American Left, From Mussolini to the Politics of Meaning*. New York: Doubleday, 2008.

_____, *The Tyranny of Cliches: How Liberals Cheat in the War of Ideas*. New York: Sentinel / Penguin, 2012.

David P. Goldman, *How Civilizations Die (And Why Islam Is Dying Too)*. Washington, D.C.: Regnery, 2011.

Paul Goodman, *Like A Conquered Province: The Moral Ambiguity of America*. New York: Random House, 1967.

Jason Goodwin, *Greenback: The Almighty Dollar and The Invention of America*. New York: John Macrae / Henry Holt and Company, 2003.

John Steele Gordon, *Hamilton's Blessing: The Extraordinary Life and Times of Our National Debt*. London: Walker Books, 2010.

Robert J. Gordon, *The Rise and Fall of American Growth: The U.S. Standard of Living Since the Civil War (The Princeton Economic History of the Western World)*. Princeton, New Jersey: Princeton University Press, 2016.
William M. Gouge, *A Short History of Paper Money and Banking in the United States*. Auburn, Alabama: Ludwig von Mises Institute, 2011.

Charles Goyette, *The Dollar Meltdown: Surviving the Impending Currency Crisis with Gold, Oil, and Other Unconventional Investments*. New York: Portfolio / Penguin, 2009.

Michael Grabell, *Money Well Spent? The Truth Behind the Trillion-Dollar Stimulus, the Biggest Economic Recovery Plan in History*. New York: PublicAffairs / Perseus Books Group, 2012.

David Graeber, *Debt: The First 5,000 Years*. Brooklyn, New York: Melville House Books, 2012.

Thomas Greco, *The End of Money and the Future of Civilization*. White River Junction, Vermont: Chelsea Green Publishing, 2009.

_____, *Money: Understanding and Creating Alternatives to Legal Tender*. White River Junction, Vermont: Chelsea Green Publishing, 2012.

Andy Greenberg, *This Machine Kills Secrets: How WikiLeakers, Cypherpunks, and Hacktivists Aim to Free the World's Information*. New York: Dutton Adult, 2012.

Alan Greenspan, *The Age of Turbulence: Adventures in a New World*. New York: Penguin Books, 2007.

William Greider, *Secrets of the Temple: How the Federal Reserve Runs the Country*. New York: Simon & Schuster, 1989.

G. Edward Griffin, *The Creature from Jekyll Island: A Second Look at the Federal Reserve*. Third Edition. Westlake Village, California: American Media, 1998.

Os Guinness, *A Free People's Suicide: Sustainable Freedom and the American Future*. Westmont, Illinois: IVP Books (InterVarsity Press), 2012.

Martin Gurn, *The Revolt of the Public and the Crisis of Authority in the New Millennium*. Seattle: Amazon Digital Publishing , 2014

Gwendolyn Hallsmith and Bernard Lietaer, *Creating Wealth: Growing Local Economies with Local Currencies*. Gabriola Island, British Columbia, Canada: New Society Publishers, 2011.

Mary Katherine Ham and Guy Benson, *End of Discussion: How the Left's Outrage Industry Shuts Down Debate, Manipulates Voters, and Makes America Less Free (and Fun)*. New York: Crown Forum, 2015.

Philip Hamburger, *Is Administrative Law Unlawful?* Chicago: University of Chicago Press, 2014.

Alexander Hamilton, James Madison and John Jay, *The Federalist Papers*. New York: Mentor Books / New American Library, 1961. For an online version of James Madison's Federalist Paper No. 44, go to this URL: http://www.constitution.org/fed/federa44.htm

Yuval Noah Harari, *Sapiens: A Brief History of Humankind*. New York: Harper, 2015.

Bob Harris, *The International Bank of Bob: Connecting Our Worlds One $25 Kiva Loan At A Time*. New York: Walker & Company, 2013.

Lawrence E. Harrison and others, *How Much Does Culture Matter?* Washington, D.C.: Cato Institute, 2007.

Keith Hart, *Money in an Unequal World*. New York: Texere, 2001.

David Harvey, *Seventeen Contradictions and the End of Capitalism*. Oxford: Oxford University Press, 2014.

Micahel V. Hayden, *Playing to the Edge: American Intelligence in the Age of Terror*. New York: Penguin Press, 2016.

Friedrich A. Hayek (Editor), *Capitalism and the Historians*. Chicago: Phoenix Books / University of Chicago Press, 1963.

_____, *Choice in Currency: A Way to Stop Inflation*. London: Institute of Economic Affairs, 1976.   This can be downloaded from the Internet at no cost from http://www.iea.org.uk/sites/default/files/publications/files/upldbook409.pdf

_____, *The Counter-Revolution of Science: Studies On The Abuse of Reason*. New York: The Free Press / Macmillan / Crowell-Collier, 1955.

_____, *The Constitution of Liberty*. The Definitive Edition, Edited by Ronald Hamowy. Chicago: University of Chicago Press, 2011.

_____, *Denationalisation of Money: The Argument Refined: An Analysis of the Theory and Practice of Concurrent Currencies. Third Edition*. London: Institute of Economic Affairs, 1990.   This can be downloaded from the Internet at no cost from http://mises.org/books/denationalisation.pdf

_____, *The Fatal Conceit: The Errors of Socialism*. Chicago: University of Chicago Press, 1991.

_____, *The Road to Serfdom*. Chicago: Phoenix Books / University of Chicago Press, 1944.

Henry Hazlitt, *The Failure of the "New Economics": An Analysis of The Keynesian Fallacies*. New Rochelle, New York: Arlington House, 1959.

_____, *From Bretton Woods to World Inflation: A Study of Causes & Consequences*. Chicago: Regnery Gateway, 1984. This can be downloaded from the Internet at no cost from http://mises.org/books/brettonwoods.pdf

James J. Hentz, *The Obligation of Empire: United States' Grand Strategy for a New Century*. Lexington, Kentucky: The University Press of Kentucky, 2004.

Arthur Herman, *To Rule the Waves: How the British Navy Shaped the Modern World*. New York: HarperCollins, 2004.

Robert L. Hetzel, *The Great Recession: Market Failure or Policy Failure? (Studies in Macroeconomic History)*. New York: Cambridge University Press, 2012.

_____, *The Monetary Policy of the Federal Reserve*. New York: Cambridge University Press, 2008.

Mike Hill and Warren Montag, *The Other Adam Smith*. Redwood City, California: Stanford University of Press, 2014.

Kim R. Holmes, *The Closing of the Liberal Mind: How Groupthink and Intolerance Define the Left*. New York: Encounter Books, 2016.

_____, *Rebound: Getting America Back to Great*. Lanham, Maryland: Rowman & Littlefield, 2013.

Hans-Hermann Hoppe, *Democracy: The God That Failed*. Piscataway, New Jersey: Transaction Publishers, 2001.

John Horgan, *The End of Science: Facing the Limits of Knowledge In The Twilight of The Scientific Age*. New York: Broadway Books, 1997.

David Horowitz and Jacob Laksin, *The New Leviathan: How the Left-Wing Money-Machine Shapes American Politics and Threatens America's Future*. New York: Crown Forum, 2012.

Michel Houellebecq, *Submission: A Novel*. New York: Farrar, Straus and Giroux, 2015.

Philip K. Howard, *The Rule of Nobody: Saving America from Dead Laws and Broken Government*. New York: W.W. Norton, 2014.

Timothy Howard, *The Mortgage Wars: Inside Fannie Mae, Big-Money Politics, and the Collapse of the American Dream*. New York: McGraw-Hill Education, 2014.

Glenn Hubbard and Tim Kane, *Balance: The Economics of Great Powers From Ancient Rome to Modern America*. New York: Simon & Schuster, 2013.

Michael Hudson, *The Bubble and Beyond: Fictitious Capital, Debt Deflation and Global Crisis*. ISLET / Open Library, 2012.

Samuel P. Huntington, *The Clash of Civilizations and the Remaking of World Order*. New York: Simon & Schuster, 2007.

W.H. Hutt, *The Keynesian Episode: A Reassessment*. Indianapolis: Liberty*Press*, 1979.

Nancy Isenberg, *White Trash: The 400-Year Untold History of Class in America*. New York: Viking Press, 2016.

Bob Ivry, *The Seven Sins of Wall Street: Big Banks, Their Washington Lackeys, and the Next Financial Crisis*. New York: PublicAffairs Press / Perseus Group, 2014.

Andrew Jackson and Ben Dyson, *Modernising Money: Why Our Monetary System Is Broken and How It Can Be Fixed*. Seattle: Positive Money/Amazon Digital Services, 2013.

Steven H. Jaffe, Jessica Lautin and the Museum of the City of New York, *Capital of Capital: Money, Banking, and Power in New York City, 1784-2012*. New York: Columbia University Press, 2014.

Chalmers Johnson, *Blowback: The Costs and Consequences of American Empire*. New York: Henry Holt, 2004.

_____, *The Sorrows of Empire: Militarism, Secrecy, and the End of the Republic*. New York: Metropolitan Books / Henry Holt, 2004.

_____, *Nemesis: The Last Days of the American Republic*. New York: Metropolitan Books / Henry Holt, 2008.

Simon Johnson and James Kwak, *13 Bankers: The Wall Street Takeover and the Next Financial Meltdown*. New York: Pantheon Books, 2010.

Garett Jones, *Hive Mind: How Your Nation's IQ Matters So Much More Than Your Own*. Redwood City, California: Stanford Economics and Finance / Stanford University Press, 2015.

Robert P. Jones, *The End of White Christian America*. New York: Simon & Schuster, 2016.

Sebastian Junger, *Tribe: On Homecoming and Belonging*. New York: Twelve / Hachette Book Group, 2016.

Robert Kagan, *The World America Made*. New York: Vintage / Random House, 2012.

Jerry Kaplan, *Humans Need Not Apply: A Guide to Wealth and Work in the Age of Artificial Intelligence*. New Haven, Connecticut: Yale University Press, 2015.

Craig Karmin, *Biography of the Dollar: How the Mighty Buck Conquered the World and Why It's Under Siege*. New York: Crown Business, 2008.

John Kay, *Other People's Money: The Real Business of Finance*. New York: PublicAffairs / Perseus Group, 2015.

Craig Karmin, *Biography of the Dollar: How the Mighty Buck Conquered the World and Why It's Under Siege*. New York: Crown Business, 2008.

Margrit Kennedy, *People Money: The Promise of Regional Currencies*. London: Triarchy Press, 2012.

Robert O. Keohane (Editor), *Neorealism and Its Critics*. New York: Columbia University Press, 1986

Charles R. Kesler, *I Am the Change: Barack Obama and the Crisis of Liberalism*. New York: Broadside Books, 2012.

John Maynard Keynes, *Essays in Persuasion*. New York: W.W. Norton, 1963.

_____, *The General Theory of Employment, Interest, and Money*. New York: Harcourt, Brace & World, 1935.

Parag Khanna, *Connectography: Mapping the Future of Global Civilization*. New York: Random House, 2016.

Brian Kilmeade and Don Yaeger, *Thomas Jefferson and the Tripoli Pirates: The Forgotten War that Changed American History*. New York: Sentinel / Penguin, 2015.

Elior Kinarthy, *The Psychology of Investing During the Chaotic Obama Years*. Bloomington, Indiana: Xlibris Publishing, 2011.

Charles P. Kindleberger and Robert Z. Aliber, *Manias, Panics and Crashes: A History of Financial Crises (Sixth Edition)*. London: Palgrave Macmillan, 2011.

Mervyn King, *The End of Alchemy: Money, Banking, and the Future of the Global Economy*. New York: W.W. Norton, 2016.

Stephen D. King, *When the Money Runs Out: The End of Western Affluence*. New Haven, Connecticut: Yale University Press, 2013.

Henry Kissinger, *World Order*. New York: Penguin Books, 2014.

Arnold Kling, *The Case for Auditing the Fed Is Obvious*. (Monograph / Briefing Paper). Washington, D.C.: Cato Institute, April 27, 2010. URL: http://www.cato.org/pubs/bp/bp118.pdf

_____, *Not What They Had In Mind: A History of Policies that Produced the Financial Crisis of 2008*. Fairfax, Virginia: Mercatus Center at George Mason University, 2009.

_____, *Specialization and Trade: A Re-introduction to Economics*. Washington, Institute, 2016.

Chuck Klosterman, *But What If We're Wrong?: Thinking About The Present As If It Were the Past*. New York: Blue Rider Press / Penguin Random House, 2016.

Knowledge @ Wharton and Ernst & Young, *Global Banking 2020: Foresight and Insights*. Seattle: Amazon Digital Services, 2012.

Gabriel Kolko, *Railroads and Regulation 1877-1916*. New York: W.W. Norton, 1970. Originally published in 1965 by Princeton University Press.

Martijn Konings, *The Emotional Logic of Capitalism: What Progressives Have Missed*. Redwood City, California: Standord University Press, 2015.

Ted Koppel, *Lights Out: A Cyberattack, A Nation Unprepared, Surviving the Aftermath*. New York: Crown, 2015.

Laurence J. Kotlikoff, *Jimmy Stewart Is Dead: Ending the World's Ongoing Financial Plague with Limited Purpose Banking*. Hoboken, New Jersey: John Wiley & Sons, 2011.

Laurence J. Kotlikoff and Scott Burns, *The Clash of Generations: Saving Ourselves, Our Kids, and Our Economy*. Cambridge, Massachusetts: The MIT Press, 2012.

_____, *The Coming Generational Storm: What You Need to Know About America's Economic Future.* Cambridge, Massachusetts: MIT Press, 2005.

Laurence J. Kotlikoff, Philip Moeller and Paul Solman, *Get What's Yours: The Secrets to Maxing Out Your Social Security*. New York: Simon & Schuster, 2015.

Paul Krugman, *The Return of Depression Economics and The Crisis of 2008*. New York: W.W. Norton, 2009.

Stanley Kurtz, *Spreading the Wealth: How Obama Is Robbing the Suburbs to Pay for the Cities*. New York: Sentinel / Penguin, 2012.

Joel Kurtzman, *The Death of Money: How the Electronic Economy Has Destabilized the World's Markets and Created Financial Chaos*. New York: Simon & Schuster, 1993.

Ray Kurzweil, *How to Create a Mind: The Secret of Human Thought Revealed*. New York: Penguin Books, 2013.

Adrian Kuzminski, *Fixing the System: A History of Populism, Ancient and Modern*. London: Bloomsbury Academic, 2008.

Kwasi Kwarteng, *War and Gold: A Five-Hundred-Year History of Empires, Adventures and Debt*. London: Bloomsbury Publishing, 2014.

Arthur B. Laffer, Stephen Moore and Peter J. Tanous, *The End of Prosperity: How Higher Taxes Will Doom the Economy – If We Let It Happen*. New York: Threshold Editions / Simon & Schuster, 2008.

Arthur B. Laffer, Stephen Moore, Rex A. Sinquefield and Travis H. Brown, *An Inquiry into the Nature and Causes of the Wealth of States: How Taxes, Energy, and Worker Freedom Change Everything*. Hoboken, New Jersey: John Wiley & Sons, 2014.

Arthur B. Laffer and Stephen Moore, *Return to Prosperity: How America Can Regain Its Economic Superpower Status*. New York: Threshold Editions / Simon & Schuster, 2010.

George Lakoff, *The Political Mind: A Cognitive Scientist's Guide to Your Brain and Its Politics*. New York: Penguin Books, 2009.

George Lakoff and Elizabeth Wehling, *The Little Blue Book: The Essential Guide to Thinking and Talking Democratic*. New York: Free Press, 2012.

John Lanchester, *I.O.U.: Why Everyone Owes Everyone and No One Can Pay*. New York: Simon & Schuster, 2010.

David S. Landes, *The Wealth and Poverty of Nations: Why Some Are So Rich and Some So Poor*. New York: W.W. Norton, 1998.

Vincent Lannoye, *The History of Money For Understanding Economics*. Seattle: CreateSpace Independent Publishing / Amazon, 2015.

Jonathan V. Last, *What to Expect When No One's Expecting: America's Coming Demographic Disaster*. New York: Encounter Books, 2013.

Adam Lebor, *Tower of Basel: The Shadowy History of the Secret Bank that Runs the World*. New York: PublicAffairs / Perseus Group, 2013.

Chris Lehmann, *The Money Cult: Capitalism, Christianity, and the Unmaking of the American Dream*. Brooklyn: Melville House Publishing, 2016.

Lewis E. Lehrman, *Money, Gold and History*. Greenwich, Connecticut: The Lehrman Institute, 2013.

_____, *The True Gold Standard – A Monetary Reform Plan Without Official Reserve Currencies*. Greenwich, Connecticut: The Lehrman Institute, 2011.

Gwendolyn Leick (Editor), *The Babylonian World*. London: Routledge, 2009. See chapter "The Egibi Family" by Cornelia Wunsch.

George Lekatis, *Understanding Basel III: What Is Different After March 2013*. Washington, D.C.: Basel III Compliance Professionals Association (BiiiCPA), 2013.

Lawrence Lessig, *Republic, Lost: How Money Corrupts Congress – and a Plan to Stop It*. New York: Twelve / Hachette Book Group, 2011.

Louise Levathes, *When China Ruled the Seas: The Treasure Fleet of the Dragon Throne, 1405-1433*. Oxford: Oxford University Press, 1997.

Mark Levin, *Plunder and Deceit*. New York: Threshold Editions / Simon & Schuster, 2015.

Yuval Levin, *The Fractured Republic: Renewing America's Social Contract in the Age of Individualism*. New York: Basic Books, 2016.

Hunter Lewis, *Crony Capitalism in America: 2008-2012*. Charlottesville, Virginia: AC2 Publishing, 2013.

Michael Lewis, *Boomerang: Travels in the New Third World*. New York: W.W. Norton, 2011.

_____, *Flash Boys: A Wall Street Revolt*. New York: W.W. Norton, 2014.

_____, *Panic: The Story of Modern Financial Insanity*. New York: W.W. Norton, 2009.

Naphtali Lewis and Meyer Reinhold (Editors), *Roman Civilization: Sourcebook II: The Empire*. New York: Harper Torchbooks, 1966.

Nathan Lewis and Addison Wiggin, *Gold: The Once and Future Money*. Hoboken, New Jersey: John Wiley & Sons, 2007.

Qiao Liang and Wang Xiangsui, *Unrestricted Warfare*. Panama City, Panama: Pan American Publishing Company, 2002.

Bernard Lietaer, *The Future of Money: Creating New Wealth, Work and a Wiser World*. London: Random House, 2001.

Bernard Lietaer and Stephen Belgin, *New Money for a New World*. Boulder, Colorado: Qiterra Press, 2011.

Bernard Lietaer and Jacqui Dunne, *Rethinking Money: How New Currencies Turn Scarcity Into Prosperity*. San Francisco: Berrett-Koehler Publishers / BK Currents, 2013.

Charles A. Lindbergh, Sr., *Lindbergh on the Federal Reserve* (Formerly titled: *The Economic Pinch*). Costa Mesa, California: Noontide Press, 1989.

Brink Lindsey (Ed.), *Understanding the Growth Slowdown*. Washington, D.C.: Cato Institute, 2015.

Lawrence B. Lindsey, *Conspiracies of the Ruling Class: How to Break Their Grip Forever*. New York: Simon & Schuster, 2016.

Julia Lovell, *The Great Wall: China Against the World, 1000 BC-AD 2000*. New York: Grove Press, 2007.

David Lukas, *Whose Future Are You Financing? What the Government And Wall Street Don't Want You To Know*. Little Rock, Arkansas: Race Publishing, 2014.

Deirdre N. McCloskey, *Bourgeois Dignity: Why Economics Can't Explain the Modern World*. Chicago: University of Chicago Press, 2010.

_____, *The Rhetoric of Economics*. Madison: University of Wisconsin Press, 1998.

Robert McCrum, Robert MacNeil, and William Cran, *The Story of English: Third Revised Edition*. New York: Penguin Books, 2002.

Heather MacDonald, *The Burden of Bad Ideas: How Modern Intellectuals Misshape Our Society*. Chicago: Ivan R. Dee, 2000.

_____, *The War on Cops: How the New Attack on Law and Order Makes Everyone Less Safe*. New York: Encounter Books, 2016.

James Macdonald, *A Free Nation Deep In Debt: The Financial Roots of Democracy*. New York: Farrar, Straus and Giroux, 2003.

Robert D. McHugh, *The Coming Economic Ice Age: Five Steps To Survive and Prosper*. London: Thomas Noble Books, 2013.

Bethany McLean and Joe Nocera, *All the Devils Are Here: The Hidden History of the Financial Crisis*. New York: Portfolio / Penguin, 2010.

John McWhorter, *Winning the Race: Beyond the Crisis in Black America*. New York: Gotham / Penguin, 2006.

Michael Magnusson, *The Land Without A Banking Law: How to Start a Bank With a Thousand Dollars*. York, England: Opus Operis Publishing, 2013.

_____, *Offshore Bank License: Seven Jurisdictions*. York, England: Opus Operis Publishing, 2013.

Michael P. Malloy, *Principles of Bank Regulation, 3rd Edition (Concise Hornbook)*. Eagan, Minnesota: West Publishing/Thompson Reuters, 2011.

Andreas Malm, *Fossil Capital: The Rise of Steam Power and the Roots of Global Warming*. London: Verso, 2016.

Felix Martin, *Gold: The Unauthorized Biography*. New York: Knopf, 2014.

James A. Marusek, *Solar Storm Threat Analysis* (Monograph). Bloomfield, Indiana: Impact, 2007. URL: http://www.breadandbutterscience.com/SSTA.pdf.

Karl Marx and Friedrich Engels, *The Communist Manifesto*. London: Penguin Classics, 1985.

Paul Mason, *Postcapitalism: A Guide to Our Future*. New York: Farrar, Straus and Giroux, 2016.

Doreen Massey and others, *The Greatest Invention: Tax and the Campaign for a Just Society*. Margate, Kent, U.K.: Commonwealth Publishing, 2015.

Philip Matyszak, *Ancient Rome on 5 Denarii a Day*. London: Thames & Hudson, 2008.

John Mauldin and Jonathan Tepper, *Code Red: How to Protect Your Savings From the Coming Crisis*. Hoboken, New Jersey: John Wiley & Sons, 2013.

_____, *Endgame: The End of the Debt Supercycle and How It Changes Everything*. Hoboken, New Jersey: John Wiley & Sons, 2011.

Martin Mayer, *The Fed: The Inside Story of How the World's Most Powerful Financial Institution Drives the Markets*. New York: Free Press, 2001.

John J. Mearsheimer, *The Tragedy of Great Power Politics* (Updated Edition). New York: W.W. Norton, 2014.

Michael Medved, *The 5 Big Lies About American Business: Combating Smears Against the Free-Market Economy*. New York: Crown Forum, 2009.

David I. Meiselman and Arthur B. Laffer (Editors), *The Phenomenon of Worldwide Inflation*. Washington, D.C.: American Enterprise Institute, 1975.

Mary Mellor, *The Future of Money: From Financial Crisis to Public Resource*. London: Pluto Press, 2010.

Gavin Menzies, *1421: The Year China Discovered America*. New York: Harper Perennial, 2002.

_____, *1434: The Year a Magnificent Chinese Fleet Sailed to Italy and Ignited the Renaissance*. New York: Harper Perennial, 2009.

Eric Metaxas, *Amazing Grace: William Wilberforce and the Heroic Campaign to End Slavery*. New York: HarperOne, 2007

_____, *Bonheoffer: Pastor, Martyr, Prophet, Spy*. Nashville, Tennessee: Thomas Nelson / HarperCollins, 2011.

_____, *If You Can Keep It: The Forgotten Promise of American Liberty*. New York: Viking Press, 2016.

_____, *Seven Men: And the Secret of Their Greatness*. Nashville, Tennessee: Thomas Nelson / HarperCollins, 2016.

Atif Mian and Amir Sufi, *House of Debt: How They (and You) Caused the Great Recession, and How We Can Prevent It from Happening Again*. Chicago: University of Chicago Press, 2014.

Norbert J. Michel, *The Financial Stability Oversight Council: Helping to Enshrine "Too Big to Fail"* (Monograph / *Backgrounder*). Washington, D.C.: The Heritage Foundation, April 1, 2014.

Willem Middlekoop, *The Big Reset: War on Gold and the Financial Endgame*. Amsterdam: Amsterdam University Press, 2014.

James D. Miller, *Singularity Rising: Surviving and Thriving in a Smarter, Richer, and More Dangerous World*. Dallas, Texas: BenBella Books, 2012.

Terry Miller, Anthony B. Kim and Kim R. Holmes, *2014 Index of Economic Freedom*. Washington, D.C.: Heritage Foundation / *Wall Street Journal*, 2014. URL for free download: http://www.heritage.org/index/download

Gregory J. Millman, *The Vandals' Crown: How Rebel Currency Traders Overthrew the World's Central Banks*. New York: Free Press, 1995.

Brendan Miniter (Ed.), *The 4% Solution: Unleashing the Economic Growth America Needs*. New York: Crown Business / George W. Bush Institute, 2012.

Hyman P. Minsky, *John Maynard Keynes*. New York: McGraw-Hill, 2008.

_____, *Stabilizing an Unstable Economy*. New York: McGraw-Hill, 2008.

Ludwig von Mises, *The Anti-Capitalist Mentality*. Princeton, New Jersey: Van Nostrand Company, 1956.

_____, *Human Action: A Treatise on Economics*. Third Revised Edition. Chicago: Contemporary Books, 1966.

_____, *On the Manipulation of Money and Credit*. Dobbs Ferry, New York: Free Market Books, 1978.

_____, *The Theory of Money and Credit*, New Edition. Irvington-on-Hudson, NY: Foundation for Economic Education, 1971.

Frederic S. Mishkin, *The Economics of Money, Banking and Financial Markets: The Business School Edition, 3rd Edition*. New York: Prentice-Hall, 2012.

Kelly Mitchell, *Gold Wars: The Battle for the Global Economy*. Atlanta, Georgia: Clarity Press, 2013.

W.F. Mitchell, *Modern Monetary Theory and Practice: An Introductory Text*. Seattle: CreateSpace Independent Publishing Platform, 2016.

Benjamin Moffitt, *The Global Rise of Populism: Performance, Political Style, and Representation*. Redwood City, California: Stanford University Press, 2016.

Stephen Moore, *How Barack Obama Is Bankrupting the U.S. Economy* (Encounter Broadside No. 4). New York: Encounter Books, 2009.

_____, *Who's the Fairest of Them All? The Truth About Opportunity, Taxes, and Wealth in America*. New York: Encounter Books, 2012.

Bethany Moreton, *To Serve God and Wal-Mart: The Making of Christian Free Enterprise*. Cambridge, Massachusetts: Harvard University Press, 2009.

Hans J. Morganthau, *Politics Among Nations: The Struggle for Power and Peace* [Third Edition]. New York: Alfred A. Knopf, 1965.

Charles R. Morris, *The Trillion Dollar Meltdown: Easy Money, High Rollers, and the Great Credit Crash*. New York: Public Affairs/Perseus, 2008.

Alan D. Morrison and William J. Wilhelm, Jr., *Investment Banking: Institutions, Politics, and Law.* New York: Oxford University Press, USA, 2008.

Warren Mosler, *Soft Currency Economics II: What Everyone Thinks That They Know About Monetary Policy Is Wrong.* Seattle: Amazon Digital Services, 2012.

Cas Muddle, *Populist Radical Right Parties in Europe.* Cambridge: Cambridge University Press, 2007.

Cullen Murphy, *Are We Rome? The Fall of an Empire and the Fate of America.* Boston: Mariner Books/Houghton Mifflin, 2007.

Robert P. Murphy, *The Politically Incorrect Guide to Capitalism.* Washington, D.C.: Regnery, 2007.

Charles Murray, *By the People: Rebuilding Liberty Without Permission.* New York: Crown Forum, 2015.

_____, *Coming Apart: The State of White America, 1960-2010.* New York: Crown Forum, 2012.

_____, *In Our Hands: A Plan to Replace The Welfare State* (Revised and updated since 2006 original). Washington, D.C.: American Enterprise Institute (AEI), 2016.

_____, *What It Means to Be a Libertarian: A Personal Interpretation.* New York: Broadway Books, 1997.

Ralph Nader, *Unstoppable: The Emerging Left-Right Alliance to Dismantle the Corporate State.* New York: Nation Books, 2014.

Moises Naim, *The End of Power: From Boardrooms to Battlefields and Churches to States, Why Being in Charge Isn't What It Used to Be.* New York: Basic Books, 2014.

Andrew P. Napolitano, *Lies the Government Told You: Myth, Power, and Deception in American History.* Nashville: Thomas Nelson, 2010.

_____, *Theodore and Woodrow: How Two American Presidents Destroyed Constitutional Freedom.* Nashville: Thomas Nelson, 2012.

Sylvia Nasar, *Grand Pursuit: The Story of Economic Genius.* New York: Simon & Schuster, 2011.

R. Nelson Nash, *Becoming Your Own Banker (Sixth Edition).* Seattle: Infinite Banking Concepts/ Amazon Digital Printing, 2012.

Paul Nathan, *The New Gold Standard: Rediscovering the Power of Gold to Protect and Grow Wealth.* Hoboken, New Jersey: Wiley & Sons, 2011.

Daniel Arthur Nelson, *The Virtue of Money: How Money Contributes to Peace, Happiness, and Goodness.* Seattle: CreateSpace Independent Publishing / Amazon, 2013.

Karen Rhea Nemet-Nejat, *Daily Life in Ancient Mesopotamia.* Ada, Michigan: Baker Academic Publishing, 2001.

Maxwell Newton, *The Fed: Inside the Federal Reserve, the Secret Power Center that Controls the American Economy.* New York: Times Books, 1983.

Robert Nisbet, *The Quest for Community: A Study in the Ethics of Order and Freedom.* Wilmington, Delaware: ISI Books . Intercollegiate Studies Institute, 2010.

Johan Norberg, *Financial Fiasco: How America's Infatuation with Home Ownership and Easy Money Created the Economic Crisis.* Washington, D.C.: Cato Institute, 2009.

Grover Norquist and John R. Lott, Jr., *Debacle: Obama's War on Jobs and Growth and What We Can Do Now to Regain Our Future.* Hoboken, New Jersey: John Wiley & Sons, 2012.

Barack Obama, *The Audacity of Hope: Thoughts on Reclaiming the American Dream.* New York: Crown, 2006.

Brian O'Brien, *The Tyranny of the Federal Reserve.* Seattle: Amazon Digital Services, 2015.

Mancur Olson, *The Logic of Collective Action: Public Goods and the Theory of Groups*, Revised Edition. Cambridge, Massachusetts: Harvard University Press, 1971.

_____, *Power and Prosperity: Outgrowing Communist and Capitalist Dictatorships.* New York: Basic Books, 2000.

_____, *The Rise and Decline of Nations: Economic Growth, Stagflation, and Social Rigidities.* New Haven, Connecticut: Yale University Press, 1984.

David Orrell and Roman Chiupaty, *The Evolution of Money.* New York: Columbia University Press, 2016.

David Osborne and Peter Hutchinson, *The Price of Government: Getting the Results We Need in an Age of Permanent Fiscal Crisis.* New York: Basic Books / Perseus Group, 2004.

James Ostrowski, *Progressivism: A Primer on the Idea Destroying America.* Cazenovia, N.Y.: Cazenovia Books, 2014.

Ronen Palan, Richard Murphy and Christian Chavagneux, *Tax Havens: How Globalization Really Works.* Ithaca, New York: Cornell University Press / Cornell Studies in Money, 2009.

Scott Patterson, *Dark Pools: The Rise of the Machine Traders and the Rigging of the U.S. Stock Market.* New York: Crown Business / Random House, 2012.

Ron Paul, *End The Fed.* New York: Grand Central Publishing / Hachette, 2009.

_____, *Liberty Defined: 50 Essential Issues That Affect Our Freedom.* New York: Grand Central Publishing / Hachette, 2011.

_____, *Pillars of Prosperity: Free Markets, Honest Money, Private Property.* Auburn, Alabama: Ludwig von Mises Institute, 2008.

_____, *The Revolution: A Manifesto.* New York: Grand Central Publishing / Hachette, 2008.

Ron Paul and Lewis Lehrman, *The Case for Gold: A Minority Report of the U.S. Gold Commission.* Ludwig von Mises Institute, 2007. This can be downloaded from the Internet at no cost from http://mises.org/books/caseforgold.pdf

John Peet and Anton La Guardia, *Unhappy Union: How the Euro Crisis – and Europe – Can Be Fixed.* London: Economist Books, 2014.

Michael G. Pento, *The Coming Bond Market Collapse: How to Survive the Demise of the U.S. Debt Market*. Hoboken, New Jersey: John Wiley & Sons, 2013.

Maria Jose Pereira, *A Banker Reflects on Money, Love, and Virtue*. Axminster, Devon, U.K.: Triarchy Press, 2015.

Peter G. Peterson, *Running On Empty: How the Democratic and Republican Parties Are Bankrupting Our Future and What Americans Can Do About It*. New York: Farrar, Straus and Giroux, 2004.

Ann Pettifor, *Just Money: How Society Can Break the Despotic Power of Finance*. Margate, Kent, U.K.: Commonwealth Publishing, 2014.

Kevin Phillips, *Bad Money: Reckless Finance, Failed Politics, and the Global Crisis of American Capitalism*. New York: Viking Press, 2008.

_____, *Boiling Point: Democrats, Republicans, and the Decline of Middle-Class Prosperity*. New York: Random House, 1993.

James Piereson, *Shattered Consensus: The Rise and Decline of America's Postwar Political Order*. New York: Encounter Books, 2015.

Paul Pierson and Jacob S. Hacker, *American Amnesia: How the War on Government Led Us to Forget What Made America Prosper*. New York: Simon & Schuster, 2016.

Thomas Piketty, *Capital in the Twenty-First Century*. Cambridge, Massachusetts: Harvard University Press, 2014.

Steven Pinker, *The Better Angels of Our Nature: Why Violence Has Declined*. New York: Penguin Books, 2012.

Federico Pistono, *Robots Will Steal Your Job, But That's OK: How to Survive the Economic Collapse and Be Happy*. Seattle, Washington: CreateSpace / Amazon, 2014.

John Plender, *Capitalism: Money, Morals and Markets*. London: Biteback Publishing, 2016.

Lowell Ponte, *The Cooling*. Englewood Cliffs, New Jersey: Prentice-Hall, 1976.

Richard A. Posner, *The Crisis of Capitalist Democracy*. Cambridge, Massachusetts: Harvard University Press, 2010.

_____, *A Failure of Capitalism: The Crisis of '08 and the Descent into Depression*. Cambridge, Massachusetts: Harvard University Press, 2009.

Charles Postel, *The Populist Vision*. Oxford: Oxford University Press, 2007.

Virginia Postrel, *The Future and Its Enemies: The Growing Conflict Over Creativity, Enterprise, and Progress*. New York: Free Press, 1998.

Sidney Powell, *Licensed to Lie: Exposing Corruption in the Department of Justice*. Dallas: Brown Books Publishing, 2014.

Kirsten Powers, *The Silencing: How the Left is Killing Free Speech*. Washington, D.C.: Regnery Publishing, 2015.

Eswar S. Prasad, *The Dollar Trap: How the U.S. Dollar Tightened Its Grip on Global Finance.* Princeton, New Jersey: Princeton University Press, 2014.

Nomi Prins, *All the Presidents' Bankers: The Hidden Alliances That Drive American Power.* New York: Nation Books, 2014.

James D. Purvis, *The Samaritan Pentateuch and the Origin of the Samaritan Sect* [Harvard Semitic Monographs, Vol. 2]. Cambridge: Harvard University Press, 1968.

John Quiggin, *Zombie Economics: How Dead Ideas Still Walk Among Us.* Princeton, New Jersey: Princeton University Press, 2012.

Carroll Quigley, *The Anglo-American Establishment.* San Diego: Dauphin Publications, 2013.

_____, *Tragedy and Hope: A History of the World in Our Time.* New York: Macmillan Company, 1974.

Alvin Rabushka, *From Adam Smith to the Wealth of Nations.* New Brunswick, New Jersey: Transaction Books 1985.

Raghuram G. Rajan, *Fault Lines: How Hidden Fractures Still Threaten the World Economy.* Princeton, New Jersey: Princeton University Press, 2010.

Madhavan Ramanujam and Georg Tacke, *Monetizing Innovation: How Smart Companies Design the Product Around the Price.* Hoboken, New Jersey: John Wiley & Sons, 2016.

Joshua Cooper Ramo, *The Age of the Unthinkable: Why the New World Disorder Constantly Surprises Us And What We Can Do About It.* New York: Little Brown / Hachette, 2009.

_____, *The Seventh Sense: Power, Fortune, and Survival in the Age of Networks.* Boston: Little, Brown and Company, 2016.

Ayn Rand, *Capitalism: The Unknown Ideal (With additional articles by Nathaniel Branden, Alan Greenspan, and Robert Hessen).* New York: Signet / New American Library, 1967.

Eric Rauchway, *The Money Makers: How Roosevelt and Keynes Ended the Depression, Defeated Fascism, and Secured a Prosperous Peace.* New York: Basic Books, 2015.

Carmen M. Reinhart and Kenneth S. Rogoff, *This Time Is Different: Eight Centuries of Financial Folly.* Princeton, New Jersey: Princeton University Press, 2009.

James Rickards, *The Big Drop: How to Grow Your Wealth During the Coming Collapse.* Baltimore: Laissez Faire Books, 2015.

_____, *Currency Wars: The Making of the Next Global Crisis.* New York: Portfolio/ Penguin, 2011.

_____, *The Death of Money: The Coming Collapse of the International Monetary System.* New York: Portfolio / Penguin, 2014.

_____, *The New Case for Gold.* New York: Portfolio / Penguin, 2016.

Jeremy Rifkin, *The Age of Access: The New Culture of Hypercapitalism, Where All of Life Is a Paid-for Experience.* New York: Jeremy P. Tarcher / Penguin, 2000.

_____, *The End of Work: The Decline of the Global Labor Force and the Dawn of the Post-Market Era*. New York: Jeremy P. Tarcher / G.P. Putnam's Sons, 1995.

_____, *The Zero Marginal Cost Society: The Internet of Things, the Collaborative Commons, and the Eclipse of Capitalism*. New York: Palgrave Macmillan, 2014.

Barry Ritzholtz with Aaron Task, *Bailout Nation: How Greed and Easy Money Corrupted Wall Street and Shook the World Economy*. Hoboken, New Jersey: John Wiley & Sons, 2009.

Keith Roberts, *The Origins of Business, Money and Markets*. New York: Columbia University Press / Columbia Business School Publishing, 2011.

Russ Roberts. *How Adam Smith Can Change Your Life: An Unexpected Guide to Human Nature and Happiness*. New York: Portfolio / Penguin Random House, 2015.

Daniel T. Rodgers, *Age of Fracture*. Cambridge, Massachusetts: Belknap Press / Harvard University Press, 2012.

Wilhelm Roepke, *A Humane Economy: The Social Framework of the Free Market*. Chicago: Henry Regnery Company, 1960. This can be downloaded from the Internet at no cost from http://mises.org/books/Humane_Economy_Ropke.pdf

Kenneth S. Rogoff, *The Curse of Cash*. Princeton, New Jersey: Princeton University Press, 2016.

Murray N. Rothbard, *America's Great Depression*. Fifth Edition. Auburn, Alabama: Ludwig von Mises Institute, 2000. This can be downloaded from the Internet at no cost from http://mises.org/rothbard/agd.pdf

_____, *The Case Against the Fed*. Second Edition. Auburn, Alabama: Ludwig von Mises Institute, 2007. A version of this book can be downloaded from the Internet at no cost from http://mises.org/books/Fed.pdf

_____, *A History of Money and Banking in the United States: The Colonial Era to World War II*. Auburn, Alabama: Ludwig von Mises Institute, 2002. This can be downloaded from the Internet at no cost from http://mises.org/Books/HistoryofMoney.pdf

_____, *The Mystery of Banking*. Second Edition. Auburn, Alabama: Ludwig von Mises Institute, 2010. This can be downloaded from the Internet at no cost from http://mises.org/Books/MysteryofBanking.pdf

_____, *What Has Government Done to Our Money?* Auburn, Alabama: Ludwig von Mises Institute, 2008. This can be downloaded from the Internet at no cost from http://mises.org/Books/Whathasgovernmentdone.pdf

_____, *For a New Liberty: The Libertarian Manifesto* (Revised Edition). New York: Collier Books / Macmillian, 1978.

Michael Rothschild, *Bionomics: The Inevitability of Capitalism*. New York: John Macrae / Henry Holt and Company, 1990.

Nouriel Roubini and Stephen Mihm, *Crisis Economics: A Crash Course in the Future of Finance*. New York: Penguin Books, 2010.

Manu Saadia, *Trekonomics: The Economics of Star Trek*. Pipertext, 2016.

Jeffrey D. Sachs, *The Price of Civilization: Reawakening American Virtues and Prosperity*. New York: Random House, 2012.

Nicholas Samuel, *Unending Recovery: A Fresh Look at the Economic Crisis, Neglected Issues, Real Solutions*. Seattle: Amazon Digital Services, 2015.

Robert J. Samuelson, *The Good Life and Its Discontents: The American Dream in the Age of Entitlement 1945-1995*. New York: Times Books, 1995.

_____, *The Great Inflation and Its Aftermath: The Past and Future of American Affluence*. New York: Random House, 2008.

Michael J. Sandel, *What Money Can't Buy: The Moral Limits of Markets*. New York: Farrar, Straus and Giroux, 2013.

Michael Savage, *Government Zero: No Borders, No Language, No Culture*. New York: Center Street / Hachette Book Group, 2015.

_____, *Scorched Earth: Restoring the Country After Obama*. New York: Center Street / Hachette Book Group, 2016.

_____, *Stop the Coming Civil War: My Savage Truth*. New York: Center Street / Hachette Book Group, 2014.

Peter D. Schiff and Andrew J. Schiff, *How an Economy Grows and Why It Crashes*. Hoboken, New Jersey: John Wiley & Sons, 2010.

Detlev S. Schlichter, *Paper Money Collapse: The Folly of Elastic Money and the Coming Monetary Breakdown*. New York: John Wiley & Sons, 2011.

Peter H. Schuck, *Why Government Fails So Often: And How It Can Do Better*. Princeton, New Jersey: Princeton University Press, 2014.

Peter H. Schuck and James Q. Wilson (Eds.), *Understanding America: The Anatomy of an Exceptional Nation*. New York: PublicAffairs / Perseus Books Group, 2009.

Robert L. Schuettinger and Eamonn F. Butler, *Forty Centuries of Wage and Price Controls: How NOT to Fight Inflation*. Washington, D.C.: Heritage Foundation, 1979. This can be downloaded from the Internet at no cost from http://mises.org/books/fortycenturies.pdf

Barry Schwartz, *The Paradox of Choice: Why More Is Less*. New York: Ecco / Harper Collins, 2004.

Peter Schweizer, *Architects of Ruin: How Big Government Liberals Wrecked the Global Economy – and How They Will Do It Again If No One Stops Them*. New York: HarperCollins, 2009.

_____, *Clinton Cash: The Untold Story of How and Why Foreign Governments and Businesses Helped Make Bill and Hillary Rich*. New York: Harper, 2015.

James C. Scott, *Seeing Like A State: How Certain Schemes to Improve the Human Condition Have Failed*. New Haven, Connecticut: Yale University Press, 1998.

George Selgin and others, *Has the Fed Been a Failure?* Revised Edition. (Monograph). Washington, D.C.: Cato Institute, 2010.

Hans F. Sennholz (Editor), *Inflation Is Theft*. Irvington-on-Hudson, New York: Foundation for Economic Education, 1994. A copy of this book may be downloaded at no cost from FEE's website at http://fee.org/wp-content/uploads/2009/11/InflationisTheft.pdf See also: Hans F. Sennholz, "Inflation Is Theft," *LewRockwell.com*, June 24, 2005. URL:

http://www.lewrockwell.com/orig6/sennholz6.html

Ben Shapiro, *Bullies: How the Left's Culture of Fear and Intimidation Silences Americans*. New York: Threshold Editions / Simon & Schuster, 2013.

Ruchir Sharma, *Breakout Nations: In Pursuit of the Next Economic Miracles*. New York: W.W. Norton, 2013.

_____, *The Rise and Fall of Nations: Forces of Change in the Post-Crisis World*. New York: W.W. Norton, 2016.

Nicholas Shaxson and John Christensen, *The Financial Curse: How Oversized Financial Sectors Attack Democracy and Corrupt Economics*. Margate, Kent, U.K.: Commonwealth Publishing, 2014.

Judy Shelton, *Fixing the Dollar Now: Why US Money Lost Its Integrity and How We Can Restore It*. Washington, D.C.: Atlas Economic Research Foundation, 2011.

_____, *Money Meltdown: Restoring Order to the Global Currency System*. New York: The Free Press / Macmillan, 1994.

Amity Shlaes, *The Forgotten Man: A New History of the Great Depression*. New York: Harper Collins, 2007.

_____, *The Greedy Hand: How Taxes Drive Americans Crazy And What to Do About It*. New York: Random House, 1999.

Fred Siegel, *The Revolt Against the Masses: How Liberalism Has Undermined the Middle Class*. New York: Encounter Books, 2014.

Justo Sierra (Mendes), *The Political Evolution of the Mexican People*.

Austin: University of Texas Press, 2014.

Julian L. Simon, *The Ultimate Resource*. Princeton, New Jersey: Princeton University Press, 1981.

David Sinclair, *The Pound: A Biography: The Story of the Currency That Ruled the World*. London: Random House UK, 2001.

Chris Skinner, *Digital Bank: Strategies to Launch or Become a Digital Bank*. Singapore: Marshall Cavendish International (Asia-Singapore) / Times Publishing, 2014.

_____, *The Future of Banking in a Globalized World*. Hoboken, New Jersey: Wiley Finance Series, 2007.

Mark Skousen, *Economics of a Pure Gold Standard*. Seattle: CreateSpace, 2010.

_____, *The Making of Modern Economics: The Lives and Ideas of the Great Thinkers*. Second Edition. Armonk, New York: M.E. Sharpe, 2009.

Nick Smicek and Alex Williams, *Inventing the Future: Postcapitalism and a World Without Work*. London: Verso, 2015.

Craig R. Smith, *Rediscovering Gold in the 21ˢᵗ Century*. Sixth Edition. Phoenix: Idea Factory Press, 2007.

_____, *The Uses of Inflation: Monetary Policy and Governance in the 21ˢᵗ Century* (Monograph). Phoenix: Swiss America Trading Corporation, 2011.

Craig R. Smith and Lowell Ponte, *Crashing the Dollar: How to Survive a Global Currency Collapse*. Phoenix: Idea Factory Press, 2010.

_____, *The Great Debasement:The 100-Year Dying of the Dollar and How to Get America's Money Back*. Phoenix: Idea Factory Press, 2012.

_____, *The Great Withdrawal:How the Progressives' 100-Year Debasement of America and the Dollar Ends*. Phoenix: Idea Factory Press, 2013.

_____, *The Inflation Deception: Six Ways Government Tricks Us…And Seven Ways to Stop It!* Phoenix: Idea Factory Press, 2011.

_____, *Re-Making Money: Ways to Restore America's Optimistic Golden Age*. Phoenix: Idea Factory Press, 2011.

Helen Smith, *Men on Strike: Why Men Are Boycotting Marriage, Fatherhood, and the American Dream – and Why It Matters*. New York: Encounter Books, 2012.

Roy C. Smith, Ingo Walter and Gayle DeLong, *Global Banking* (Third Edition). Oxford: Oxford University Press, 2012.

Vera C. Smith, *The Rationale of Central Banking and the Free Banking Alternative*. Indianapolis, Indiana: Liberty Press / Liberty Fund, 1990.

Jacob Soll, *The Reckoning: Financial Accountability and the Rise and Fall of Nations*. New York: Basic Books, 2014.

Ilya Somin, *The Grasping Hand: Kelo v. City of New London and the Limitis of Eminent Domain*. Chicago: University of Chicago Press, 2015.

Guy Sorman, *Economics Does Not Lie: A Defense of the Free Market in a Time of Crisis*. New York: Encounter Books, 2009.

George Soros, *The Age of Fallibility: Consequences of the War on Terror*. New York: PublicAffairs / Perseus Books Group, 2007.

_____, *The Bubble of American Supremacy: The Costs of Bush's War in Iraq*. London: Weidenfeld & Nicolson, 2004.

_____, *George Soros on Globalization*. New York: PublicAffairs / Perseus Books Group, 2005.

_____, *The New Paradigm for Financial Markets: The Credit Crisis of 2008 and What It Means*. New York: PublicAffairs / Perseus Books Group, 2008.

_____, *Open Society: Reforming Global Capitalism*. New York: Public Affairs, 2000.

_____, *The Soros Lectures at the Central European University.* New York: Public Affairs, 2010.

Thomas Sowell, *Basic Economics: A Common Sense Guide to the Economy.* Third Edition. New York: Basic Books/Perseus Books Group, 2007.

_____, *A Conflict of Visions: Ideological Origins of Political Struggles.* New York: William Morrow, 1987.

_____, *Dismantling America.* New York: Basic Books, 2010.

_____, *Economic Facts and Fallacies.* Second Edition. New York: Basic Books, 2011.

_____, *The Housing Boom and Bust.* Revised Edition. New York: Basic Books, 2010.

_____, *Intellectuals and Society.* New York: Basic Books/Perseus Books, 2009.

_____, *Marxism: Philosophy and Economics.* New York: William Morrow, 1985.

_____, *On Classical Economics.* New Haven, Connecticut: Yale University Press, 2007.

_____, *The Quest for Cosmic Justice.* New York: Free Press/Simon & Schuster, 1999.

_____, *The Vision of the Anointed: Self-Congratulation as a Basis for Social Policy.* BasicBooks HarperCollins, 1995.

_____, *Wealth, Poverty and Politics: An International Perspective.* New York: Basic Books, 2015.

Dimitri Speck, *The Gold Cartel: Government Intervention on Gold, the Mega Bubble in Paper, and What This Means for Your Future.* New York: Palgrave Macmillan, 2013.

Paul Sperry, *The Great American Bank Robbery: The Unauthorized Report About What Really Caused the Great Recession.* Nashville, Tennessee: Thomas Nelson / HarperCollins Christian Publishing, 2011.

Henry William Spiegel and Ann Hubbard (Editors), *The Growth of Economic Thought (3rd Edition).* Durham, North Carolina: Duke University Press, 1991.

Guy Standing, *A Precariat Charter: From Denizens to Citizens.* London: Bloomsbury Academic, 2014.

_____, *The Precariat: The New Dangerous Class.* London: Bloomsbury Academic, 2011.

Andy Stern, *Raising the Floor: How a Universal Basic Income Can Renew Our Economy and Rebuild the American Dream.* New York: PublicAffairs / Perseus Books Group, 2016.

Mark Steyn, *After America: Get Ready for Armageddon.* Washington, D.C.: Regnery, 2011.

_____, *America Alone: The End of the World As We Know It.* Washington, D.C.: Regnery, 2008. *[Full Disclosure: Steyn quotes Lowell Ponte in this book.]*

Joseph E. Stiglitz, *The Euro: How a Common Currency Threatens the Future of Europe.* New York:: W.W. Norton, 2016.

_____, *Freefall: America, Free Markets, and the Sinking of the World Economy.* New York: W.W. Norton, 2010.

_____, *Globalization and Its Discontents*. New York: W.W. Norton, 2002.

_____, *Making Globalization Work*. New York: W.W. Norton, 2007.

David A. Stockman, *The Great Deformation: The Corruption of Capitalism in America*. New York: PublicAffairs/Perseus Books Group, 2013.

Susan C. Stokes and others, *Brokers, Voters, and Clientelism: The Puzzle of Distributive Politics*. Cambridge: Cambridge University Press, 2013.

John F. Stover, *History of the Baltimore and Ohio Railroad*. West Lafayette, Indiana: Purdue University Press, 1995.

Kimberly Strassel, *The Intimidation Game: How the Left Is Silencing Free Speech*. New York: Twelve / Hachette Book Group, 2016.

Wolfgang Streeck, *Buying Time: The Delayed Crisis of Democratic Capitalism*. London: Verso, 2014.

Paola Subacchi and John Driffill (Editors), *Beyond the Dollar: Rethinking the International Monetary System*. London: Chatham House / Royal Institute of International Affairs, 2010. URL: http://www.chathamhouse.org/sites/default/files/public/Research/International%20Economics/ r0310_ims.pdf

Arun Sundararajan, *The Sharing Economy: The End of Employment and the Rise of Crowd-Based Capitalism*. Cambridge, Massachusetts: MIT Press, 2016.

Cass R. Sunstein, *A Constitution of Many Minds: Why the Founding Document Doesn't Mean What It Meant Before*. Princeton, New Jersey: Princeton University Press, 2011.

_____, *Simpler: The Future of Government*. New York: Simon & Schuster, 2013.

Ron Suskind, *Confidence Men: Wall Street, Washington, and the Education of a President*. New York: Harper Collins, 2011.

Bob Swarup, *Money Mania: Booms, Panics, and Busts from Ancient Rome to the Great Meltdown*. London: Bloomsbury Press, 2014.

Charles J. Sykes, *A Nation of Moochers: America's Addiction to Getting Something for Nothing*. New York: St. Martin's Press, 2012.

Nassim Nicholas Taleb, *Antifragile: Things That Gain from Disorder*. New York: Random House, 2012.

_____, *The Bed of Procrustes: Philosophical and Practical Aphorisms*. New York: Random House, 2010.

_____, *The Black Swan: Second Edition: The Impact of the Highly Improbable: With a New Section: "On Robustness and Fragility."* New York: Random House, 2010.

_____, *Fooled by Randomness: The Hidden Role of Chance in Life and in the Markets*. New York: Random House, 2005.

Peter J. Tanous and Jeff Cox, *Debt, Deficits and the Demise of the American Economy*. Hoboken, New Jersey: John Wiley & Sons, 2011.

Daniel K. Tarullo, *Banking on Basel: The Future of International Financial Regulation.* Washington, D.C.: The Peterson Institute for International Economics, 2008.

Frederick Taylor, *The Downfall of Money: Germany's Hyperinflation and the Destruction of the Middle Class.* New York: Bloomsbury Press, 2013.

Richard H. Thaler, *Misbehaving: The Making of Behavioral Economics.* New York: W.W. Norton, 2015.

Richard H. Thaler and Cass R. Sunstein, *Nudge: Improving Decisions About Health, Wealth, and Happiness.* New York: Penguin Books, 2009.

Adam Thierer, *Permissionless Innovation: The Continuing Case for Comprehensive Freedom.* Fairfax, Virginia: Mercator Center at George Mason University, 2016.

J.A. Thompson, *The Bible and Archeology.* Grand Rapids, Michigan: William B. Eerdmans Publishing, 1962.

Frank Trentmann, *Empire of Things: How We Became a World of Consumers, from the Fifteenth Century to the Twenty-First.* New York: HarperCollins, 2016.

James Turk and John Rubino, *The Money Bubble: What to Do Before It Pops.* Moscow, Idaho: DollarCollapse Press, 2013.

Adair Turner, *Between Debt and the Devil: Money, Credit, and Fixing Global Finance.* Princeton, New Jersey: Princeton University Press, 2015.

Walter Tyndale, *Fundamentals of Offshore Banking: How to Open Accounts Almost Anywhere.* Seattle, Washington: CreateSpace/Amazon Publishing, 2009.

United States Government Accountability Office, *Offshore Tax Evasion: IRS Has Collected Billions of Dollars, but May be Missing Continued Evasion* (Report). Washington, D.C.: GAO, March 2013. URL: http://www.gao.gov/assets/660/653369.pdf

Richard Vague, *The Next Economic Disaster: Why It's Coming and How to Avoid It.* Philadelphia: University of Pennsylvania Press, 2014.

Johan Van Overtveldt, *Bernanke's Test: Ben Bernanke, Alan Greenspan and the Drama of the Central Banker.* Chicago: B2 Books/Agate Publishing, 2009.

Harry C. Veryser, *It Didn't Have to Be This Way: Why Boom and Bust Is Unnecessary – and How the Austrian School of Economics Breaks the Cycle.* Wilmington, Delaware: ISI Books / Intercollegiate Studies Institute, 2012.

Damon Vickers, *The Day After the Dollar Crashes: A Survival Guide for the Rise of the New World Order.* Hoboken, New Jersey: John Wiley & Sons, 2011.

William Voegeli, *Never Enough: America's Limitless Welfare State.* New York: Encounter Books, 2010.

Joseph Vogl, *The Specter of Capital.* Redwood City, California: Stanford University Press, 2014.

M.W. Walbert, *The Coming Battle: A Complete History of the National Banking Money Power in the United States.* Chicago: W.B. Conkey Company, 1899. Reprinted by Walter Publishing & Research, Merlin, Oregon, 1997.

David M. Walker, *Comeback America: Turning the Country Around and Restoring Fiscal Responsibility*. New York: Random House, 2009.

Jude Wanniski, *The Way the World Works*. New York: Touchstone / Simon & Schuster, 1978.

Jack Weatherford, *The History of Money: From Sandstone to Cyberspace*. New York: Crown Publishers, 1997.

Carolyn Webber and Aaron Wildavsky, *A History of Taxation and Expenditure in the Western World*. New York: Simon & Schuster, 1986.

Janine R. Wedel, *Shadow Elite: How the World's New Power Brokers Undermine Democracy, Government and the Free Market*. New York: Basic Books / Perseus Books Group, 2009.

Eric J. Weiner, *The Shadow Market: How a Group of Wealthy Nations and Powerful Investors Secretly Dominate the World*. New York: Scribner, 2010.

David Wessel, *In Fed We Trust: Ben Bernanke's War on the Great Panic: How the Federal Reserve Became the Fourth Branch of Government*. New York: Crown Business, 2009.

Diana West, *American Betrayal: The Secret Assault on Our Nation's Character*. New York: St. Martin's Press, 2013.

_____, *The Death of the Grown-Up: How America's Arrested Development Is Bringing Down Western Civilization*. New York: St. Martin's Press, 2007.

Drew Westen, *The Political Brain: The Role of Emotion in Deciding the Fate of the Nation*. New York: PublicAffairs / Perseus Books Group, 2008.

R. Christopher Whalen, *Inflated: How Money and Debt Built the American Dream*. Hoboken, New Jersey: John Wiley & Sons, 2010.

Charles Wheelan, *Naked Economics: Undressing the Dismal Science* (Revised Edition). New York: W.W. Norton, 2010.

_____, *Naked Money: What It Is and Why It Matters*. New York: W.W. Norton, 2016.

Lawrence H. White, *The Clash of Economic Ideas: The Great Policy Debates and Experiments of the Last Hundred Years*. Cambridge: Cambridge University Press, 2012.

_____, *Is The Gold Standard Still the Gold Standard among Monetary Systems?* (Monograph). Washington, D.C.: Cato Institute, February 8, 2008. URL: http://www.cato.org/pubs/bp/bp100.pdf

John W. Whitehead, *A Government of Wolves: The Emerging American Police State*. New York: SelectBooks, 2013.

_____, *Battlefield America: The War On The American People*. New York: SelectBooks, 2015.

Meredith Whitney, *Fate of the States: The New Geography of American Prosperity*. New York: Portfolio, 2013.

Peter C. Whybrow, *American Mania: When More Is Not Enough*. New York: W.W. Norton, 2005.

Addison Wiggin and William Bonner, *Financial Reckoning Day Fallout: Surviving Today's Global Depression.* Hoboken, New Jersey: John Wiley & Sons, 2009.

Addison Wiggin and Kate Incontrera, *I.O.U.S.A.: One Nation. Under Stress. In Debt.* Hoboken, New Jersey: John Wiley & Sons, 2008.

Benjamin Wiker, *Worshipping the State: How Liberalism Became Our State Religion.* Washington, D.C.: Regnery, 2013.

Aaron Wildavsky, *How to Limit Government Spending...,* Berkeley, California: University of California Press, 1980.

John Williams, *Hyperinflation 2012: Special Commentary Number 414. Shadow Government Statistics (Shadowstats)*, January 25, 2012. URL: http://www.shadowstats.com/article/no-414-hyperinflation-special-report-2012

Jonathan Williams (Editor), *Money: A History.* New York: St. Martin's Press, 1997.

Ruth Wodak, *Right-Wing Populism In Europe.* London: Bloomsbury Academic, 2013.

Naomi Wolf, *The End of America: Letter of Warning to a Young Patriot.* White River Junction, Vermont: Chelsea Green Publishing, 2007.

David Wolman, *The End of Money: Counterfeiters, Preachers, Techies, Dreamers – and the Coming Cashless Society.* Boston: Da Capo Press / Perseus Books, 2012.

Gordon S. Wood, *Empire of Liberty: A History of the Early Republic, 1789-1815.* New York: Oxford University Press, 2009.

Thomas E. Woods, Jr., *Meltdown: A Free-Market Look at Why the Stock Market Collapsed, the Economy Tanked, and Government Bailouts Will Make Things Worse.* Washington, D.C.: Regnery Publishing, 2009.

_____, *Nullification: How to Resist Federal Tyranny in the 21st Century.* Washington, D.C.: Regnery Publishing, 2010.

_____, *Rollback: Repealing Big Government Before the Coming Fiscal Collapse.* Washington, D.C.: Regnery Publishing, 2011.

Thomas E. Woods, Jr., and Kevin R.C. Gutzman, *Who Killed the Constitution?: The Federal Government vs. American Liberty From WWI to Barack Obama.* New York: Three Rivers Press, 2009.

Bob Woodward, *Maestro: Greenspan's Fed and the American Boom.* New York: Simon & Schuster, 2000.

_____, *The Power of Politics.* New York: Simon & Schuster, 2012.

L. Randall Wray, *Modern Money Theory: A Primer on Macroeconomics for Sovereign Monetary Systems.* London: Palgrave Macmillan, 2012.

_____, *Understanding Modern Money: The Key to Full Employment and Price Stability.* Northampton, Massachusetts: Edward Elgar Publishing, 2006.

Pamela Yellen, *The Bank On Yourself Revolution: Fire Your Banker, Bypass Wall Street, and Take Control of Your Own Financial Future.* Ben Bella Books, 2014.

Noam Yuran, *What Money Wants: An Economy of Desire*. Redwood City, California: Stanford University Press, 2014.

Fareed Zakaria, *The Future of Freedom: Illiberal Democracy at Home and Abroad*. New York: W.W. Norton, 2003.

_____, *The Post-American World*. New York: W.W. Norton, 2009.

Gabriel Zucman, *The Hidden Wealth of Nations: The Scourge of Tax Havens*. Chicago: University of Chicago Press, 2015.

Luigi Zingales, *A Capitalism for the People: Recapturing the Lost Genius of American Prosperity*. New York: Basic Books / Perseus Books Group, 2012.

Todd J. Zywicki, *The Economics and Regulation of Network Branded Prepaid Cards* (Working Paper). Arlington, Virginia: Mercatus Center / George Mason University, January 2013. URL: http://mercatus.org/sites/default/files/Zywicki_Prepaid_v2.pdf